KINGS' DAUGHTERS

KINGS' DAUGHTERS

BY

JANETTA C. SORLEY

CAMBRIDGE
AT THE UNIVERSITY PRESS
1937

CAMBRIDGE
UNIVERSITY PRESS

University Printing House, Cambridge CB2 8BS, United Kingdom

Published in the United States of America by Cambridge University Press, New York

Cambridge University Press is part of the University of Cambridge.

It furthers the University's mission by disseminating knowledge in the pursuit of
education, learning and research at the highest international levels of excellence.

www.cambridge.org
Information on this title: www.cambridge.org/9781107415980

First published 1937
First paperback edition 2014

A catalogue record for this publication is available from the British Library

ISBN 978-1-107-41598-0 Paperback

IN MEMORY

of

W. R. S.

V f T

CONTENTS

"'Old things need not be therefore true',
O brother men, nor yet the new;
Ah! still awhile the old thought retain,
And yet consider it again!"

PREFACE

This book does not pretend to be a history of the University of Cambridge except when that is concerned with the lives of those who brought some of its Colleges into being.

In the century that held the lives and deaths of St Francis and St Clara, when Charity was born again and walked with simplicity, ere yet she had learned the uses of advertisement or the manners of the highwayman, one of the queens of England gave to the University fifty marks "for the use of poor scholars". How far that little candle shed its ray we may learn from the long list of the University's benefactors, among whom appear certain honourable women who thus proved themselves spiritually as some of them were actually the descendants and kinswomen of the Queen. I have thought it worth while to trace this gracious succession and to inquire not only what manner of persons these were but also what prompted them to this special form of "personal munificence".

I wish gratefully to acknowledge my debt to the staff of the University Library and to the readers of the University Press for ready and constant help; also to certain of my friends who will recognise themselves when I remind them that without their encouragement and criticism the work could not have been accomplished.

J. C. S.

Cambridge
June 1936

CHAPTER I

ELEANOR OF CASTILE

"Kings' daughters were among thy honourable women;
on thy right hand did stand the Queen."

I

She was born in the year 1240, one of the daughters of 1240
Ferdinand III, King of Castile, a mountainous land ringed
round by the forts which gave it its name. Her mother was
his second wife Jeanne de Ponthieu of the royal house of
France; her birthplace was Burgos where her great-grandfather Alfonso the Noble had built a palace for his queen
Eleonora of England on the spur of a hill above the meeting
of two rivers. Two of their daughters Berenguela and Blanche
became the mothers of those fighting saints King Ferdinand
and King Louis. Berenguela's son was stern and high like the
mountain on whose breast he was born, but not, like it, barren,
for he had a powerful vision of the next world and a super-
abundant sense of his duty in this one which led him to make
war on all those within his dominions whom he counted unbelievers. His queen, as the custom was, followed him about
on his unending crusades while the care of the family was the
affair of the grandmother in rocky Burgos. Time was when
Berenguela had "armed her fair head and issued from the
walls, nor feared nor shunned a soldier's death"; but when
that was no longer required of her she thankfully retired to
Burgos to live a woman's life.

In this she would have the help of the Cistercian nuns of the
neighbouring convent founded by her father and mother for

the shelter of pilgrims on their way westward to Compostela and for the cure of the sick in the good highland air—Las Huelgas, House of Health and Refreshment which indeed it was for the King's children too. A homely, happy place where they early learned the secrets of farm life, wondered at the pilgrims' stories, helped with the sick and incidentally received such teaching in religion and letters as the convent afforded. They would understand enough of Latin for religious purposes, the French language and their own musical Castilian, to this day the classical Spanish.

"To read in my psalter, to broider in gold and silk,
    To hear about Thebes and Troy or sound a lay on the harp,
    To checkmate another at chess or to strike my bird on my wrist";

so does a singer of her day relate how a girl of Eleanor's degree passed her time. Trojans and Thebans sound remote, but Roderigo de Diaz, called by Arabs the Cid, who was born at Burgos not so very long before Eleanor herself, was already a heroic figure, as also was Roland, the tale of whose glory was first told for the entertainment of the pilgrims to Compostela.

King Ferdinand's family had a strong hereditary leaning towards religion and the things of the mind; Sancho and Beatrice were dedicated to the church; Alfonso the eldest was a seeker after truth by way of the stars in their courses. He had an independent mind and spoke it freely; he must have been an interesting if alarming element in the family. At a time when the inhabitants of this earth held the comfortable belief that it was the centre of the universe, he was heard to observe that he thought somehow there must be another and a better way of ordering it. But when he succeeded his father as King of

Castile and Leon his business was clearly with this planet and his own particular piece of it, one of his more immediate duties being the finding of a husband for his half-sister Eleanor.

In those days a marriage between two persons of high degree was considered less for their mutual help and comfort than for that of the states they represented. Alfonso had a powerful neighbour in King Henry of England, the overlord of Gascony, whose people's game was fighting and who were then seeking Alfonso's support in a quarrel they had with Henry. But the kings had good reasons for not making war on each other; Alfonso desired Henry's support in the bid he was to make for the Empire, and Henry thought that the dowry which Alfonso's sister would ultimately inherit from her mother would add considerably to his interest in France and his possessions there, which already were greater than his whole realm of England. So the two made up a marriage between Edward, Henry's heir, and Alfonso's sister Eleanor.

As he was fourth and she fifth in descent from Henry II of England, the union was within the forbidden degrees of matrimony; but papal objection was a matter of form when the peace of provinces and great possessions were in question. Eleanor being her father's child and the daughter of her generation would take as a matter of course her pawn's part in the game of politics; but romance was never yet denied its share in a wedding. Eighty years earlier an Eleanor of England had come to Leon as queen; legends of her land would be revived with the wedding fineries for the encouragement of the child who was now to travel thither. Minstrel or pilgrim could tell the tale of the comet that heralded the prince's birth with flames before but smoke and ruin behind, foretelling for Edward a path of glory, albeit calamity for him who should come after him; but who at the moment would believe that part of the prophecy?

King Alfonso made one condition, his star-gazing not having wholly blinded him to this world's ways: the bridegroom must present himself at Burgos five weeks before the date fixed for the wedding else it should not take place. His father had been a laggard in love, one of the ladies whom he had jilted at the last moment being none other than Eleanor's mother Jeanne de Ponthieu.

But the son proved himself in this as in other ways a better man than his father for he came to Burgos not five but eight weeks before Michaelmas, eagerly so that there might be the more time for courting. He was accompanied by his mother Eleanor of Provence, wishful no doubt to have a look at the lady she had supplanted, and a whole army of relations and lords, one of whom was Richard de Clare, the head of a family that busied itself much with the King's affairs. Henry had remained at his city of Bordeaux perhaps grateful for the etiquette which did not require his presence at the wedding.

Eleanor must have thought when she saw her prince that the half had not been told her, for he was comely and yellow-haired, shapely and tall with the long arms and flat thighs of a horseman, excelling in all manly sports; the blemish of a drooping eyelid giving only a pleasing touch of mystery to a countenance otherwise frank and happy. Their common spoken language was the French in which, on an emperor's authority, it becomes a lover to address his lady. Eleanor's pawnhood was over.

Their hands were joined at Michaelmas by her brother Sancho in the convent of Las Huelgas of which her sister Beatrice was now Abbess, and there was a tournament at Burgos when

4

the bridegroom was knighted by King Alfonso. It is to be hoped that the motherly nuns who dressed the bride and armed her knight for his vigil in their chapel had a part in the festivities. Then Eleanor set out on the first of many journeys

> "to that new world which is the old.
> Over the hills and far away,
> Beyond their utmost purple rim,
> And deep into the dying day
> Through all the world she followed him."

II

At Bordeaux they were abundantly welcomed by King Henry who may amiably have thought thus to atone for his remissness in the matter of Eleanor's mother. Indeed all along he treated this daughter-in-law with affection and generosity if so it can be called when the means were generally supplied by others. He promised to increase his son's allowance, and created him Prince of Wales with command to conquer that unsubdued principality; he gladly gave him Ireland also, and, of his French possessions, Aquitaine, land of water and wine, which included Gascony; thus in the lightness of his heart, he dowered this pair of children with the most troublesome parts of his dominions on both sides of the sea. He gave a great banquet in their honour—at a cost of three hundred thousand marks—and then took them to Paris to be presented to King Louis IX, cousin of both Eleanor's parents. As they rode to the palace on the Isle in the Seine, they were greeted by the townspeople, "and especially by the scholars of the University most of whom were English". The Holy Chapel beside the palace was then in all its fresh glory; the architect Pierre de Montreuil came from one of Eleanor's dower-towns; on the walls were portrayed the towers of her own Castile, for King Louis's mother also was a daughter of that land.

Again King Henry broke out with a still more splendid entertainment called the Feast of Kings from the number of royal personages who partook of it. King Louis, who, like his cousin Ferdinand, really earned his title of saint, tried to put the giver of the feast in the chief place; but Henry would not because he was the other's vassal in France, whereat Louis softly said, "Would that all might come by their own without offence".

Here were changed days for the child of thrifty and dignified Castile. At a family council it was decreed she should pass over to England while her husband returned to Aquitaine to learn his business under his uncle Simon de Montfort the viceroy there. Edward was but a boy of sixteen, a new-made knight with money in his hand; what wonder if he took his pleasure in tourneys, and in the hunting and hawking for which Gascony was famous? It was moreover a sure way to popularity there; as one of its own poets has said "In following noble sport and the chase, a man flees from the seven deadly sins to the great profit and salvation of his soul; for he that is a good sportsman will have joys and delights in this world and afterwards again in Paradise".

Oct. 13 1255 But Eleanor came obediently to England where she was royally welcomed at Dover by the Lord Warden; then, riding the palfrey King Henry sent to greet her, by "holy crosses where she kneeled and prayed for happy wedlock hours", she came gently though the autumn land to London. The King and his Court met and escorted her to the new Temple by the Fleet brook where already was lodged her brother Sancho the

Pope's Legate, come on a mission about the marriage of the King's daughter Beatrice to the son of the Duke of Brittany.

But the red cloth the citizens had hung out to greet Eleanor could not smother their grumbles about many a cause of offence. Her name to begin with was ominous, neither of her predecessors who bore it having endeared themselves to the people. If, as was said of her mother-in-law Eleanor of Provence, "she had no equal as far as Constantinople", the fame of her gifts and graces had not followed her to the North. She came from the mutual admiration society of her father's Court with a train of relations to plant out in the high places of her husband's kingdom; one of them, Peter of Savoy, has left his name on London to this day. She was an able woman but insensitive with the stupidity of the self-centred which made her blind and deaf to a spirit of nationality just then becoming aware of itself and, like all things young and callow, deeply suspicious especially of foreigners and their ways. "These Englishmen most commonly have ever great envy at strangers" said the Lord of Hainault seventy years later; it may be this national virtue has not yet died from amongst us.

Now here came another foreign woman with a Spanish priest of a brother and an outlandish train of men and beasts, for their mules, poor creatures, gave offence, uncouthly floundering in the filthy mud of the riverside causeways. Eleanor's personal wardrobe was simple and even scanty; but she and her brother had innocently brought with them the house comforts to which they were used in windy Spain—curtains hung tentwise round the draughty walls, and rugs on the floors instead of rushes. "Wanton Southern luxury!" said the Londoners who had heard, too, of banquets at Bordeaux and Paris and knew only too well who would have to pay the cost. And what about those three greedy leopards in the Tower (an embarrassing gift to the King from his cousin the Emperor), not to speak of the silly white bear for whose food the King had already taken three hundred marks from the citizens besides a groat a day for its collar and chain when it should be minded to go a-fishing in the river? And that silver alms-dish the King gave the Princess to offer before St Thomas's shrine in Canterbury Church? Even now they heard he was preparing for her at Guildford a bower with a raised hearth and a chimney and a fine painted window in the oriel. "It is we who shall have to pay for all these fancies" murmured the people telling over a jumble of grievances real and imagined but credited to the account of the new-comer. And as there is no acid so pervasive as disapproval, be sure that it penetrated to Eleanor who understood and shaped her course accordingly, not in silly resentment but with sense and sympathy. After brother Sancho had accomplished his mission and blessed the oriel—L-shaped for Leonora—in the thickness of the wall at Guildford Castle, there was no more of him. Homesick at times she must have been; but there is little trace of any promotion or even natural encouragement of her countrymen or kindred. At one time she had the services of a Spanish doctor; and long years after her first coming to England when a ship from Seville came into Portsmouth one Easter Monday, it is on record that the Queen sent for some of her native fruits, "dates, raisins, figs, citrons, pomegranates and seven oranges".

1255   In November Edward came to London where one of his first duties was to settle a quarrel about port dues between the King's officers and the Bordeaux wine-merchants in favour of the latter which somewhat allayed the citizens' joy at his return; they looked yet more askance when he increased his household and rode with two hundred horse. But such things were as bubbles on the surface of a sea of real troubles that were threatening the country whose resources were being exploited for their own ends by the imported relations of the King and Queen, till Simon de Montfort also returned from Gascony and there was a day of reckoning. Then followed nearly ten years of bitter struggle from which emerged the beginnings of England as one nation. Simon de Montfort died in the doing of it and Edward his godson had the increase. The slow stirring current of nationality set to him and he did not miss the signal.

Meanwhile his wife was with his mother in France, seeing life at her cousin's Court (silently noting from the example of the elder Eleanor how not to do it when her turn should come), or with her own mother in Ponthieu. That marshy country so-named from its many bridges might not have seemed such a desirable dowry to King Henry had it not neighboured Normandy and been joined up with Montreuil, a fortified port on the Calais sea-board. The name Ponthieu has died, but the place in these latter days has come alive again for us as the land of the Somme.

Eleanor returned to England when she was twenty-three to 1264 begin the business of her life. During the next four years she produced three children, Eleanor, John and Henry, born in the fastness of Windsor from which, however, she had once to flee for safety to Westminster. The boys' births so delighted the King that, undismayed by his own desperate position and the state of the country, he gaily increased the mother's allowance.

There came a day when the rebel barons surrendered to 1267 Edward at Ely and the worried land had peace for a space.

Then he was a boy again holding tournaments and playing at the strife that had lately been real. In the next year, after the fashion of his time, he took the Cross and was invited by King Louis to follow it with him to Palestine. That fighting saint had realised the soldier sense in this young kinsman to whom he now offered financial help to enable him to make the Crusade. The prince was to join King Louis not as heir of England but as peer of France and to leave one of his sons there as a hostage during the pilgrimage. The terms were accepted and Edward prepared to fulfil his vow.

His wife took for granted that she was to accompany him. For several years she had seen little enough of him and perhaps too much of some of his family; here was a chance of having him to herself and sharing his adventures. People in those days travelled less for the sake of their bodies than their souls; but though the making of a pilgrimage might be a good investment for the life of the world to come it offered also a chance of seeing this one and enjoying the sun. Eleanor's example inspired her sister-in-law Beatrice to bestow her young family in Windsor Castle with their cousins and follow her lord Red John of Brittany and his father, one of the peers of France, who also went on this Crusade.

Three-year-old Henry was duly taken as hostage to Paris, a case of touch-and-remit, for after King Louis had tenderly received and blessed the child he returned him to his father who took him home while his mother went on to Bordeaux. Edward remained in England till the day "when King Henry did translate with great solemnity the body of King Edward the Confessor that before lay in the side of the quire where the monks did sing at Westminster into a new chapel at the back of the high altar which he hath prepared for him of a marvellous workmanship". One of the poles of the King's devotion was the Confessor after whom he had named his eldest son.

In April of this year Edward had accompanied the King to Cambridge where "being informed of the contentions and disputes constantly occurring between the burgesses and the scholars the Prince undertook to act as medium between them". Henry was wise in leaving this difficulty to his son, whose remarkably just and reasonable suggestions as to a solution may be read in the Annals of the town.

Edward then joined his wife and, reversing the order of their first journey together, they travelled up to Burgos. King Ferdinand's son and successor had not carried on his crusades; he had a way of his own with heretics and had skilfully rendered his kingdom independent of papal control by a law for dealing with them which left him free to use the keen intellects of Arabs and Jews for peaceful research in science. He re-founded the University of Salamanca where later the Copernican system was taught before it was recognised by other European seats of learning; the Alphonsine Tables were at this very time being prepared at Toledo. There was also in the making a chronicle of the kingdom and a code of its laws which had a special interest for Edward in whom the lawyer was joined with the soldier; indeed the whole atmosphere of Alfonso's Court must have been stimulating to the alert mind of his brother-in-law. Eleanor the while could take her ease in the home of her youth, bridging the years with her brothers and Abbess Beatrice and glorifying her absent children to the nuns of Las Huelgas.

She and Edward spent their wedding day at Aigues Mortes near which weird fortress lay the ships that took them to Tunis, where they learned that six weeks earlier King Louis their leader had died, calling upon Jerusalem. With him had died also the life of the Crusade, for Edward found the other peers of France—three of whom were the King's sons—already making terms with the Saracens. "By the blood of God," thundered the Englishman, "though you should all desert me and I enter Acre alone with Fowen my groom yet will I keep my word and my oath to the dead." So he served himself heir to the personality that had initiated the Crusade and took command of it.

This was counted to him for righteousness and the high favour of heaven when all except the English ships were driven from their anchorage and wrecked in one of the sudden Mediterranean storms which fell upon the expedition quartered for the winter at Trapani in the heel of Italy, the good seamanship of the English not having the credit.

Then "Edward the King's son with his brother Edmund and many other nobles sayling into Asia against the Infidels by his policy and manly acts so demeaned himself that oftimes he put the Turks to great disworship". His headquarters were Acre where his wife and sister were bestowed in the great Citadel looking across the bay to Carmel. After nearly two years, on the evening of Edward's birthday, came overtures of peace from the Emir of Jaffa. As the prince, bare-headed and lightly clad for the sultry weather, sat musing over the letter, the messenger made as if to take another from his girdle but drew a knife instead and aimed a blow at the prince who raised his arm in defence and received a deep wound on the right shoulder. But he laid the wretch low with a kick, seized the knife and drove it home in the grovelling body. The prince's minstrel dashed out the brains with his stool, but was sharply rebuked by the prince for striking the dead. There were others ready with real help in the way of salves and drugs, but the wound turned black and ugly showing poison was at work. A surgeon who was an Englishman proposed then and there to cut away the affected part, promising that if this were done the prince should be able to mount and manage his horse in a fortnight's time. Edward consented, was shriven and made his will, a brief, soldierly affair. But Eleanor vehemently protested and forbade the use of the knife till she was carried away weeping and struggling and the surgeon did his work. A hundred and fifty years later, a romancing Spaniard, ignoring his countrywoman's sounder claims to heroism, made up the tale that she sucked the poison from her husband's wound. There is no foundation for this film story; the poor lady's behaviour at this time was the more natural because only a few weeks later she bore her fourth child. At the date promised by the surgeon the prince was able to mount and manage his horse, and in due course received in his arms his child of the Crusade.

It was suspected that the murderer was an agent of the mysterious Old Man of the Mountains, head of the fanatic sect of the Assassins, so-called from the drug hashish which they used in their secret rites. They came from Persia to a mountain fastness in Syria and were nominally followers of Islam, but they had long abandoned religion for politics wherein they practised terrorism and "the use of murder as an avowed political weapon". The Saracen princes often though secretly found them useful for dirty work. Thus, when the Sultan with professions of friendship and admiration for a noble foe renewed his proposals of peace Prince Edward received them with words not new in the land of Palestine: "This people honoureth me with their lips, but their heart is far from me".

1272   Nevertheless he made a truce for ten years with the Sultan, and then with all his following set sail for Europe which they reached after a voyage of seven weeks, cooped up—men, women, children, horses, armour—in small sailing ships. In these our days of swift and luxurious transit through the world, when every possible alleviation of disgust and discomfort is forthcoming, do we ever give a thought to the sufferings of all who travelled by sea in the brave days of old? A heartless ballad of that time indicates that sea-sickness is one of the world's oldest jokes; in the hundred and seventh Psalm, the life histories of the prophet Jonah, the apostle Paul and the Sieur de Joinville there are glimpses of the minor horrors of such journeys. But, as a rule, an admirable reserve is maintained. "They commended themselves unto the keeping of God and took their passage by sea", and so came to Sicily.

1272   While they rested there with cousin Charles, the king, news came from England of the death of King Henry. Edward having gone out a peer of France was to come back King of England, his first and last Crusade occurring between the deaths of the two men who were more to him than any others. For now he fell into a passion of grief to the amazement of those about him, especially of his light-hearted host, who once upon a time had not let the news of a brother's death interrupt a game of backgammon. The messengers from England had to tell next of the death of the young prince John, but his father seemed so little moved by this that his cousin remarked "though you are now a king, you refuse to be comforted for the death of him whereby you are made great while you take small heed of your son's", to which Edward answered with all his father's simplicity, "God can easily give me another son, but not another father". The mother's lips were sealed.

14

Misrule, broken pledges and wasted revenues make up the record of Henry III's reign, yet it should be remembered that he was only fourteen when, the child of parents of whom we know nothing that is good, he came into a bankrupt inheritance. And he became the father of children who redeemed the honour of his house.

> "King of the simple life
> More honoured in his issue than himself"

is how Dante, that ruthless awarder of blame and faint praise, judges Henry III. He had a certain piety towards God and a loving understanding of beauty by which he re-created the Westminster Abbey we know. And in a ferocious age he kept a tenderness of nature which "becomes the throned monarch better than his crown"; it is said that his favourite son was not Edward straight and shapely but Edmund who was called Crouchback. Yet Edward wept for him on his death as for a friend.

It is remarkable that in a time of fights and factions, Edward did not hurry to take his kingdom. He may have realised that once he got home there would be enough doing to keep him there; now he was on the road to Rome where he had business with the Pope Gregory X, Teobaldo of Liége who had been with him in Palestine as Bishop of Acre. New Pope, new King and Queen, they all met again at Orvieto the papal city of refuge when Rome was inhospitable; there they could mark the beginnings of the great church building in commemoration of the miracle of the blood that fell from the uplifted Host to convince a doubting monk. (What were the thoughts of King Alfonso's sister?) Feb. 1273

Pope Gregory took them to Rome where he gave Edward

authority to tithe the English clergy and religious houses for three years so as to pay the expenses of the Crusade. A better plan this than to grind the faces of the poor as King Henry in his time had done; but Eleanor may have thought on the answer of her father when it was suggested the Church should help to pay for his holy wars: "I ask nothing but their prayers from my clergy", said Ferdinand. No wonder they hailed him Saint.

Eleanor too had business in the Holy City, for there she bore that "other son whom God can easily give", naming him Alfonso for her brother. In the spring they turned northwards, pausing at Bologna and attaching one of the teachers in the great school of law who came back with them to help Edward to do for England what Alfonso had done for the laws of Castile. Then, travelling gently because of the young children, they passed safely through the storied land of the Patient Griselda, that model wife, "a long and lusty country full of castles and towns and adorned with woods, meadows, rivers, vines, hayfields and ploughed fields". They must have scattered good largesse, for the peasants from their terraced crofts acclaimed the King as Emperor, giving him the highest title they knew. So over the Alps into Savoy, full of Edward's relations, and on to Châlons where they paused for an interval of sport and chivalric exercises with the Count. In Paris Edward swore homage to King Philip for Aquitaine where now the Gascons were joyfully stirring up strife, taking advantage of the fact that both their overlords were new to their work. For nearly a year Edward remained there to make himself felt, and he and Eleanor again visited Castile where they left little Joanna of Acre with the grandmother after whom she was named. Then 1274 they returned to their kingdom when they were about thirty-five years old.

III

For the Queen it was a home-coming and very different from the day when she first rode into London, the foreign wife of an untried boy who like his parents passed his time amusing himself. Now he was "a man of such noble and valiant courage that he never fainted in most dangerous enterprises; of excellent wit and great towardnesse", besides namely as a sportsman which did him no harm with the people. She had borne him five fair children and showed that the heart of her husband could safely trust in her. They came to those that wanted them with a lively desire to be friends.

For all this time wonders were never ceasing. That youthful spirit of nationality which had kicked at everything to which it was not used was now, after the manner of all healthy, natural growths, absorbing whatever suited it in the foreign elements that came its way. Instinctive and unconscious but all the surer for that, this corporate spirit was making one of what had hitherto been diverse, and the king was ready for it. One of its manifestations was the foundation in Oxford University 1265 by the Chancellor of the kingdom, Walter de Merton, of a house for poor scholars where, in their own country and under secular rule, they would receive education of a more liberal sort than had hitherto been possible.

But the King and Queen had their difficulties. Though Alexander of Scotland had sworn fealty for his English fiefs, not so had Llewellyn of Wales, vassal though he was and contracted to Eleanor de Montfort, the King's cousin. Like another turbulent vassal of the King he held that "to God alone do I owe homage for my land and to no other be he duke, count or king".

The Queen's hands were full arranging disputes among the poor relations who brought their grievances to be redressed by the new order—every Court had its Adullam—and she had also to avert or to mitigate the demands made upon the King by his mother, the storm centre of the family, who after the manner of distinguished dowagers had retreated to a convent at Amesbury. The children had to be settled in their new quarters, a part of the palace of Westminster called Maiden Hall, where their mother instituted the harmless and agreeable habit she had acquired in the East of warm baths, no doubt to the affronting of her household much as when she scandalised the London citizens by her curtains and carpets. But now she was Queen indeed, and might do what she would; and the people took knowledge of her that "to our nation she was a loving mother, the column and pillar of the realm, a godly, modest and merciful princess; in her time the English nation was not harassed by foreigners nor the country people by the purveyors of the Crown; the sorrowful she consoled as became her dignity and she made them friends that were at discord".

One sure though quite adventitious cause of her popularity was the steady and punctual increase of her family. Then it was commendation enough to call a woman "fruitful", irrespective of whether or how the fruit matured. From parents of the mettle of this couple, men children only might have been expected, yet of their family of twelve only four were sons, of whom but one survived childhood. Four of their eight daughters died young, and only one of all the family attained middle age.

It is hard to see how their mother could have had any leisure. The King gave her a set of chessmen curiously wrought in jasper and amber, one of the trophies of their travels, and chess is only for those who have time on their hands. She certainly took pleasure in beautiful things and encouraged the employment of artists in France and England, for she lived in a happy time for Art, which had lately been loosed from prison to find men waiting and worthy to express it in many lovely forms. But all that she did was done quietly and naturally for she was "a modest princess", not like her mother-in-law, the trumpeter of her own activities.

One art understood by the King was holiday-making, usually tinctured by pious observance. One April day "when 1275 longen folk to go on pilgrimages" he set forth with the Queen for the shrine of St Edmund in Suffolk to fulfil a vow made in Palestine. Hoof and harness of horse and palfrey would ring pleasantly by the slow waterways and quick windmills of the Fen country; and if the going at times were rough or weary, the King could lighten it with tales of his shifts and skirmishes and triumphs on the road to Ely nine years ago. At this time Ely's bishop was Hugh de Balsham, a sturdy and successful example of the national English spirit. From the office of sub-prior in the monastery he had fought his way, backed by his brethren, to the bishop's seat in spite of the opposition of the late king and queen who had favoured first one and then another foreigner. He simplified matters by going himself quietly to Rome where the Pope secured to him the mitre for his own head and, for those of his monks, the right "to wear caps suited to their order during service in the church because Ely is set on a hill and exposed to cold and sharp winds".

The royal pilgrims were wise if they turned a little out of their way to rest beneath the roof of this comfortable prelate; and as no travellers worth their salt are indifferent to their fellows on the road, so they might ask the Bishop about the sturdy beggars, poor scholars from the neighbouring University who acclaimed them and craved largesse. At this time the University was in his jurisdiction as Bishop of Ely; and he was one who took note of his responsibilities. If he did entertain the King and Queen on their way to St Edmundsbury, he may have opened his mind to them about a scheme he had of a foundation for the poor scholars of Cambridge after the pattern of Walter de Merton's house at Oxford.

Soon after this the trouble in Wales became acute, and the King made Shrewsbury the headquarters of the Government, the Queen going there with him; he then passed to Chester, clearing the country of forest and building castles along the border. After nearly three years Llewellyn gave in, swore fealty to the King and kept Christmas with the family at Westminster. His promised bride, Eleanor de Montfort the King's cousin and ward, had meanwhile been sheltered in Maiden Hall with the King's children as a hostage; those years were probably the happiest of her brief, tragic life. When the Queen returned from France, whither she had gone to pay homage for her dower lands on the death of her mother, there was a fine wedding in Worcester Cathedral. "Gone to be married, gone to swear a peace"; this princess was done with peace when she cast in her lot with Llewellyn, and not thus could Edward establish his supremacy in Wales. By this marriage with a descendant of King John, Llewellyn had reckoned that his children would have a claim on the crown of England; so he was soon up again and over the border, his homage forsworn. But he fell fighting by the Wye; his head was struck off and exposed as a traitor's by the Tower of London, while the gold circlet—King Arthur's crown—it had once worn was offered at the shrine of St Edward in Westminster Abbey by Prince Alfonso, the heir of England. The little orphan Gwenllian was hurried from her mountains to a convent in the Fens where she spent a long life as a nun. King Edward was not taking any chances of a Welsh succession.

During a breathing space in the Welsh campaign the King and Queen, suitably accompanied by the Archbishop of Canterbury, went to Glastonbury "when the King had the tomb of King Arthur opened whose bones he caused to be removed so as to behold the length and bigness of them". It could do Edward Longshanks no harm to look for once upon a bigger man than himself.

Christmas of that year was kept at St Edmundsbury where 1280 the King signed letters patent permitting Hugh Bishop of Ely "to put into his hospital of St John at Cambridge in lieu of the secular brethren there, studious scholars who shall in everything live together as students of the University of Cambridge according to the rule of the scholars at Oxford called of Merton".

It is well seen that Queen Eleanor was a hardy traveller; wherever the King went, whatever the season or her state of health, in peace or war, this soldier's wife and daughter followed the flag. Sometimes along with her went the young Eleanor, and Joanna (already a far-travelled child), Margaret and Mary, encouraged in a love of change and adventure which they never lost. Their childhood was a very different matter from their mother's in the highlands of Castile of which wild Wales may have put her in mind. She seems to have had no fear of its strange people though the King revived and enforced an old law by which "those shall be punished who shall push or strike the Queen or snatch anything from her hand".

The Welsh campaign did not consist so much in field warfare as in punitive sallies and skirmishes having for their base

one or other of the castles with which the border was now fortified. These were never meant either for splendour or domestic
occasions; yet in them the Queen too had her struggles and
1283 her triumphs. In Rhuddlan Castle one summer morning,
she bore her ninth child and fifth daughter Elizabeth, hence
called the Welshwoman. The following spring she moved to
the new castle of Caernarvon before it was quite finished; there,
in a narrow dark chamber in the thickness of the wall, in conditions that would appal a modern midwife, her fourth son was
1284 born. He was called Edward, and one Mary of Caernarvon
nourished him.

It may be that his birth on the soil of Wales, under the brow
of Snowdon, was a stroke of policy on the part of the King; but
more was to depend on this infant than the principality
of Wales. In August of that year he became the heir of all
England by the death of his brother Alfonso, the son whom
God had given in Rome twelve years before. To add to the
Queen's grief came news from Spain of the death of her
brother the elder Alfonso.

The end of that "bright, particular star" was inglorious. The
fact of his descent from Philip, the Emperor, had roused in him
imperial longings which to realise he had debased the currency
of the kingdom and overtaxed his subjects. When they rebelled,
his sister Eleanor and her husband tried to mediate and mend
matters but in vain; Alfonso was deposed and his son set up in
his place, the Church the while looking on coldly, for this
son of holy Ferdinand had yoked himself with unbelievers.
Besides there was that unlucky remark about a better ordering
of the universe which has traversed the ages to sound in our
ears as a truism, though then a blasphemy. So this man of
vigorous mind and whimsical humour fell by Lucifer's sin,

22

though not into a bottomless pit but a peaceful retreat in flowery Seville—no bad close to the life of a philosopher.

About this time Archbishop Kilwardby, who had crowned the King and Queen, bespoke their help for the Friars Preachers who were moving from the outskirts of the City to a new settlement nearer the river Thames. Now St Dominic who first sent them forth to preach the Gospel in all lands was a Castilian and had lived at the Court of Alfonso the Noble, great-grandfather of the Queen. Amongst her earliest memories of Las Huelgas must have been a picture on one of its walls of Alfonso, his queen Eleanor and their descendants (including the infant saints Louis and Ferdinand), with St Dominic in a corner blessing them all. So the Queen re-founded the house of the Black Friars; and the tomb of her child Alfonso was ordered there. The picture has long faded from the convent wall in Castile; and by London river remains only the name of the Black Friars; but the Word passes not away.

In May of this year the Bishop of Ely asked and obtained 1284 from the King a charter whereby his scholars in the University of Cambridge were separated from the rule of the brethren of the Hospital and of the White Canons and given "two hostels by the churchyard of St Peter without the Trumpenton Gate together with the church itself and the tithes of the mills". Thus was Peterhouse the first-born of the University; though its foundations were laid in sorrow for the brave bishop "who at this time deceased at his manor of Downham".

The next year saw the completion of "the new work of the Church of Westminster by which season it appears to have been re-edifying about the space of sixty years".

As Wales was sullenly settling down, so was Gascony beginning to ferment; the King and Queen therefore went to Aquitaine where they stayed for three years and did much business. Eleanor their eldest child was contracted to Alfonso the young King of Aragon, the Queen bore yet two more daughters, all Jews were banished from the territory, and the King took the Cross at Bordeaux with the idea, at forty-five, of making another Crusade. But his English barons protested by the mouth of their chief, Gilbert de Clare, and summoned him home or supplies would be stopped. Return he did but he took his own time. With wife and daughters and Mary of Brittany his niece, he made a patriarchal progress through Kent, Essex and Suffolk to Dereham in Norfolk where "with four stout mariners of Spalding" the party took the water and travelled by way of Ely to Fen Ditton near Cambridge where they disembarked. For dwellers on the banks of the river Cam it is cheering to find that Fen Ditton was used later by this family as a health resort.

The Queen brought back from Gascony the orphan son of a knight of the country and installed him as a companion to her little brotherless Edward; his name was Piers Gaveston. About this time also she arranged the marriage of her kinswoman, Margaret de Fiennes, with Edmund de Mortimer; their son was Roger de Mortimer. Thus from two innocent acts of kindness was bred the ruin and confusion that was to follow the comet's career—as foretold by the seers at the King's birth.

The King's mother was ready for him on his return with two of her bright ideas, one for the salvation of the kingdom, the other of the family. Encouraged by the expulsion of the Jews from Aquitaine, she required him to do the same in England by the people she herself had brought there and to whom she was at this time deeply in debt. Having first secured the Pope's permission to keep her dowry, she had taken the veil in the convent of her retreat at Amesbury; now she exhorted her son to emulate her piety and give one of his many daughters to the Church. So much did she pester both parents that, in spite of the mother's intense reluctance, ten-year-old Mary was professed in the same convent as her grand-mother. She had a grant from the King of the forest of Saver-nake to furnish wood for her chamber fire, and the dues of Southampton port provided wine and oil for her table.

In the shadow of this parting the Queen must arrange for the worldly weddings of two of Mary's elder sisters—Joanna to the Earl of Gloucester and Margaret to John, Duke of Brabant. Joanna's wedding banquet was calculated to impress the foreign bridegroom and be worthy of the English one who was richer than any of them. In the dull list of gold and silver plate that furnished forth the marriage tables there is one bright spot when, almost with awe, it is recorded that forks were used. To meet the cost of these festive occasions the King, with a touch of his mother's financial craft, levied an extra tax on all new knights "pour filles marier". But while Joan and Meg pranced off with their fine husbands, did not the mother's heart go out to Moll the novice of Amesbury?

Before going to Gascony the King had arranged the betrothal of his son to Margaret of Norway, the heiress of her grand-father King Alexander III of Scotland; she was also Edward's great-niece. After King Alexander's death there was much to-do with the Scots about the conditions of the alliance, that wary people being on their guard lest the kind uncle trespass on their independence. But one of them, having heard a rumour that the little queen was ailing, sent secretly to Edward coun-selling him to be near the Border "to prevent bloodshed and

1286

enable the faithful [*sic*] men of the realm to choose for their king him that ought to be so ". So the autumn Parliament was summoned to meet at Clipstone in Sherwood Forest, where also was plentiful good hunting, and by August the Court was at Northampton.

Queen Eleanor was now nearly fifty years old and about to journey to a wilder, stranger country than any she had yet known. This or the fact that her splendid health showed signs of failing may have been the reason why she arranged her affairs. It is now that the Queen's Grace remembers the poor scholars of Cambridge and gives to the University fifty marks for their use. She is the first royal person to make such a gift. More than sixty years before this, King Henry III had so far shown he was aware of his Universities as to invite a migration of students from Paris to Oxford and Cambridge, but he was the last to concern himself with the means of their maintenance. His daughter-in-law had a quick sense of the needs of poor people and her own ways of finding them out. Her will is taken up not so much with provision for her comfort in the next world as with motherly remembrance of many who had served her in this one.

In the early days of September she became sick of a fever and stayed her journey at Herdeby, close to the Great North Road, where she was received into the house of a gentleman whose son was one of her knights. The young King of Aragon who was engaged to marry her eldest daughter sent her his physician; it is thought that the priest who ministered to her was also from her own country.

By the end of the month came news of the death of the little Maid of Norway while on the way to take her kingdom. Still the King made no hurry to go to the North, for the

Queen who had never failed him before was now to journey forth alone. Well was he to remember Scotland's patron saint, for on Tuesday in the Octave of St Andrew died "the lady Alianore, Queen of England, our consort to whom we were joined in the days of childhood". Nov. 1290

> "He loved her well and it was meet,
> For young she was when given to him.
> So did they use their love for each other
> That more than sister unto brother,
> Their two hearts joined in one good will,
> For joy or grief, for good or ill."

After the body of St Louis was brought home, fair stone crosses were raised where the bier rested on the road between St Denis and Paris. Edward and Eleanor must have seen them and kneeled before them; and he now took this way of commemorating her who was a loving mother to his people. Before or since it was never so done in England; very differently when his time came was the King to order the manner of his own obsequies. The artists he employed for the Queen's crosses were, with one exception, English; some of them were variously gifted like Alexander the Imaginator who was an artist in metal and also the painter of the cloth that covered her coffin.

The Queen's heart was laid beside her child Alfonso in the Black Friars' Church of her founding; her body was carried to Westminster Abbey to rest amidst the glowing mosaics of the Chapel of St Edward at the feet of King Henry to whom in life she was a loving and comfortable daughter. Her effigy designed and fashioned in metal by the Englishman William Torrell has life and character besides being exquisite in itself.

27

The tombs were once inlaid with gems brought for the purpose from Palestine by the royal pilgrims; none of them ever shone so fair as two lines from the Queen's epitaph which used to hang at the side:

> "She did increase her husband's friends
> And also enlarged his honour."

In all her life there was nothing to hide and little to explain or excuse. She took it as it came neither missing nor straining the chances it gave her "all noble hearts to encourage for ensample and matter of honour".

CHAPTER II

ELIZABETH DE BURGH

The Lady of Clare

I

When Edward I came to England as King in the autumn of the year 1274, he and his family rested on the road from Dover to London at Tonbridge Castle, of which the lord was Gilbert de Clare, called the Red, Earl of Gloucester and Hertford, one of the three men who kept the country together after the death of King Henry and secured a peaceful succession for his son. The Red Earl was descended from one of two brothers, who came to England with their kinsman, Duke William of Normandy, and were among the "wise men at Gloucester with whom he held deep speech" resulting in that survey of the country's resources known as Doomsday Book. The Conqueror gave his kinsmen large gifts of land which they shared roughly after the way of Abraham and Lot, Baldwin going to the West and Richard, called Bienfaite, to the East, where among the Saxon kingdoms was the castle and market town of Clare. One of his sons returned to the West country and founded Tintern Abbey, another was Prior of Ely, a third held Tonbridge Castle against William Rufus; their sister was wife to William Tyrrell who sped the arrow that killed that king. Clare was taken as the family name by Bienfaite's grandson, the father of Strongbow, who carried it to Ireland and planted it there; seventh in descent from Bienfaite was Richard who with his son Gilbert joined the other barons in securing the rights of the Great

Charter. Thus, alternating Richards and Gilberts, the Clares passed down the years taking foremost places in the country's annals, the while by timely service and wisely directed matrimonial affections they managed so to enlarge their scope as to become the first family of the baronage.

The Red Earl was contracted in marriage when a child of nine to Alice of Angoulême, one of a band of young ladies brought into England by King Henry's half-brothers as likely wives for some of the nobles; she was older than Gilbert, there was no son of the marriage, and both parties desired its dissolution. At the time he entertained the King and Queen he was waiting for the necessary papal dispensation; when, after fifteen years he obtained it, he sued for the hand of the King's second daughter Joanna of Acre.

She had been already twice disappointed of matrimony by the deaths of one and another foreign princeling to whom she was betrothed before she could speak. Here was an Englishman "after the King most mighty in deed and discourse, prudent in counsel, vigorous in arms and very bold in defence of his rights". If there were a drawback, it was the fact that he was three times her age; but he was the richest of her father's subjects and she was one of several daughters. They were married in the beginning of May in Westminster Abbey where the three chevrons of Clare glowed on the wall beside the coat of arms of St Louis the King. The couple remained at Court till July when her sister Margaret was married to John of Brabant, and the Red Earl gave a fine party in the house of the Knights Hospitallers of St John at Clerkenwell.

Queen Eleanor who liked to keep her family about her tried to attach Joanna by the gift of five horses for her chariot; but Joanna not unnaturally used them to ride away bag and baggage on a tour about her husband's estates. First to Tonbridge, then to the West, where at Wynchcombe by Tewkesbury she bore a son and called him—not Richard as he should have been—but Gilbert for his father. This was after the death of Queen Eleanor who never knew a grandchild. In that year also died the Queen dowager at Amesbury. 1292

The next year at her husband's new castle of Caerphilly in Glamorgan Joanna bore a daughter who was naturally named Eleanor. Thereafter with all her mother's punctuality and despatch, Joanna produced two more daughters; but the fierce light that beats upon a throne has not revealed either the birth-places or birthdays of these two grandchildren of the King. They were named respectively Margaret and Elizabeth, the younger having the name of her aunt the Welshwoman.

When giving his consent to the marriage of Joanna with the Red Earl, the Pope had expressed a fatherly hope that he would join the Crusade which Archbishop Peckham was then preaching in England, for Acre had fallen to the Saracens who were driving the Christians out of Palestine. Twenty years earlier Gilbert de Clare had been one of the band of brothers who took the Cross at Northampton with Prince Edward; but he sent his brother Thomas to Palestine in his place. "If I wished to do what was pleasing to God I should remain to aid and defend my people for if I risked my person in the adventures of the Cross I saw clearly it would be for the hurt and damage of my people", was Joinville's answer to King Louis on the same occasion and Gilbert de Clare seems to have agreed with him; they were both careful men. If Joanna had any sentimental desire to visit the land of her birth it was not encouraged by her lord; and, truth to tell, crusading was going out of fashion. But something had to be done, so they generously endowed the

Austin Friars at Clare in Suffolk and Kirkham in Yorkshire, thereby atoning in some degree for the depredations on the Church's property committed by the wicked uncle of the family aptly called Bogo. Earl Gilbert busied himself more than ever with politics and frequent misunderstandings with his father-in-law who got rid of him for a little by appointing him captain of the forces in Ireland. Thither he and his wife went for a year and there it is likely that Elizabeth their youngest child was born.

On their return they found their Welsh tenants in revolt, perhaps because Earl Gilbert had caused some land to be enclosed for preserving game; once before they had tried to poison him. He does not seem to have had the gift of popularity as they have not who know their own minds, go their 1295 own way and leave their mark. In December he died leaving Joanna a widow at twenty-three with four children under six years. Like her grandmother Eleanor of Provence, she had been dowered by the fairies in her cradle with one of their most-to-be-coveted gifts, supreme belief in herself, and she was one of the richest women in the land. The King lost no time in setting about the business of a second marriage for her, but she was before him there. Soon after her husband's death she took occasion to present to the King one Ralph de Monthermer for knighthood on the score of his services as squire of the body to the Red Earl; before long it became known 1297 that they were man and wife.

There are times in the lives of every one of us when our world seems to fall in ruins about us; so it was with the King at the moment. Wales and Scotland would not cease from troubling; King Philip his overlord in France showed signs of holding on to Aquitaine like one of its own leopards. While

Edward himself was seeking a second wife in Blanche of France, Philip the Fair (and false), having more dazzling prospects for her, passed off upon the elderly Jacob her more homely sister Margaret. Within the family, his only son gave the King cause for uneasiness; now here was his desirable Joanna not content to settle down with a second advantageous husband and bring up a possible heir to the throne but secretly marrying one of her household and cheating the King into knighting the fellow.

About this time the keeper of the privy purse had to pay "for making good a large ruby and emerald lost out of the coronet of the bride—the Countess of Holland—when the King's Grace was pleased to throw it behind the fire". The marriage of Elizabeth the Welshwoman was then proceeding; she was a good girl and reliable in the midst of a perverse generation, meekly marrying the husband provided for her; it could not have been her behaviour that caused this expensive damage to her father's temper.

The King's anger had other manifestations; Joanna's son was removed from her custody, she was deprived of her estates—except Tonbridge Castle which her devoted seneschal refused to give up even to the King—and her husband was imprisoned in her own castle of Bristol. But she was Edward's own child in resourcefulness and instinct for success. She rallied to her cause such persons of influence as her young stepmother the new Queen, her cousin Joanna the Countess of Pembroke and Anthony de Bek the gallant Bishop of Durham, though her surest allies were her own wits. Once a squire of low degree loved the king's daughter of Hungary; and there was that lord of Saluzzo who took Griselda a peasant girl to wife. By the mouth of the Bishop Joanna told her father that "as it was no disgrace for a great and mighty earl to wed a poor woman in lawful union so it could not be blame-worthy for a countess to advance a capable young man, which answer pleased the King and his anger was appeased". He may have had a weakness for his child of the Crusade. Monthermer was released and accepted for the good soldier and honest man he was, and the loves of Joanna and her knight were sung by minstrels in hall and barn throughout the country.

At first Joanna and her family lived in Marlborough Castle, her husband who was one of the wardens of Scotland going to and fro. The triumphant Countess bore him a daughter Mary and two sons Thomas and Edward. The custody of Gilbert de Clare remained in the hands of Queen Margaret; though a good deal younger than his uncle Edward he was admitted to his companionship and that of Piers Gaveston from which, however, he does not appear to have taken any harm. When his mother who must be in the midst of whatever was afoot joined her husband in Scotland, the rest of her family—Clares and Monthermers—were bestowed in one of the houses in Windsor Castle granted by the King to Joanna on her widowhood.

We know little of their childhood except that it was brief, for, at the age when our children are still at school, they were on the verge of matrimony or knighthood or both. With regard to the most serious affairs of life their future was ordered for them from their earliest years when they were strange little beings in hampering clothes that were but copies of their elders'. They lived among a throng of relations coming and going which always helps to quicken the wits; there is this to be said for King Henry III and his queen, that they seem to have bred in their descendants a sense of family obligation and tolerance. They were continually jaunting about visiting each other. The King's eldest child Eleanor followed abroad the tragic fortunes of her husband the Comte de Bar and clave to him; but Elizabeth the Welshwoman returned from Holland when she became a widow, speedily re-married and added her successive babies to the nurseries in Windsor Castle. Margaret did sometimes visit Brabant her husband's country but preferred taking a hand with Joanna in the civilising of Scotland or joining their brother who with Piers Gaveston kept open house at King's Langley and Mortlake. These daughters of the King would not readily forget their father's house. Chief among them was the nun Mary whose spiritual ancestor was not so much St Ferdinand as King Henry. Like him she belonged to "the large and generous class of borrowers", and, like him, she had a soul above repayment. Though amply provided for by her father, she never had any money; lightly, happily, naturally, she borrowed from her brothers and sisters or at a pinch from her grooms, with whom, if none better offered, she would throw a main, for she loved gambling. So it was not for her, like her decorous cousin Eleanor of Britanny, to come at last to be Abbess; but when there was friction between her house of Amesbury and its parent of Fontevraud in France she was a pleasant mediator and could be trusted to get the King's good ear. Always ready to oblige with her company the expectant mothers among her relations, she was a merry lady and must have been a welcome visitor at the house in the inner bailey of Windsor Castle.

Athwart the mysteries veiling the overheard talk of the grown-up children, the little pitchers would gather notions of what was going on in that curious upper world; the new Queen's chances of popularity, the pity of the great fire in

Westminster Palace so that she must keep her state at the Tower where there was danger of infection from a disfiguring disease brought by the pilgrims from Syria and now rife in the city: the strange cure for it by the Queen's physician who caused one patient "to be enveloped in scarlet cloth, his bed and all the furniture of his chamber of a bright red colour", in spite of which he disconcertingly recovered with not a mark of the pox on him.

1298   News would filter through from Scotland of the great victory at Falkirk where Joanna's champion Bishop Anthony de Bek had himself led five hundred men; and the London citizens went mad with joy of the victory, especially (and mysteriously) the Guild of Fishmongers who devised a pageant of knights glittering in gold and silver "like great salmon and luces of the sea".

In time there came to Windsor the Queen's babies to be played with and led into mischief as when "Martinet the tabourer, making minstrelsy for the Lords Thomas and Edmund the King's sons, claims seven shillings for the repairing of his tabour broken by them". The music of the time, even of dances and love-songs, being of the most piercing and unbearable melancholy, who shall blame the poor infants?

Certainly not the King whose meteoric appearances meant junketing and fun save when he fell into strange fits of passion about some new devilry of Piers' devising. Sometimes it was muttered that the mother of that impish Gascon orphan had been burned for a witch, and that he had inherited her spells for "with his conversation all the world was, as it were, infected". Not Prince Edward only but his sisters took Piers' part against the King and secretly helped him out of many a scrape.

Their cousin the young Robert de Brus Earl of Carrick came South in these days to be married to a daughter of the King's friend (and creditor for Edward too was a borrower) Richard de Burgh, the greatest man in Ireland; the bands of marriage were constantly and not unskilfully used by the King to secure more firmly the allegiance of his vassals. He kept his Christmas at Dunfermline where he had news that the rebel Wallace had been trapped at last. So in Westminster Great Hall, with a mocking crown of laurel on his head, he was tried and condemned to die a traitor's death, though there were some who held he was no traitor for he had never taken the oath of homage to King Edward. But of Robert de Brus it were shame even to speak, for not only did he kill the King's Regent on the very steps of God's altar, but while living free and friendly at the Court he had caused to be fashioned secretly "a coronal of gold for a fitting occasion. For this heavy trespass and malefaction of Geoffrey de Coigners the goldsmith" Queen Margaret had obtained his pardon from the King. But for staunch Countess Isabella of Buchan whose eager hands placed that coronal on the head "of the King's rebel and enemy in Scotland", there was none to plead, for she was shut up in a cage on the walls of Berwick. "So let all thine enemies perish, O King", would be the natural comment of Edward's following.

Before long it was whispered that Piers Gaveston had incited the lord Edward to ask the King for Ponthieu, Queen Eleanor's dowry, that he might give it to Piers, and that the two young men were summoned to Lanercost whither they went with a gay following of foreign fiddlers and soft diversions to appear before the gaunt King and his hard-bitten fighting men. The dreadful news came back that Piers the gay companion had been banished from the kingdom and the Prince was broken-hearted.

Wallace's noble head was stark on Tower Hill and Isabella of Buchan had died on the walls of Berwick when King Edward returned to keep Christmas in his Palace of Westminster re-built and resplendent after the fire. He brought as hostage in his train the Bruce's wife who being the daughter of an important ally must be gently treated. She was a cynical half-hearted lady, soured by the life she had led since her marriage to him she called "a summer king"; she did not hold with spiders nor any who encouraged him in his strange passion for that comfortless land. While he was hunted about its wintry hills and glens by men who had been his friends and brothers in arms, she shared in the festivities at Westminster. There was a great tourney, and the King's son was knighted with two hundred other young nobles, giving fine choice of husbands for the King's granddaughters. Eleanor de Clare was betrothed to Hugh le Dispenser, one of a vigorous, upstart family from the Welsh border, and Elizabeth to John de Burgh the heir of the Earl of Ulster; Margaret the middle one was biding her time and with her mother's connivance. Joan the little Damoiselle de Bar who had come to England an orphan and found a friend for life in Elizabeth de Clare was betrothed to Earl Warren and married in May on the same day as Eleanor de Clare whose brother Gilbert was then knighted by the King.

The next year at the age of thirty-five their mother died and was magnificently buried—not in Tewkesbury Abbey the Clares' long home but at Clare in the Church of the Austin Friars. Because of her generosities to that and other foundations she was called a "full holy woman", which may be true enough but is hardly an apt description of such a complete child of this world as was Joanna of Acre. Her father died a few months later on Solway Sands in sight of that ungrateful country which owed him much, for, as has been said, he hammered its people into a nation.

II

To many who had thriven under his shelter the death of Edward I must have seemed the end of all things, but to others a relief, and his son would be among these. At least from him came no wild burst of grief and the world rolled on not at all in the old King's way. It has been noticed that the childhood of such as Edward II was brief, but not so was his, for all his life he was a child and a spoiled one, taken up with toys of which the chief was his kingdom. One of his first acts was to recall Piers Gaveston on whom he heaped principalities and powers snatched from worthier men, adding in the end his richly dowered niece Margaret de Clare in marriage.

The family's hereditary tendency to matrimony was having full play. Gilbert de Clare having received "license to marry whom he would" his grandfather had carefully arranged he should take to wife Maud de Burgh, said to be the fairest of Ulster's daughters. Before the King departed to France for his own marriage, he was present at his nephew's in Waltham Abbey where at the same time his niece Elizabeth fulfilled her Michael-contract with John de Burgh. mas 1308

They were all of the Conqueror's kin, and the Ulster family was a branch of that of Hubert de Burgh, King John's Chancellor, with which the Clares had intermarried. It may once and for all be taken for granted that almost if not all persons of

rank at this time were related to the King or to each other or
to both.

If Elizabeth now went to Ireland with her husband she was
probably returning to the land of her birth and would find that
a large part of it bore her family name brought by Strongbow
and fastened later by her uncle Thomas de Clare. Her husband
was heir to about half of the country; as one of "the obedient
English in Ireland" he held his possessions at his sword's point
and was constantly in and out of strife with the native chiefs.
During the year after his marriage the place was surprisingly
peaceful although the King's Lord Deputy was Piers Gaveston;
but to give him his due the Gascon was one of Ireland's successful governors. Three years later Elizabeth came to England for
the birth of her son who as a descendant of one of the first
Edward's daughters had his own small place in the succession
to the throne. The King had special information of the birth
from his sister, the nun Mary, who was obliging her niece with
her good company on the occasion.

What a store of gossip she would bring!—the beauty of the
young Queen Isabelle, her splendid Paris trousseau—the fruit
of the spoiling of the Templars—the discontent of her critical
French uncles at Piers' mismanagement of the Coronation, the
banquet being served so late to the starving guests that all the
food was spoiled; but Piers' honours had gone to his head and
he put everyone past patience with his airs and the play he gave
to his loose, witty tongue; not that the King seemed to care and
the King's sister was content and enjoyed the outing, for her
brother paid all her charges as their father used to do and sent
her away with a gift in her hand. The inner history of Piers'
disgrace would come out, only Aymer de Valence and young
Earl Gilbert countenancing him, and the King was frantic

about his murder, but if the Queen's expected child should be a boy he might be in a measure comforted; Piers' glories had been stripped from his widow, but their little daughter's future was assured for she was now a novice and would be veiled at Amesbury; the pity of Queen Isabelle's temper, Queen Margaret, "good without lack", being the only one who could rule her when she was vexed; she could not abide Eleanor's husband Hugh Dispenser, and though the King too had seemed to hate him he was now taking him to his bosom in Piers' room, while the Queen would rather advance Roger de Mortimer their kinsman. So might the two women talk over the cradle of young William de Burgh while dragons' teeth were sowing.

When the child was a year old his father died in Ireland 1313 and he thus became his grandfather's heir; an uncle had custody of him for a while; later, he was returned to his mother.

Next year about the feast of Pentecost the King went North with the flower of his kingdom to relieve the beleaguered English garrison in Stirling Castle. When his father was dying he had charged him as he hoped for victory to lay his bones— not in the Abbey—but in a black bull's skin and carry them at the head of the army when it marched against the Scots. In this as in many other respects the grand old savage was not obeyed, and his son now the father of a third Edward rode through the spring land in the conqueror's vein, "to make and mar the foolish Fates". But Gilbert de Clare who was to lead the van of the army knew better; he had not been one of the wardens of Scotland for nothing, and the soldiers knew that the Bruce had said he feared the bones of the dead father more than the living son.

On the eve of St John Baptist's Day the English camped under Stirling Castle over against the Scots; then Gilbert de Clare advised his uncle to give the army a rest over the Saint's day. The pettish King answered with accusations of cowardice and treachery, the Bruce and Gilbert being both cousins and brothers-in-law. To such taunts there was but one answer. The next day when the battle was joined "the Earl of Gloucester threw himself upon the Scots like a wild boar making his sword drunk with their blood". But his horse stumbled and threw him; helpless in his armour he was overwhelmed and lost. His body pierced by many lances was found afterwards by a Franciscan friar and carried to the King of Scots who sent it to King Edward with all honourable observance and words of grief for the death of so brave a man.

With him ended the bright promise of his house for he left no living son. He was laid in Tewkesbury Abbey beside his 1315 father; a year later his little widow Maud de Burgh came to rest beside them, the end of a gallant story. Yet not so, for upon her tomb are the words:

"We seek that which is to come."

Gilbert de Clare's three sisters "of the whole blood" were declared his heirs, excluding his father's daughters by the first wife, and the Monthermers. Eleanor le Dispenser had the honour of Gloucester, Margaret now the wife of Lord Audley the honour of Tonbridge and Elizabeth de Burgh the honour of Clare and of Usk.

The disaster of Bannockburn would appal the English people, used as they were to the conquering habits of the old King; and hard upon its heels came famine, nor was the kingdom at peace within itself. "If one looks upon the land behold

darkness and sorrow; and the light is quenched in the heavens."
The tale of the comet was remembered that heralded the birth
of the King's father; and the murky confusion that was to
follow it. Nevertheless, as people will, they went on marrying
and giving in marriage, particularly the widow de Burgh who
early in the next year was taken to wife by her second cousin
Theobald de Verdun.

He was descended from the lords of Verdun on the Meuse,
one of whom had come to England as butler to the Conqueror.
From him the family had large estates in Ireland, of which
country Theobald was lieutenant justiciar at this time. His
grandfather had followed the Cross with Edward I, his father
was foremost in that prince's counsels, he himself had a
brilliant record of service in France and Scotland. He had
three daughters by his first wife who was a sister of Roger de
Mortimer; thus by both marriages he was closely enmeshed
in the web of kinship that knitted the Court about. He and
Elizabeth de Burgh were married "secretly", that is without
the knowledge of the King whose ward she was, but who,
when the fact became known, received it pleasantly as an uncle
should; at any rate, on this occasion, the Crown jewels did not
suffer. Like her mother Elizabeth may have thought this time
to take her own way and marry for love; though it was not
given to her to hold it long for within a year Theobald de
Verdun died.

Again the nun princess came to the rescue and sheltered her   1316
niece in the convent at Amesbury where, three months later,
a daughter was born and christened Isabelle after the Queen.

In the following May her undaunted mother essayed
matrimony for the third time, with Sir Roger d'Amory of
Bletchington in Oxfordshire. Strangely enough he does not

seem to have been related to her though, like her first husband, he was one of that "band of brothers" knighted on New Year's Day 1306. This marriage took place with the consent and high approval of the King who gave the couple three manors—one of them Vauxhall—in consideration of d'Amory's services at Bannockburn.

The next year a daughter was born to them in a time of alarms and confusions. After the death of Queen Margaret, who had kept some check on her niece's violent temper, the quarrels between the King and Queen, fanned by the Dispensers and the Mortimers, flamed into war. Lord d'Amory cast in his lot with Thomas of Lancaster the leader of the Queen's party, he having like many others no use for Hugh the younger Dispenser. In a fighting retreat after the battle of Boroughbridge, Amory was wounded and died a prisoner in Tutbury Castle 1322 on March 14.

For his share in the struggles that rent the country he had been frequently respited and forgiven by the King his wife's uncle; yet two days after his death she and her young son William de Burgh were imprisoned in the Abbey of Barking and forced "under stress and fear of death for herself and him" to give up her valuable Welsh estates to Hugh Dispenser and his wife because five years previously she had married Theobald de Verdun without the King's knowledge or consent. As the marriage took place at Bristol of which Eleanor Dispenser had the honour, it was no doubt with the knowledge if not the connivance of her and her husband.

The following Christmas Elizabeth was held captive at York, again at his instance, until she signed a bond promising "not to marry or dispose of any of her lands without the King's license on pain of forfeiting all she possessed".

Truly she was not happy in her brothers-in-law nor does the story reflect pleasantly on sister Eleanor. Piers Gaveston was his own worst enemy; but the other "though in body very comely was in spirit proud and in action most wicked, whose covetousness and ambition by the disinheriting of widows and strangers, brought the death of the nobles, the fall of the King with the bitter destruction of himself and his father".

After which the widow of Lord d'Amory naturally retrieved her property; and in the first Parliament of the next reign the bond she had signed at York was annulled "as against law and all reason". However, she had already taken a vow of perpetual chastity, being done with matrimony for herself.

III

Behold her then, at the age of twenty-eight a widow indeed with the children God had given her, one by each husband: William de Burgh aged ten, Isabel de Verdun aged six, and Elizabeth d'Amory not quite four. Hers was not an age of portraiture and there is no authentic presentment of her; but since three gentlemen had her to wife, it may be supposed that, as was sung of another granddaughter of Eleanor of Castile,

> "She was sweet and debonnaire,
> Courteous, homely, pleasant and fair."

Though Theobald de Verdun and Roger d'Amory were peers their families did not rank as high as that of her first husband which is why she went back to his name; her title she took from Clare of which she had inherited the honour. "An Honour", says Cokayne, "was a great Barony held in chief of the Crown of which inferior baronies formed the parts, every

honour having a *caput* or chief seat commonly called a castle."
Clare Castle in Suffolk was then her chief seat and home from
which she administered her children's properties and such of
her own as had not then been reft from her.

At that time widowhood and inheritance did not necessarily
mean a sudden call to the direction of affairs; for while the
lord was absent, as he mostly was, in the King's business, or in
prison, it was the lady's part to abide by the stuff and cherish it
so that, if return he ever did, it should not be to panic and
emptiness. Elizabeth's three husbands had been active soldiers
as well as owners of property; so her hand was used to the
helm. Her inheritances were diverse and complicated; but in
her was joined the long head of the Clares with the light heart
and happy temper of her mother's family, and the strong will
common to both: besides she had the *Rules of St Robert* to help
her. Fifty years before she was born, a great scholar and father
in God had given them to her great-grandmother the Countess
of Lincoln, like herself a rich young widow with a son in his
minority. "Whosoever will keep these rules will be able to
live on his means and keep himself and those belonging to
him", says Robert Grosseteste who is said to have been "in
housekeeping liberal and in corporate refection plentiful".
Besides giving clear, practical direction about everything to
do with the cultivation of land, he does not disdain to treat
particularly of such anxious matters within the castle as the
laying of the table, the manner of serving food and drink,
the ordering of servants, their holidays, the practice of good
manners on the part of employer and employed, fault finding
to be given and taken with cheerfulness, "and if any who keep
office in your house will not serve your will and pleasure send
them away and get others who will—of whom you will find

enough"—a statement which cannot but excite a certain wistful envy in the breast of the harassed housekeeper of to-day.

But the beginning and end of St Robert's Rules is the value of personal knowledge and supervision by the lord or lady; that this was understood and practised by the Lady of Clare is clear from her will and her household accounts which reflect the interests and activities of her life. Though she had a council for the direction of her manors and the usual officers of a great household—stewards, constables, marshalls, bailiffs—besides a host of lesser serving men and women, she did not merely "cook her head and order folk about" as has been said of some of her modern counterparts. Punctually she visited her manors scattered over half England, examining into the harvest returns, grain for the mill and malting house, seed for the field, the supply of good water, the breeding of stock, the repair of thatch and bridge and causeway. If it is remembered that each manor was self-contained and that those who worked the land had to be fed by the land, that being held from the King it must supply its quota of men to fight for him, then it may be realised that

> "Vacant heart and brain and eye,
> Easy live and quiet die"

was not the lot of this young woman.

She was a merciful mistress, keeping her servants long, nor forsaking them in their old age; their children grew up under her wing, some of them being sent to Oxford or Canterbury to be educated at her expense for clerkly posts in her household; a clever boy on one of her manors whose wits had outgrown the village school had his fees paid by her at Clare burgh school. *She* had no doubt as to who was her neighbour; by her orders the leaking roof of the holy man's cottage at Thaxted was repaired; as she rode by the gaols of Bury and Colchester she thought upon the sighing of the prisoners within and sent them comforts, remembering the bitter weeks of her own captivity. When the Queen mother fell into disgrace she was not forgotten by this kinswoman who sent that poor Jezebel some of the good sea bream from her Essex fisheries. The executors of her will are charged to remember the needs of "poor religious, women as well as men and others who have fallen on evil days as poor gentlewomen with children, poor pupils of the parish schools, poor traders who through ill chance have lost all and poor prisoners"—echoes of the wars on land and sea from which she never knew her country free.

She had two carriages, one for her own use and another for her damsels, both copiously cushioned, but being innocent of springs or tyres, they must have been vehicles of little ease on the sort of roads they had to travel. For safety as for comfort the horse was the traveller's best friend; the stables of Clare Castle were filled with palfreys and geldings for the Lady and her suite as well as stout rounceys to pull the carts that went before her on her journeys with plenishing for her quarters at nightfall in one of her manors or an approved religious house. Then she would not forget to give thanks for grandfather Edward who first ordained that the King's highway be cleared of all cover except high trees for forty feet on either side so that his lieges might the more safely pass to and fro on their lawful occasions.

The only estates she did not visit personally were the Irish ones which were administered by notaries and so, perhaps, 1326 wastefully. Nor would her son when he became Earl of Ulster and took seisin of his lands have any freedom to look after them. As one of his own vassals said "When strength and courage of valiant men may be found never will I by the grace of God seek to lurk behind dead walls; my fort shall be wherever young blood is stirring and where I can find room to fight in".

"That was their game
To fight with men and storms and it was grand."

But there was another side to it, for when William de Burgh was twenty-one he was "barbarously murdered near Carrickfergus by Richard de Mandeville and others". They must have done him to death with peculiar savagery for the native people of the country rose against them in vain effort to avenge him. As long as his cousin and comrade Edward III was King a sinister saving clause appeared in any amnesty granted in Ireland to malefactors: "always excepting the murderers of William de Burgh".

Not long before this he had married his cousin Maud, daughter of the Earl of Lancaster; so once again in the family of Clare there was a young widow with a child in her arms, and again for Elizabeth the light of her eyes went out in violence. At a time when a strong man armed was hard put to it to keep his goods, she had caused hers to increase and might reasonably have looked for the natural, happy perpetuation of her great name. Yet there was shown to her a more excellent way.

IV

On their manor of Great Baddow in Essex there lived a family, members of that great company of faithful people who go on from father to son down the history of their country quietly and inconspicuously doing their duty. One of them named Richard chose a scholar's life at Cambridge and became Chancellor of the University. Like Hugh de Balsham he was a humane man who was grieved by the difficulties with which his students had to struggle in the pursuit of learning; as Fuller puts it "they could not live to study who could only study to live". So he bought two houses in Mill Street near the marshy river but presumably healthy since they had been a physician's. In them he installed a principal and a number of students who lived at their own charges but were assured of an ordered life and suitable companionship. This hostel called University Hall was not the first of its kind in Cambridge. The house of St Peter, Hugh de Balsham's foundation, had existed for forty years; in 1317 Edward II had placed his King's Scholars in a hired house between High Street and Mill Street. He had also gone to the rescue of St Mary's House of Scholars at Oxford which was refounded by him and later named Oriel College (the first house of learning to have that designation), so that Badew could not ask the King's help when he was busy about University Hall. A third hostel in Cambridge was Michael House, founded at 1326 this time by Canon Hervey de Stanton in the interests of the Church.

These hostels were for residence and discipline only (teaching being given in the churches), and, like most of the dwelling-houses in walled towns, were of wood with thatched roofs which made them liable to the danger of fire. St Bene't's Church in Cambridge still preserves the long-handled hooks for dragging the thatch off burning houses. University Hall 1336 was burnt down after about sixteen years; undauntedly the Chancellor looked about for help to build it up again. The King and Queen had already pre-occupations of the kind,

Edward being the patron of King's Hall while Philippa had her settlements of Flemish weavers at Norwich; but near at hand was a cousin of the King's reputed one of the richest of his subjects. Badew as Chancellor would be aware of her grandmother's gift to the University for the use of poor scholars; Walter de Thaxted the Master of University Hall came from one of the Clare manors and knew the Lady as neighbourly and approachable. So approach her they did and in a good hour.

Her well-dowered daughters and step-daughters were by this time suitably married; her granddaughter Elizabeth as orphan Countess of Ulster was a ward of the King, and Queen Philippa had custody of her. The Lady herself was now forty, an age when an intelligent woman who has fulfilled creditably the functions of wife and mother may reasonably look about her for some fresh interest which shall be more than a pastime. Here a new family was offering itself to her without the perils and complications of matrimony, yet with almost as alluring an aspect of novelty and adventure. Not that the idea was new in the history of her family; her grandfather Richard de Clare gave two of his West Country manors to his vassal Walter de Merton for his foundation for poor scholars at Oxford and her father confirmed the gift. But as yet in England, with the exception of Balliol Hall, no house of learning owed its life to a woman.

She made a ready response. In March she petitioned the 1336 King for licence to give to the Master and Scholars of University Hall in Cambridge the advowson of the church of Litlington in that county; a month later she signed the deed of gift at her manor at Anglesey. From that time a period of every two years marks her successive benefactions to the Hall

1346 and her position as its patroness till in June 1346 she bestowed
the advowsons of the churches of Great Gransden and of Dux-
ford upon the Master and Scholars of *Clare* Hall in the University of Cambridge. The Master and Richard de Badew having
surrendered to her all rights in the Hall, she was now established
as its foundress and changed its name to the most beautiful as
well as the most English of the many that were hers.

Three years previously on finding herself the last surviving
child of Gilbert de Clare and Joanna of Acre, she had planned
a pilgrimage to the land of her mother's birth or, which was
almost as profitable for merit, to the shrine of St James of
Compostela the guardian saint of Castile. But the Pope permitted her to commute the pilgrimage for other good works
"as she was over forty and could not hope to accomplish it".
Good works in the Pope's sense were already to her a matter of
course. At Croweshouse the Castle gate by the Nethergate of
the town of Clare a host of poor persons daily received a penny
each whether the Lady were in residence or no. A Franciscan
Friary was founded by her at Walsingham one year when the
harvest was plentiful and her granges overflowed, What-
shall-I-render? being her response to such challenges. East and
West religious houses of every sort of order fed of her bounty
and she did her duty too by the pet charities of her relations.
As a family they piously "took in each other's washing" in
this respect; though when urged by Queen Philippa the Lady
sent oaks from her park at Hunsden "to repair the houses of the
Scholars whom the King maintains at Cambridge", it does not
appear that there was any response in kind from King or
Queen for the benefit of Clare Hall.

King's Hall was for a special class of scholar: the sons or de-
pendants of prosperous persons holding office about the Court

for whom posts were certain in some department of the state. But Hervey de Stanton required that the Fellows of Michael House "men of good moral character and learned" should be "moreover indigent", and in Clare Hall also there was an insistence upon the claims of poverty. There were to be continually "ten poor scholars, docile, proper, respectable youths the poorest that could be found": they were not, however, "to be sent too often into the town by the Fellows on their errands". It was also suggested that the Fellows "be sparing of inviting guests into College so as not to be burdensome to the rest", from which it may be inferred that the entertainment of their foundress was not often required of them. As the earliest records of the society were destroyed in repeated fires, it is not possible to tell if or when she visited Cambridge after 1336, but there is no doubt she was on comfortable terms with her new family. It would be the easier for her to follow its early fortunes since Henry de Motelot, one of the Fellows elected after 1336—and probably at her instance— was an officer of her household, and later, one of the chief executors of her will. He bought wine and attended markets for her and conveyed the great salmon across the country from the Usk fisheries to Bardfield Manor in Essex for salting. Three fish-days in the week was the diet rule in the Castle except in Advent and Lent when it was six.

In Clare Hall as in Clare Castle the laymen were in the majority; of the Master and Fellows who altogether numbered twenty a third was required to be in priest's orders. That the scope and purpose of education were broadening seems to have been realised by the Lady and her advisers. It may be remarked that in the year that she adopted University Hall, 1336 a law came into force forbidding the Friars, by whom most of the teaching was done, to receive into their Orders any man under the age of eighteen.

In spite of war, poor harvests and the claims of her several foundations, the Lady kept open house at Clare and Usk for her friends and relations whether of the whole or the half blood. Thomas de Monthermer, a soldier like his father, used the castle as his home, while Edward, feeble in mind or body or both, was sheltered there by this half-sister for eighteen years till he was laid beside their mother in the church of the Austin Friars. One Hugh de Burgh, who later became a chief baron of the Exchequer in Ireland, learned his job when managing the Lady's accounts in the Auditestour of the Castle. She was sensitive to the ties of blood; when Queen Isabelle thinking to patch up matters with the Scots made a marriage between her baby daughter Joan of the Tower and David the son of the Bruce, William de Burgh was sent to Berwick with two golden zones and a purse of gold, his mother's wedding gifts to the contracting infants. But she never frequented her uncle's Court whence as he himself is supposed to have said "Wisdom and wit have flown, and beauty vanishéd." Nor in the next reign was she one of "three hundred ladies and damsels all of noble lineage and apparelled accordingly" who attended 1344 Queen Philippa at Windsor on St George's Day when the Order and Brotherhood of the Garter were instituted by the King; but her cousin Joan the Countess Warenne was there and would tell her all about it. For a time one of her sons-in-law was the King's chamberlain; one step-daughter Elizabeth de Verdun married into the notable family of Burghersh who were in the Prince of Wales's battalion at Crecy and were hard pressed but lived to fight again and triumph at Poitiers. Henry de Burghersh the Bishop of Lincoln was a true friend, for he

stored wine for her in the cellars that were Grosseteste's, whence
it was conveyed to Clare by the brothers Motelot on occasions
like the great feasts of the Church or if the King were expected.
For if she went not to Court it came to her; there was a
King's room in the Castle. He was the same age as her son;
they were knighted on the same day by their cousin Wry-neck
great Henry of Lancaster.

With his grandfather's eye for a match the King early
arranged one between his second son Lionel of Antwerp and
Elizabeth of Ulster the Lady's heiress; once again the Clare
blood was to mingle with the King's. Until they should be of
an age to marry the children were brought up together in the
Queen's household, Elizabeth doubtless bringing up fair and
fat Lionel for she was six years his senior. She came often into
Suffolk to see her mother Maud of Lancaster now a nun at
Campsey, and her grandmother at Clare, sometimes bringing
with her her friend Isabelle the King's elder daughter, a girl of
character. She did not marry till the mature age of thirty, re-
acting like her eldest brother from matrimonial policing; those
two took their time and chose for themselves, which must have
considerably bothered Queen Philippa.

As in the fairy tales it was the youngest of the three Clare
sisters who came to the greatest honour; but all the forces of
convention and conformity which rule the lives of such as she
could not avail to press her into a mould and turn her out to
pattern. Something escapes which is herself; and none were
quicker to realise this than the youth of the flock. Like her
aunt the nun Mary she was the sort who are valued "as their
age increases by their nephews and nieces" for they came in
troops about her. Even the children of her persecutor Hugh le
Dispenser were among them. Hugh the third deserved her

notice for he redeemed the honour of his name at Crecy where he was in the King's retinue. Her sister Margaret had picked up her life again in a marriage with Lord Audley; their sons and the Burghershs, beloved of Froissart for their valour and good counsel, would keep the Lady in news about the war that flickered and flamed up and down Flanders and Artois. The names of many an inconsiderable hamlet and port over the water would be as familiar to her then as they have become to us for the same reason six hundred years later. And her men-at-arms, ready in case of invasion, were watching the Essex shores for the pirates who harried the home-coasts.

King, bishops, soldiers, courtiers—the whole chess-board came to Clare and were free of Clarette the great hall of the Castle. "Command strictly", says St Robert, "that all your guests secular and religious be quickly, courteously, and with cheer received by the seneschal from the porters, ushers and marshals and by all be courteously addressed and in the same way honoured and served within your presence and without for in so doing can they show particularly that they wish what you wish. As far as possible constrain yourself to eat in the hall before your people for this shall bring great honour and benefit to you. Forbid dinners and suppers out of the hall in secret and in privy rooms for from this arises waste and no honour to the lord or lady."

But the Lady had a privy room, probably an oratory, "new 1347 fashioned for herself with a window, a chair and bed of bord". Which way did it look—down to the church of the Austin Friars where lay some of her dead or over Essex to the sea?

Among the host of her friends there were three who were dearest to her: in the order of time her cousins Joanna de Bar, the Lady Warenne, and Henry de Grosmont Earl of Lancaster, the brother-in-law of her son; in order of love Marie de St Pol the Countess of Pembroke, widow of another cousin Aymer de Valence, the only one of her friends in whose house she would visit. These three had with her that commerce of interests and enthusiasms without which friendship is a poor affair. It may be noted that at the time Clare Hall was finally adopted and so named by Elizabeth de Burgh, Pembroke Hall was founded by Valence Marie; the same year saw also the beginnings of the College of Corpus Christi by that "honest man, brave soldier, and skilful diplomat" Henry of Grosmont. 1346

When, ten years afterwards, he was created Duke of Lancaster his cousin Elizabeth gave a party for him in her town house by Aldgate which she rented from the Convent of Minoresses there. His grandparents Edmund Crouchback and Blanche of Navarre had founded this religious house so Elizabeth asked the Abbess and all the nuns to meet him— thus bringing together some of the actual and the spiritual kin of St Louis the king whose sister Blessed Isabelle was the first Minoress.

What the Court poet sang of the Duke's daughter Blanche is as true of her elderly cousin:

"And thereto could she be so gay,
At pleasure I will dare to say,
That she was like a torch so bright,
That every man might take its light,
An yet it never shines the less,"

for the Lady of Clare was good at a party and had, besides, what that entails—a strong interest in dress. He was a wise man who observed that "the consciousness of being well dressed gives to a woman a consolation that even religion cannot afford"; many and various were the opportunities this one allowed herself. Her clothes were beautiful even to our ideas, cut as most of them were in long, graceful lines; they were often "three piece" arrangements—a close-fitting under-dress, a sleeveless robe and the mantle, a magnificent, heraldic affair. Then as now the renewal of one's wardrobe was regulated by the feasts of the Church, especially Easter, Whitsuntide and Assumption. Materials ranged from the lustrous velvet new come from Italy to tyretein (tartan?), a useful homespun made in Florence but perhaps deriving its name from Tyre. One dress of russet cloth was such a success that the Lady must have another just like it made for the Countess of Pembroke; the two cost five pounds, nine shillings inclusive of two shillings and fourpence halfpenny "for the shearing" or shaving of threads and thrums that often started on the face of the cloth.

"Your robes purchase at St Ives", advised neighbourly St Robert who had a house at Buckden close by; but his spiritual daughters would take leave to please themselves in this respect. Not long since, another great scholar was challenged to guess the weight of a girl's dancing frock; he put it at half a pound but it did not turn the scale at two ounces. Some of Lady Clare's robes would have been nearer his mark embroidered as they were with gold and gems; she could tell Joanna de Bar how once she had wondered at the hundred and twenty buttons of gold on a dress Joanna's mother had for Assumption.

"Weird" might be the word by which the girl of to-day would describe the hairdressing of that time though the fashion of a snail couchant on each ear was prevalent then as now. Some of the caps and hoods were pointed and fanciful like a jester's; others copied the helmet and gorget of a knight.

An interesting study might be made of women's dress down the ages showing how and when it has imitated—often to advantage—that of men.

The Middle Age was indeed gorgeous at this time and one of the chief figures of the pageant was "that most victorious monarch who reigned in great glory for the space of fifty years; he slew two kings in one day and routed a third, had two kings his prisoners at one time; he had the offer of the Empire though he refused it. He took Calais from the French and instituted the Famous Order of the Garter." "Never had this island brought forth a Prince of such Mature Vertue at so unripe an age." These words of two later chroniclers are quoted here because they express how a large number of his subjects such as the Lady of Clare regarded King Edward III. His business was to fight and slay and desire to have; theirs to help and admire but never to criticise or complain; their King could do no wrong. But from those whose blood and sweat had to pay for all the glory which they could not share there were ominous volcanic mutterings; wandering on the Malvern Hills at this time dreaming dreams and seeing visions there was a man who was soon to make vocal that inarticulate misery. Meanwhile the King went on in his arrogant striving for the lilies of France, doing for its people—if he had only known it— what, far beyond his guess, his grandfather did for the Scots.

Then the blast of the Black Death fell on the shuddering 1349 country "and there was not a house wherein there was not one dead". The King's daughter Joan had it for her bridegroom and was carried to her grave instead of her bridal at Bayonne. Isabelle de Verdun, the child who was cradled and christened in Amesbury Priory after the death of her father, died at this time; she was the widow of Lord Ferrers of Groby and left a daughter Elizabeth who now joined her grandmother's large miscellaneous family in Clare Castle. She was soon married off to David of Strathbogie called Earl of Atholl, a young English lord with a purloined Scots title.

Of the Lady's own three children only the youngest was now left, Elizabeth d'Amory wife of John Bardolf, Lord of Wormegay. His mother came from Switzerland; he seems to have been fond of music and something of a mystic. His were the "pair of organs" lent to the Lady on solemn occasions; it was another of John Motelot's duties to bring them carefully from Bardfield to Clare. When Lord Wormegay became a widower, he went to live at Assisi where the curious English tourist may still be shown the grave of this "great English milord of long, long ago".

After Lady Ferrers's death he and his family lived with the Lady or she with them, sometimes at Bardfield but mostly at Clare.

The next event in the family was the marriage of Elizabeth of Ulster with Lionel the King's second son, a White Prince "with lockes crull as they were layed in presse", a gentle, Flemish giant who may have had musical tastes, but was certainly fond of food and drink, and perhaps rather stupid. In this young couple there is not much to interest us except the fact that Geoffrey Chaucer was a page in their service; bullied by the varlets, petted by the damsels, early noticed by the alert Queen, his own fancy stirred and fed by the passing show of Eltham Palace where he first beheld one of the objects of his worship—beautiful Blanche of Lancaster who later married his lord's brother John of Gaunt.

In the next year a daughter was born to Lionel and Elizabeth, a great-grandchild for the Lady of Clare. She was named

Philippa after the Queen who took custody of her. "The shadow of a monarch's crown is softened in her hair" for eventually, by her marriage with Edmund de Mortimer, this child became one of the ancestresses of Edward IV and of the royal houses of Tudor, Stuart and Windsor. But that is a far cry from her birth at Eltham in 1357 after which her mother never recovered her health. When two years after the Lady of Clare, Elizabeth of Ulster died, her husband was created Duke of Clarence in which title was incorporated the name and honour of Clare.

When the marriage of her chief heiress with Lionel of Antwerp was consummated, Lady Clare set about making her will, a form of exercise which it is evident she much enjoyed for she metes out her possessions with the zest of a child marshalling its birthday presents. The document is in the French of her daily speech (though hardly of Paris); not yet awhile could English be called the mother-tongue. A large part of her will is taken up with bequests to her servants past and present who had eaten her salt and ministered to her and eased through the long years the strain of her busy life. Each one is named and remembered not by money alone but by gifts to the choice of which she must have given much thought, which matters are far more interesting than the manors and masses of plate bestowed upon relations and religious houses. Her damsels and waiting women had most of her clothes from "Susan de Neketon my first best dress" to Alison de Wodeham (for whom one feels rather sorry) "my sixth best dress what is left of it". Two sisters called Drucys had the tyretein robes; the favourite russet was left to the Abbess of the Minoresses without Aldgate. Richard Coachman had the small carriage of the damsels with its harness and cushions; the Lady's own carriage was kept in the family, Lady Bardolf getting it along with the great bed and its green velvet hangings shot with crimson, and the cover embroidered in blue cockerels and popinjays like a king's pavilion. Lady Atholl being only a granddaughter had one of the second best beds and the Bardolf girls the others along with a lot of plate "to help them to marry". But who had the Lady's "bed of bord"?

To the Duke of Lancaster she left a piece of the true Cross, to the Countess of Pembroke two rings and a small golden cross with a sapphire in its heart, to Joanna the Countess Warenne, that gay Court lady, an image in gold of St John Baptist in the desert.

As became a patroness of learning she had a library which was for the time considerable—antiphoners, missals, Legends of the Saints, Bibles, "one book of the Questions, three volumes of the Decretals and thirty-two quires of a work called 'The Cause of God against Pelagienos'"—all these along with many silver vessels for religious and secular use were left naturally "to my Hall of Clare at Cambridge".

1359   Three years later she gave it a Charter and Statutes when the Master and Henry de Motelot must journey to the Castle, for it is not likely that the Lady went to Cambridge, her years being now heavy on her. Robert the Marshal represented her at Wormegay when Agnes Bardolf was married there that year.

The Statutes provide for every possible contingency in the life and routine of the College as it is now called for the first time, and so must be of great interest to its sons and to the academic historian; but the Preamble which has an echo of the Lady's voice should be enough for us. We may blame "the experts my advisors" for a certain pomposity, but there is not a trace of the motive openly and complacently alleged by her cousin the King in a similar document: "it is a good way of merchandise whereby with a happy bartering transitory things are exchanged for Eternal", said that royal merchant, when founding his College and Chapel of Windsor. Elizabeth de Burgo the Lady of Clare desires only "to advance Divine Learning and to benefit the State; and seeing that a large number of men have been carried off by the onslaught of the plague, this knowledge is now beginning to be lamentably lacking among men, we are therefore turning the eyes of our mind to the University of Cambridge in the diocese of Ely and to a Hall therein hitherto commonly known as University Hall which already exists by our foundation and which we wish to be called Clare Hall and by no other name for evermore. Out of the wealth given to us by God we have caused it to increase in its revenues and in the number of its students so that the Precious Pearl of Knowledge found and kept by them through study and learning may not be hidden under a bushel but revealed even farther and give light to those who walk in the dark lanes of ignorance; and that the Scholars may pursue their studies more freely through the benefit of concord and the protection of more lasting peace."

"The dark lanes of ignorance" recalls the words of her ancestor Alfonso the Noble who in founding the Academy of Palentia "called wise men from Gaul and the Indies that the wholesome discipline of learning might never be absent from the Kingdom". She was proud of her Castilian ancestry and its intellectual traditions; on the exquisite seal which she gave to the College at this time—one of the very few of her gifts which escaped the envious tooth of time—the castles of Castile were quartered with the three leopards of England.

"The protection of more lasting peace": throughout her

long life this woman had lived in none but houses of defence; the men she held most dear had died by violence, her children were born and cradled amidst the rumours of war by whose chances indeed she had acquired the major part of her great inheritance. So she used it to help her country to gain what was not granted to herself and having seen her children's

Nov. 4 children, she died persuaded of the complete fulfilment of the
1360 promise.

CHAPTER III

MARIE DE ST POL

Countess of Pembroke

I

When Eleanor of Castile first arrived in England she found at her lodging in the New Temple her brother Sancho the bishop come from the Pope to sanction the marriage of Beatrice the King's daughter to John the Red of Brittany. This couple had a family of which one called Mary became the wife of Guy de Châtillon the Count of St Pol in Artois. As the Clare family in England so was his in France, often mating with royalty and providing one of its members to stand at the King's right hand in council and war. Such was County Guy whose place at Court was immediately after the princes of the Fleur de Lys; at one time he was granted the right to have money struck with the arms of St Pol for use within his own domain. He and Mary of Brittany had two sons and six daughters, three of whom he saw well married before his death which occurred when the fourth called Mary was thirteen. Three years later Aymer de Valence a great lord of England came to sue for her hand.   1317

He was fifty years old and a widower but rich and a man of mark with his king and peers; the Countess of St Pol with two daughters still to settle in life may have been glad of him. Nor was he a stranger but near of kin to both her husband and herself for they were all descended from Isabella of Angoulême but by different husbands—Mary from King John, Guy and Aymer from Hugo de Lusignan. After the Pope's sanction

1321 had been obtained the marriage took place in Paris; in July Aymer de Valence brought his bride to London "and there came to greet her the earls and barons who had come to the King's Parliament".

So far all was fair seeming but they went armed to that Parliament; a storm was brewing that broke some months later over Ledes Castle and ravaged the whole country for the rest of Marie de St Pol's married life, if so it can be called when she had little of the company of her husband who was in the thick of the struggle.

He came of a family of adventurers, the half-brothers of Henry III, brought by him out of Poitou into England where they made themselves at home, managing to steer through its vexed politics a course convenient to themselves and generally prosperous. Like their cousins the Clares they feathered the family nest by judicious matrimony, acquiring indeed the palatinate earldom of Pembroke through an alliance with Strongbow's daughter. After which "the Earls of Pembroke were as absolute princes of themselves". Aymer de Valence was foremost in the service of the two first Edwards; for a time he was one of the Guardians of Scotland where he built a fair hunting-lodge in the Forest of Selkirk; this may have been one of the reasons why he was hated by the Scots, game-laws and their enforcement seldom making for popularity. He was one of the executors of the old King's will; at Edward II's coronation he carried the left boot, but he was trusted with even weightier matters being a guardian of the Kingdom in the King's absence and one of the justiciars at the trial of Thomas of Lancaster. In appearance he is said to have been tall and spare with a long pale face; to Piers Gaveston who abounded in opprobrious nicknames, especially for those who were trying to help him, he was Joseph the Jew. He may very likely have pressed the Gascon for the return of a loan for he guided his affairs with care and prospered—though hardly in the manner of Friday's bairn by loving and giving.

Three years after his second marriage he was sent to France on a mission from the King ostensibly to report on the royal tombs at Fontevraud, but really, it is thought, to make terms with Roger Mortimer now escaped over the water from captivity in the Tower. Roger went on his wicked way without hindrance and the tomb of Cœur de Lion is still at Fontevraud for Aymer de Valence died "very suddenly" at Compiègne aged fifty-three.   1324

Though there is about him no misleading haze of romance, yet his young wife must have found in him something to justify her steadfastness in remaining (as the beautiful phrase of the time goes) "the companion of my very dear and true lord" to the end of her life. She never put off her widowhood; both prudently and generously she administered his wealth and always associated his name with the use she made of it.

For the bringing of his body from France and its burial with due worship she petitioned the King in a letter which has an undertone of anxiety as if Edward, already beginning to lose himself in the shallows and miseries of his own life, had at first ignored her petition. "As such a thing cannot be done without the consent and order of you to whom he was akin and whom he served in the way you know, grant that his body be buried at Westminster." At last she got her way, and had a beautiful tomb fashioned whereon go the martlets that tell he was the fourth son of his father.

He was also the seventh child and his wife too came out of a large family, yet they were childless nor was there any issue of his first marriage; after his sisters had had their portions of the estate there were none to share the residue with her. She had £2000 a year and much landed property in England, Ireland and France where were her dower lands: thus she was the vassal of two kings (who during her life were constantly at war with each other) and had the burdens consequent on such a position. She is a touching figure, like the little mermaid of the story with the cumbersome oysters, signs of her rank and importance, clinging to her tail. There were many waiting to rid her of them. The younger Hugh Dispenser did his best, that devourer of widows' houses, "framing mischief as a law"; but though she lost three castles and all her husband's personal possessions she managed to keep most of her lands and goods. After the Dispensers' downfall, an outrageous attempt was made to marry her to that other poisoner of the kingdom's peace, Roger Mortimer, but this she firmly resisted. From the hour of her young widowhood, in a foreign land and a miserable time of strife and intrigue, this girl of twenty showed such strength of character and capacity for affairs that when she went later to France to see to her property there she was entrusted also "with the King's business". This may have been one of the bright ideas of Queen Philippa who was welcomed on her arrival in England as a bride by the Countess of Pembroke. The two were related and doubtless already well known to each other, Hainault and Artois being neighbours, and the Queen had the royal scent for a good servant; this one could be trusted to gauge the feeling in the French Court—full as it was of their near relations—as to any delicate matters that might be in suspense between the councils of the two kingdoms. Froissart the chronicler being occupied chiefly with the shows of things takes no heed of her who seems quietly to have established herself with the powers that be as one who counts and may be counted upon. They showed their gratitude in their own way: early in his reign the King gave her his manor of Denny in Cambridgeshire; when she had ceased her travels for a time, she took charge of his five-year-old daughter Joan of Woodstock, and was rewarded by the manor of Stroode in Kent.

In 1336 the grant of Denny was confirmed "to the Countess of Pembroke and her heirs for ever out of consideration for her good service". But she paid two hundred and fifty pounds for it which sounds as if she wanted it; certainly the countryside has a great look of her home in Artois. The Priory of Ely had had an offspring or cell at Denny which after passing through several hands reverted to the King who may have found it embarrassing. Close by in the fen at Waterbeach was a religious house of the Poor Clares or Minoresses founded forty years before by Dionysia de Munchensy a kinswoman of Aymer de Valence—a disappointed woman who may have found comfort for a sore heart in this good work. "She was probably the initiator of the whole English branch of the Minoresses" says a recent historian of this Order, which soon became a favourite if not fashionable focus for the charitable attentions of the pious.

This Waterbeach house was situated unhealthily, "strait, low and otherwise insufficient", and the nuns suffered from fever and ague; Denny like Ely its parent stands out of the fen on an "isle" of good land, easy of access from Aikman Street, one of the old grassy ridgeways. The Countess of Pembroke had that thrifty instinct which is all for strengthening the weak by the development of what lies to hand. She improved and enlarged the existing buildings at Denny and having done all things legally and in order she set wide the door and bade the shivering virgins of Waterbeach welcome.

Some of them were wise and came in, led by the Abbess; but, though the lot at Waterbeach was not laid in a fair ground, a number remained there stubborn and comfortless except for that sense of martyrdom so sustaining to the heart of woman. Why should they be secondary to a new, upstart house who were the first of their Order in England, deriving straight from the House of the Blessed Isabelle sister to St Louis the King, she who may well have spoken with Holy Clara herself. So they flouted Denny, choosing another Abbess from among themselves and enlisting the support of the friars who were their ministers. There was strife and heart-burning, the high-handed ways of Denny's Abbess Katherine de Bolwyk having much to do with this anti-Franciscan not to say un-Christian state of things. It challenged the Countess's forces; she appealed to principalities spiritual and temporal, most of whom "began with one accord to make excuse". At last, being one of those people who do nothing by halves, she took advantage of a lull in the war and departed for France to lay her case before the Pope himself now "exiled at Avignon". But in spite of her sisters (according to the flesh) who were set in high places, the affairs of a little nunnery in a far corner of a misty northern island were not of pressing importance in a country now at war with itself over the succession of Brittany; so, except for family sympathy, the Countess returned unsatisfied and the Waterbeach nuns continued in frowardness.

II

When as a bride of sixteen Marie de St Pol came to England she found it a friendly land, full of her kindred beginning with the King himself; and she too had an aunt in the Amesbury nunnery, though Eleanor of Brittany followed the rule more straitly than her cousin Mary and eventually became Abbess of Fontevraud the parent house. Eleanor's brother John the Duke of Brittany was also as Earl of Richmond a baron of England where he spent much of his time; he had no children and seems to have treated his niece Marie like a daughter. She had Fotheringay Castle from him and her town house in that part of the City still called Little Britain, John being another foreign uncle who has left his title on the stones of London. Her mother Mary of Brittany who was born in England had spent most of her girlhood with her cousins Eleanor and Joanna and indeed followed the drum with them and their mother; it was to the mother of Aymer de Valence in Pembroke Castle that Joanna Countess of Clare fled for support on the discovery of her secret second marriage. All these matters would be recalled by Joanna's daughter Elizabeth de Clare when their cousin Aymer brought his bride home. Fragrant memories of ancient kindness, their husbands' comradeship in arms and politics, their own experience of persecution by the same lawless despoiler—here was much to draw two young women together. But why try to analyse the mysterious elixir of friendship? Enough that of all those who were embraced by the eager heart of Elizabeth de Clare the closest was Valence Marie which may somewhat illumine for us the character of that elusive lady.

The difference in their ages was of no account—at least not to Elizabeth who hesitated not to present an exact copy of one of her dresses to a woman nearly ten years her junior. Theirs was the sort of friendship that becomes a matter of course and yet is new every morning. The habit of letter-writing for pleasure as we restlessly practise it was not yet born; in any case it is doubtful whether either of these ladies could write much more than her name. Like Charlemagne they might know how to read in several languages without being able to put pen to parchment; why should they when trained, clerkly persons were there to do it for them? But they visited often and long in each other's country homes, and their town houses were not far apart, the Countess's as was fitting by St Paul's Church and Lady Clare's at Aldgate. The Countess would be one of the first to hear about the adoption of University Hall by her friend; the contrast between that band of sober, studious, grateful men and the nest of nervous, squabbling women at Waterbeach must have appealed to her.

1346   It was after Clare Hall was established that she acquired a site in Cambridge "without the Trumpenton Gate"; by the next Christmas she had the King's licence to endow there a house of scholars and in the following summer the foundation charter of the House of Valence Marie was drafted "for a Master and thirty scolars or more". For their lodging she
1348 bought University Hostel, also by the Trumpington Gate, from the Chancellor and Regents of the University.

1343   Some years previously a visionary gentleman called Robert d'Eglesfield inspired by the fact of the King's Hall of Scholars at Cambridge had founded at Oxford the College of the Queen with the motto "Queens shall be thy nursing mothers". He was chaplain to Queen Philippa who took the hint so far as to endow the College with twenty marks a year during her life while making clear she was its patroness only, not its foundress. Still hers was a generous response, for it seems on the authority of a recent writer on economics that the queens of England are like other women in this: their private incomes are never sufficient for the claims made upon them.

A healthy spirit of emulation may have had something to do with this patronage of poor scholars by great ladies; for, though we tend to embalm them in a deadly perfection, labelling and encasing them like museum pieces, yet those women had their inspirations, follies, triumphs, discouragements, and quick, passionate hearts like ourselves. But also a freedom of spirit and a high reserve; what we call boredom they called Accidie and a deadly sin.

It should be noted that Pembroke Hall was a new foundation, not, like Clare, the renewal of one already in existence. The Countess had had enough of that at Denny whose welfare, however, she was far from neglecting. About this time she sought the King's leave to obtain from the neighbouring Abbot and convent of St Andrew's, Chesterton, the advowson of their church and a piece of land "for the benefit of the Sisters Minoresses of Denny". The royal grant of permission is written not on parchment but on paper (which still endures), then just beginning to be used in England.

The struggle about Denny had gone on for about fifteen years; but at last the veterans of the old guard, twenty in number, were carried, still protesting, over the threshold of the Abbey after the manner of a primitive wedding, and the 1350 Waterbeach house fell into ruin.

Meanwhile the Countess's estates in France had need of that searching eye which she brought to bear on all her affairs. Her agents there had taken advantage of the war and the fact that for a time she was dispossessed of her French lands "being resident with the enemy". As there was now a brief truce and she was apparently one of those gifted beings for whom sea-travel has no terrors, she asked King Edward in whom as she says "I put my trust for all things earthly" to give her a safe-conduct to France, failing permission delayed or denied from France's new King, John II. Her retinue of "knights and others with the great horses, harness and baggage" was held up at Dover in idleness, a waste of time and money that vexed her careful soul. She would need an impressive escort though she had no fear of venturing into a country which even when free from war was at the mercy of lawless freebooters, French and English. But it was her own land and there she stayed without let or hindrance for the best part of five years.

Her mother was dead but one of her brothers and three of her sisters were still living. Isabelle had married the Sieur de Coucy lord of the finest castle in the world; Blanche de Valois her niece, wife of the so-called Emperor Charles IV, was as one historian relates with unction, "the sister, aunt, mother or grandmother of almost all those reigning in Europe at this time". The Seigneur de Châtillon was Master of the King's Household. Wherever she went the Countess found her kin were people of importance. It is not clear whether at any time she lodged in Paris in what had been the family house—the Hôtel de St Pol—but she had a house of her own at St Germain-des-Prés on the left bank of the river. Edward of England was not the only claimant for the lilies of France by right of his mother; Charles of Navarre (called the Bad and with good reason) was making a bid for them too. He had a strong party among the citizens and a persuasive tongue, so there was a good deal of "preachment" by the several political factions from the platform beside the Church of St Germain. About a mile away on the slope of Mont Ste Geneviève, the Countess could see the old College of Robert de Sorbonne and next to it the Collège de France, founded by Queen Jeanne in the year of her birth. In the dark little streets that twisted about the

University lived and learned and loved and fought the Four
Nations of Students who came to Paris from all over the world
of Europe; the left bank has ever been a home for the restless
mind of man. Not far away in the Rue Lourcine was the Poor
Clares' convent of St Marcel where it is thought she made a
retreat for a time; one of her books of Hours was given her by
the "Lourcine Sisters". Her house was opposite the Isle of the
Palace and the Holy Chapel; on the farther bank is the dark
Louvre that held the key of the river; at certain times of the
year as she came from Mass, she could mark the sunrise behind
the towers of Nôtre Dame. There is not much else left of the
Paris she knew. A great boulevard now roars by the church of
St Germain-des-Prés; the meadows are covered by its sprawling
progeny of little streets; one of the biggest shops of Paris is
piled high where the great fair used to spread itself; the Palais de
Nesle where King John sometimes kept his state for a change is
now swallowed up by the Institute of France. Paris cares for
little in her past before Napoleon.

Among the Countess's friends at Court were Charles the
Dauphin—the first Child of France to bear that title—and his
wife Jeanne de Bourbon (remembered now on the left bank by
the Rue Dauphine). The age was one that freely bandied nicknames more or less conventional and often misleading; but this
Charles really was the wise man they named him. Too frail of
body to bear armour in the field, he had yet a strong spirit and
acute mind which saved his distracted country from dissolution
and won back most of what England had been gradually
acquiring through the years. But his real interests were elsewhere; like our Henry VI (his great-grandson) he took refuge
from the troubles besetting a kingly state in the things of the
spirit. He it was who first made the Louvre from a fortress

prison into a treasure house of the Arts and a great library. His wife was another of his consolations; lovely and pleasant in herself she was joined with him in all he did, especially in the love and encouragement of beauty. One of its manifestations at this time was the illustration by monks (who were gifted artists and mostly remain nameless) of missals and breviaries; one such was given by the Dauphine to the Countess of Pembroke—a Franciscan book of Hours, now happily one of the treasures of the Cambridge University Library. So after nearly six hundred years we too can enjoy the exquisite thing— the touch of the vellum soft and fresh as the lips of an infant, the clear luminous letters, the tiny conceits scattered on the margins—a girl with hawk on wrist, a boy who plays on a bagpipe, children on a see-saw, a watchman gazing from a tower—and the glowing vignettes for Saints' Days. The finest of these is the one for St Cecilia's Day in which the kneeling figure is supposed to be a portrait of the Countess. It is of a comely lady in the prime of life, wearing an under-dress of bright cherry colour with pointed sleeves to the elbows, leaving bare the rest of the beautiful arms and clasped hands; over this is a sleeveless robe of cloth of gold and a dark blue mantle like a knight's embroidered with the arms of Valence and St Pol, which covers the right shoulder and falls from the waist in front. The fair hair in a cherry-coloured net is softly arranged to frame a face open and serene as of one whose mind is a kingdom at peace within itself; the background is azure and argent, the colours of Aymer de Valence. In contrast with this radiant figure that of the saint who offers her a white book seems withdrawn and dim spite of halo and palm. Why St Cecilia? it may be the gift was made on her day November 22nd.

The Countess's own dower-lands were in the North of France which was more or less in English hands at this time; but her other estates were in that part of the country harried by the Black Prince—as the French were now calling the Prince of Wales. At last he brought matters to a head among the gardens of Maupertuis seven miles from Poitiers which has taken the name and fame of the victory. After the battle it would be easier for the Countess to visit the Valence country and arrange her affairs. In the following autumn she returned to England where she remained for the rest of her life.

Sept. 19 1356

III

King John II of France, called the Good, though, as one of his countrymen acidly remarks, less because of his virtues than his misfortunes, knew how to turn these to advantage and appear after Poitiers a romantic figure of captivity in England. He made no very great efforts for a ransom, finding himself agreeably entertained by Queen Philippa and her family in the Palace of the Savoy. So too was the irresistible Enguerrand de Coucy, the Countess of Pembroke's great-nephew, who in his turn made a captive of King Edward's sole remaining daughter —a relief to the Queen for the lady Isabelle was getting on for thirty and had flouted or been flouted by several suitors already. Her brother Lionel had not long been married to her friend the heiress of the Lady of Clare.

But it was far otherwise with brave du Guesclin and Guy de Châtillon the Count of St Pol who were galled by the unwholesome idleness of captivity: indeed Guy de St Pol later died of it.

This influx of kin and countrymen brought the Queen Mother Isabelle out of the retirement in which it is to be hoped she had repented of her sins, negligences and arrogances; at any rate she now appeared as a reformed character graciously anxious to alleviate the captives' lot. Whether or no her motives were really pious or only political, she took care to enlist the help of two other daughters of France who were above suspicion—Marie the Countess of Pembroke and Joan the Countess Warenne. The former who never went to Court worked behind the scenes as usual for the welfare of messengers, men-at-arms and the like and so was frequently at Hertford Castle, a strange return after many years to what had been her husband's; it was one of those reft from her by Hugh Dispenser and not restored to her but reverting to the Crown. Queen Isabelle took up her abode there in a belated access of motherly love, as it was now the refuge of her daughter Joan, whose chances of happiness she had blasted for ever when she married her at seven years old to David Bruce the heir of Scotland who seems to have inherited only the crooked qualities of his father King Robert along with the hard heart of his selfish mother. But the child of Edward II and Isabelle of France grew up true and fair, as a fragrant lily may spring out of mire. For twenty years she bore loyally with the treacheries of her unworthy husband; when at last she could no more, her brother and kind Queen Philippa received and sheltered her in Hertford Castle where she was a centre for the love and admiration of the whole connection. She was gentle and dutiful to the mother who had deeply wronged her and to whom she was almost a stranger; for Queen Isabelle who did not appreciate daughters early placed hers in the care of Ralph de Monthermer and his second wife the sister of Aymer de Valence. There are indications that

78

Valence Marie and Queen Joan were friends in spite of a considerable difference in their ages; the spirit of love and of a sound mind was in both. As Joan was the first queen of Scotland to be crowned and anointed she never ceased from her efforts for the welfare of its people; they hated their King but loved her whom in bitter jest they had at first called Joan Makepeace. For she took this title and wore it as a crown; she obtained various commercial concessions for the Scots from her brother —for instance that the coinage of each country should pass current in the other—and this grandchild of Eleanor of Castile was specially taken up with the reception and well-being of Scottish students at the English Universities when there were as yet none in their own country. In fact she may be said to have initiated the peaceful penetration of England by Scotsmen.

About this time some poor scholars of Oxford made bold to approach her mother with a petition for help; but they do not appear to have been successful.

Meanwhile the Countess of Pembroke was coming and going to Cambridge, looking to the ruling of her two foundations. If, in its early days, she gave her Hall its statutes they have not survived; those of 1366 are taken as hers. Like the statutes of Clare Hall they provide for a liberal plan of study in arts and theology without too much insistence on what has been venomously styled by a modern historian "the soul-destroying study of Canon and Civil Law": there is the same stipulation for poverty on the part of the Fellows and scholars and a like preponderance of the lay element in the society. The Countess kept a certain jurisdiction over it while she lived and provided in her will for two rectors to succeed her as visitors and court of appeal; one of these must be a Franciscan. In one important respect the House of Valence Marie differed from the other foundations then existing in the University: she was determined to obtain for it "the privilege of a private chapel" and in time she achieved this. Her countryman Pope Urban V, still at Avignon, confirmed his predecessor's permission for the erection within the College "of a proper and suitable Chapel or Oratory for the celebration of divine service in the presence of the Master and Fellows or any of them, or so there be any one of the Society within the College". The building of the chapel and a bell-turret was begun in the following year; then she who thought of everything and was concerned as well for the physical refreshment of her scholars, bought an acre of meadow to serve as an orchard—the nucleus of the beautiful Fellows' Garden that we know. The charter by which this was conveyed to the College bears the signature of the Mayor of Cambridge as a witness.

Denny Abbey was now a mother-house. At the request of the King's son Lionel of Clarence, thirteen of the nuns were sent to help the new house of Minoresses at Bruisyard in Suffolk where his wife's mother the Countess of Ulster was after a second widowhood following the religious life.

The Countess Marie, now approaching her seventieth year, is like the sheaf of ripe corn figured on her father's coinage of St Pol. But a lonely woman who had outlived most of her generation and friends: Elizabeth de Clare, Joan de Bar, Henry of Lancaster and Queen Joan who "deceased without issue but it is better to leave an honourable report than children behind", declared the chronicler as though it were not possible to do both like Queen Philippa that admirable mother and steadfast friend. She was the last of the group of friends to die; before long only the King was left, foolish and sick and old before his time. The Countess always had a kindness for him; Aymer de

Valence was one of his seven godfathers. She had seen the reigns of ten kings in the countries of her allegiance—three in England, seven in France—and eight popes, seven of whom ruled Christendom not from Rome but Avignon. Of change which is to some the salt of life she had known enough; did she realise that it was bringing the denial and decay of much she was used to accept as imperishable? Not only were strange new engines of war coming into use to make of no avail the defences in which man had hitherto trusted, but his own vital spirit was questioning, challenging, defying authority in Church and State.

"Hold the high road, the spirit guiding thee,
And doubt it not: the Truth shall make thee free"

said the poet of her day. So she went on her way, in the world though not of it, building a house not made with hands to give light to the ignorant and them that are out of the way. Had she been in her London house on a certain day of February in the year 1377, the noise the people were making at St Paul's Cross must have drawn her to the window to see the Lord Marshall's men clearing a way for the King's son John who was bringing Dr Wycliffe to the church for his trial before the bishops. But she was at her manor of Brasted in Essex peacefully making her will.

This is a brief and business-like affair unadorned by the picturesque detail and without the gusto of her friend Elizabeth's; she had borne her burdens too long. There are however certain points of resemblance, such as the remembrance of poor prisoners and friendless women and many religious houses throughout the country especially those of the Franciscans. And the Countess too kept her servants till they became her friends (and perhaps her rulers), notably Wilcock her confidential factotum and Mabel du Bois who was in her service for forty years; she and two members of the College are to be honoured and remembered in its prayers in perpetuity along with the foundress and her husband and nearest relations. She devised a gift of money to each of "my scholars at Cambridge"; and to the whole society any amount of plate, hangings and rich stuffs besides "what I have already devised which is recorded and will be found in the sealed place where I have bestowed it"; (we are told that her muniment chests were in beautiful order). To her Franciscan confessor she naturally left the breviary "which my Queen gave me"; it had probably been cherished for use on special occasions, while "my book of hours which was the Queen of Scots' in which I say my things" was left to the Queen of France along with an image of John the Baptist and a finger-bone of that saint. The passion for relics (with a difference) has endured to our own enlightened day only we call them by a different name.

She did not forget the great church of her name in whose shelter she had lived; it had "one of my gold cups to show" and an image of St Paul in silver gilt.

To Charles the Dauphin now the King of France "I devise a sword which I have which is without a point; my friend Willecok of my chamber will take it to him and tell him of its meaning". So again does she hide herself from us.

Her wealth was given back to the country from which most of it came; but there is no doubt that towards the close of her life her untravelled heart turned to her own land; "my Queen" was neither Philippa nor Isabelle nor Joan Makepeace but Jeanne de Bourbon. In the first statutes of Pembroke

College there was a clause which gave preference to scholars of French birth; whether any such have profited by it is not clear. But, as one of her most distinguished biographers records, the House of Valence Marie was deserted of its sons in 1914 for five years when they rallied to the defence of her two countries allied on the field of honour.

On March 16, 1377, at the age of seventy-three, she died at Denny Abbey and was buried as she directed in the habit of a Poor Clare, and "without outrageous expense", by the high altar of the church. Not for her was the tomb with the martlets at Westminster, but "where the kneeling hamlet drains the chalice of the grapes of God" is her last home. Over it for centuries has gone the traffic of a farmyard so that its exact position is now unknown; and even in death she is elusive. But what does it matter? Of far more significance is the fact that her college to whose members she commended the care of her other family "having from her a common origin with them" is now happily the possessor of Denny Abbey, and this is surely as she would have it.

Two slender pillars of weathered stone on the right-hand side of the road to Ely mark a cart track that leads to what seems an ordinary Fen farmhouse till you see here a soaring arch, there a sculptured corbel or a mason's mark on the deep firm embrasure of a window. It is a ghostly place but the ghosts are friendly and homely; Benedictines, Hospitallers, Poor Clares— countless generations of nameless men and women, and beasts, have served and loved and left Denny still beautiful. As we rounded the old boundary wall and marked the faint trace of an outlook tower, the remnant of the moat and the grassy floor of Aikman Street—far kinder to weary feet than the hard, restless Ely Road—"It's better living here nor in London, d'ye think?" said the young farmer shyly adding "and it's good to have the College looking after us". Here ploughing and seed time and harvest and that pride in the work that brings forth content; there, seven miles away, the unending search after truth and the noble strife of mind with mind. In both, the promise and the renewal of life.

CHAPTER IV

MARGARET OF ANJOU
Queen Consort of King Henry VI
of England

"Margaret my name and daughter to a king"

I

In spite of the promise of his name, René the father of Margaret was not born a king but the second son of Louis II Duke of Anjou. He was doubly allied to the Valois family at this time keeping a precarious hold upon the throne of France, for his father was a grandson and his mother Yolande of Aragon a great-granddaughter of King John II the Prisoner of Poitiers. An earlier ancestor of his mother was Henri de Bar who in 1298 married Eleanor child of Edward I of England and Eleanor of Castile.

René was not very old before his wise mother arranged that he should be accepted by her uncle Louis Cardinal and Duke of Bar as his heir, the Cardinal undertaking the boy's education. The next event in his life was his marriage at the age of ten to a girl of nine, Isabelle the heiress of the Cardinal's neighbour Duke Charles of Lorraine.

In course of time and then in quick succession there was a family of three sons and two daughters. The youngest was Margaret, born either at Pont-au-Mousson in Bar or, more 1429 likely, in her mother's home the castle of Nanci in Lorraine on March 23, 1429, a critical time in her country's history which may account for the uncertainty about her birthplace. Her cousin Charles the Dauphin, rightful heir to the empty throne, had an unnatural mother who would not own him as a son of the king; ten years earlier she had sold his birthright to England who was now claiming it for her king a child of seven. The matter had long passed beyond the region of parleys and treaties, and was being desperately fought out round the beleaguered city of Orleans which held out for France and the Dauphin against the unholy alliance of Burgundy and England. France lay bleeding where her mighty sons by their treasons and divisions had cast her "at the proud foot of a conqueror" till a farmer's daughter came out of Lorraine to lift her up.

On her way to Orleans the Maid paused at Nanci to ask help from Duke Charles her feudal lord, who received her gladly for he had heard she had magical powers and he hoped she would cure him of the gout. But she denied such gifts with horror, speaking to him rather of his soul's health that was in peril through his manner of life. And she said "Give me René your son with his men to bring me into France, and I will pray God to cure you"; at which he laughed and forgot her and took his son-in-law to fight the men of Metz about a trifling matter.

The other man who had a right to direct René's actions neither laughed at the Maid nor asked a sign from her though he pondered long whether it were wiser to support her and the Fleur-de-Lys or to cast in his lot with Burgundy his powerful neighbour and the ally of England. At last Cardinal Louis went to Paris and did homage for himself as Duke of Bar and also for René his heir to King Henry as king of France in the person of the regent Bedford—one of whose purloined titles was Duke of Anjou.

But the Cardinal had reckoned without René, son of a house which could have no alliance with Burgundy. His brothers, Louis the real Duke of Anjou and Charles Count of Maine, were with the army of France before Orleans; their mother, one of the Maid's staunchest supporters, was at Blois with their sister the Dauphine. Why then René asked himself was he in Lorraine quarrelling about a hamper of apples? The news of his uncle's doings in Paris decided him; he returned to Bar, collected the men for whom the Maid had begged and followed her into France. Too late for the triumph of Orleans; but he stood by her in her supreme hour when the true King was crowned in Rheims cathedral. Afterwards, with his brothers, he did homage to Charles VII, redeeming his honour and repudiating his uncle's action.

When the Maid set her face for Paris he followed and was one of those who rescued her when she fell wounded at the Porte St Honoré. Then he was jerked back to Champagne for another of the petty wars that were draining the life of France. It is to be hoped that he made peace with his uncle for the Cardinal died in that year; and soon after Duke Charles died 1430 also adjuring his heirs to keep friends with Burgundy.

All those lords and ladies of the seigneuries scattered about the shifting frontier of the Empire were not only in the exacting relation of neighbours but were also kindred in varying degrees by the tangled marriages and re-marriages of many generations. The strongest element in their regard for each other seems to have been the honest conviction that each had a better right to the other's possessions than the actual owner thereof; hence on the death of any of them divisions and claims which dragged on in the law-courts or were fought out in the field. Now the chief villain of the piece Duke Philip of

Burgundy (called the Good) stirred up his vassal Anthony de Vaudemont, the uncle of René's wife, to contest her right of succession to the duchy of Lorraine. René was defeated in battle and delivered to Philip who shut him up in the high tower at Dijon that still bears his name.

His wife the Duchess Isabelle, now twenty-one, first secured the safety of their children with her mother Duchess Margaret in the castle of Nanci, then held on to their inheritance, defying the looming power of Burgundy the while she had to cast about to raise ransom for her husband from territories exhausted by war and the other extravagances of her ancestors. She was set to climb a hill of glass in shoes of iron like the man in the fable.

Lorraine and Bar were as Naboth's vineyard to Philip, always in the way between him and his subject counties of Luxembourg and Flanders and a continual menace to his dream of the sovereignty of Eastern France. War was wasteful and vain; he would try the means of peace. René was released on parole to discuss terms with his captors. He consented to the betrothal of his elder daughter Yolande to Ferry de Vaudemont son of Count Anthony but refused to contract Margaret aged three to Philip's son Charles of Charolais aged one year. René bore his cousin no grudge as he showed later when he beguiled the weariness of his captive state by painting a portrait of Philip which must have been flattering for there was a touching scene of reconciliation over it. The feud between them originating in at least two murders and a broken marriage contract was not personal but concerned the honour of their families and had been augmented latterly by Burgundy's alliance with England. But the ransom money being as yet afar off, René was returned to prison and with him John his eldest son, perhaps nine years old.

About this time the Duchess Margaret died; the child Yolande was absorbed by the Vaudemonts to be brought up with her future husband after the manner of the times and Margaret with her nurse was sent to the other grandmother in Anjou.

Tiphaine the nurse also has her place in history. She had been the foster-mother of René and his sister Queen Marie and took on the cherishing of his children as naturally as their mother bore them. In return she had his friendship and observance all her life, and at her death a beautiful tomb (of which she probably saw the beginnings) with a fine epitaph in her own town of Saumur—the sort of reward that still appeals to one of her class and race.

Anjou has lost both its duke and its musical name; for all practical purposes it is now known as the department of Maine-and-Loire. To the tourist, casual and fleeting, it is "the châteaux country"; but, as one of its lovers has said, "it has the finest feminine qualities of quiet and dignity with a touch of mystery expressed in the simplest and most gracious form. . . nothing heavy or magnificent but a very wise, mature country patient and inwardly beautiful". A contrast to restless, warfaring Lorraine; for Duchess Yolande (now styled Queen of Sicily) while regent for her son Louis III kept the English out of Anjou though it lay between the territories of Guienne and Normandy which were in their occupation.

Such a countryside where René was born would be full of songs and tales that Tiphaine could tell to his child; and to a daughter of Lorraine she must have told the story of a girl of the people, nowise royal or noble, who left caring for her father's sheep and went like King David to help her country, accomplishing gloriously what princes and wise men could not do. And Queen Yolande knew she was sent from Heaven and believed in her and tried to save her from the burning.

Indeed Queen Yolande had sold her jewels to equip the convoy which took food to the starving garrison of Orleans—not the only time that she sacrificed her substance for the aid and defence of the realm. Like another King's Daughter who also came out of Spain she was "a merciful princess and a loving mother to the nation", winning the people's hearts by her consideration of the poor and those that have no helper. (It may also be noted here that this descendant of Eleanor of Castile benefited Angers University and enlarged its scope.) Not the least valuable part of her dowry was what her son's biographer calls a quality of honesty; one would like to think she helped to clear the discredit brought upon the Anjou family by the behaviour of her father-in-law Louis I when regent of France. Her counsels were faithfulness and truth at a time when those in high places would spend and pawn and borrow and spend again, laying grievous taxes on the people and driving their creditors with whips from their doors. And if the times brought forth such as Isabelle of Bavaria, Louis of Orleans and the two Joannas of Naples who gave themselves up to a vicious luxury that has been called bestial, it was also the age of the author of *The Imitation of Christ*, of Jeanne d'Arc, of King Henry VI, of Queen Yolande.

There was little doing in the affairs of the kingdom of France about which her counsel was not sought since the day when she rescued the King's younger children from the state of misery and destitution they were sharing with their poor, mad father. Nervous little Charles of Ponthieu the fourth son she took straightway into her own family; he was born old, a prey from his youth to the doubts and hesitations that are the penalties of age. She could not endue him with the sweet blood and natural Christianity of her own children, but she married him to one of them and roused in him the beginnings of self-respect and a sense of duty towards his country.

In the shelter of this woman Margaret too was brought up. Not at St Louis's great fortress whose seventeen towers dominate Angers did Queen Yolande keep her state but in the neighbouring château of Saumur on an island in the river, or for change of air at Baugé whose castle she altered and made homelike. This family had a passion for building and renovating; in René's case the wonder grows as to where the money came from for all he did. From all over Europe to the little Court of Anjou came people of importance; Margaret early learned how to bear herself before them and gracefully to manage elaborate head-dress and stiff robe of state. She was twelve when "arrayed in cloth of gold on violet shot with crimson she received the ambassadors of the Emperor". Here too, as in that older tale of a king's daughter whose clothing was of wrought gold, the ready writer is so taken up with it that he forgets to tell us what the wearer looked like. As on the princess of the fairy tale so also on Margaret of Anjou tradition liberally bestows blue eyes and golden hair; but somehow I incline to share with one of her countrywomen— —even Mme Tussaud—the fancy that she was a nut-brown maid.

"In these delicate vessels is borne onward through the ages the treasure of human affections", so exquisitely does a wise woman reflect upon the girls of her day and ours. To Margaret and her like was committed also the more fearful burden of the passions and ambitions that are the stuff of history; we learn how they were trained to the work from the voluminous writings of one who died about the time of Margaret's birth, Christine de Pisan daughter of the secretary of King Charles V of France at whose court she was brought up. A woman of the world and a born schoolmistress she is intent on the edification not only of that world but of the whole human race. Though herself a woman of learning she does not advise it for those of her sex whose lives are to be lived in the world of affairs; let the boys have it in plenty, but their sisters should have enough to do studying the characters and the well-being of the human creatures among whom they have to live. *Noblesse oblige* is the beginning and end of her educational theories; she never heard of self-expression and self-determination. Neither was that blessed word Psychology with all its uses and abuses yet born or thought of, though it was thoroughly if unconsciously practised by the great company of women whose business it was to form the characters and guide the conduct of the daughters of the great. After Tiphaine the Nurse came the gouvernante, the duenna for whom there is no exact English word, often chief priestess of the family hierarchy, necessarily a lady of birth and breeding, irreproachable reputation and discreet age. Christine who studies perfection requires also the motherly šense that takes in confidences and gives out encouragement; and, as the young should have comely people about them, a certain measure of good looks is desirable but not in abundance for there should be no risk of her becoming the rival of her charge. As to the line to be taken with her, nothing so obvious or tiresome as the "little store of maxims preaching down a daughter's heart", but delicate, adroit insinuation and a play of fancy by which the husband and the prospect of her life with him is made interesting and even vaguely romantic to the wistful child. Is he young, handsome, ardent, or bashful and cold, or old and ugly, known or unknown, near or far? For every contingency Christine hands out her recipes—(except that simple one prescribed by the gouvernante of a later day: Priez pour elles et au bon Dieu laissez le reste). It was not a bad system if we are to judge by results; though now and then it is pleasing to find a couple who managed the matter for themselves and made a job of it.

Meanwhile to René the captive came news of the death of 1435 his brother Louis III by which he became Duke of Anjou in the West and Count of Provence in the South of France. Lorraine and Bar being in the North-East, it will be seen that his territories were scattered wide over the map of France, and well separated from each other by lands in English occupation. A few months later by the death of Joanna II of Naples whose heir his brother was he became King of the Two Sicilies, of Hungary and of Jerusalem, titles that fill the mouth and take the fancy but which brought him nothing but strife and vainglory; only his beloved Provence never failed him. Thither at this time went his gallant wife—now styled Queen—on her way to establish his rights in Naples where already was another claimant, his cousin Alfonso of Aragon, while Queen Yolande held the fort in Anjou. It was René's good fortune to have a mother and a wife who were much abler than he at managing his affairs.

Two years later, when he was twenty-eight, he was released 1437 for the collection of ransom and came to Anjou and then to the château of Tocé where were his mother and the little daughter of eight years who had been an infant in Tiphaine's arms when he was taken away. What did she think of him bowed and "hollow as a ghost", bearded and blear-eyed? could this be the glorious princely father of whom Tiphaine had boasted to her? But though six years of prison had dimmed his eyes they had not availed to quench the brightness of his spirit nor his delight in beauty and talent for expressing it. For this he was despised by his peers but adored by his subjects; he had all the qualities that capture the imagination of simple people, and not of his own time only. Round this gay, gracious, unworldly man, "the king without a kingdom" (save the hearts of his fellow-creatures), have gathered the most vivid legends which ring true to character though they may not all have foundation in actual fact.

It is true and no legend that when he went to take his kingdom of Naples and had to fight not only Alfonso of Aragon but plague and famine, he shared the miseries of the people, helping to tend the sick and himself carrying food to the starving when a ship from his allies brought relief to the beleaguered city. After five years of this unusual kingship he came to Angers a beaten man as much by the intrigues of the shifty Neapolitans as by his cousin of Aragon. His mother who had ruled Anjou for her sons during twenty-six years had gone to her rest; of his children, who had numbered nine, three were left: John of Calabria married to Marie de Bourbon, Yolande betrothed to Ferry de Vaudemont, and Margaret whose marriage must now be settled for she was thirteen.

Her prospects were by no means so straightforward as her sister's. After Charles of Charolais was refused she was betrothed to a son of the Count of St Pol whose family was now merged in that of Luxembourg; he again was ousted by the elderly Count of Nevers, another of Burgundy's kinsmen. In spite of this, Nevers's suit was not favoured by the Duchess of Burgundy, Isabella of Portugal. She like Queen Yolande was one of the notable women of the time who used her talents in the service of her generation; especially was she bent on bringing to an end the weary war between France and the country of her fathers. For she was a granddaughter of John of Gaunt and Duchess Blanche of Lancaster; her cousin was the reigning King of England and his chancellor was her uncle Cardinal Beaufort a man of power in the councils of Europe. Although or perhaps because he was soldier as well as priest he also was of the peace party and was willing to join forces with his niece. She could not receive him at Dijon for her husband Philip had shed his alliance with England; by the fires of Rouen in 1431 were Herod and Pilate strangely made friends together; and they sealed the bond in the usual way by the betrothal of King Charles's eldest daughter to Charles of Charolais. So Isabella took occasion to display a little family piety and met her uncle the Cardinal on English ground at Calais whence arose the idea of the marriage of King Henry 1439 to a daughter of France.

There could be no question of one of King Charles's daughters though he had several more coming on (that patient Griselda Queen Marie bore him ten children, most of them during the years that Agnès Sorel reigned over him). But they were King Henry's first cousins, and the grandfather they had in common had been insane; besides, two of King Charles's sisters had been queens in England without any happy results either to France or to them. But an alliance of the sort seemed expedient; the English occupation was threatening Anjou and King René's affairs needed regulating. He had an eligible daughter whose energy of character was remarked by King Charles during the year she had recently spent at Court; she should mate with his gentle, dreamy nephew and keep the Fleur-de-Lys above the Rose.

It is not likely that the affair could have originated without the co-operation of Queen Yolande, but it is a strange paradox of politics by which the future of Anjou's daughter was planned by Burgundy's Duchess.

King Henry was amiably responsive to the idea of a French alliance and had already commissioned a reluctant bishop to report on the charms of the Count of Armagnac's daughters, stipulating, however, for a sight of their portraits "painted in their kirtles simple and their visages as ye see them". Whether the ladies were granted a picture of the suitor is not clear; in any case the bishop's mission did not prosper. The alliance does not seem to have been eagerly desired by France. For a hundred years the kings of England had to her cost been claiming her as theirs; now this Henry of Windsor was called her king by two crownings. But neither was at Rheims where alone her true king may become so; the ceremonies at Westminster and Paris meant nothing at all to the French people. In Nôtre Dame an English bishop poured the holy oil on Henry's head; of the twelve peers of France there were none to do him homage but only English lords with stolen titles like his own. As he went to his crowning in Paris he halted his company to ask who was the old woman at a window of the Hôtel of St Pol watching and feverishly signalling; when he heard it was his grandmother the dowager Queen Isabella, he saluted her in all simpleness and duty. But the people took it ill, and indeed it was ominous; they hated her for her wickedness and the sale of their country to England. And there was no release of prisoners nor remission of taxes nor scattering of largesse that December day in Paris; "if only one of ourselves were getting his daughter married surely he would order the business better than this", said the Paris townsfolk for whom the words "stupid" and "English" were become synonymous.

In the spring of the year 1444, King Charles VII holding his court at Tours, came "the Marquess of Suffolk with his wife and other honourable personages as well of men as of women" to sue for a truce that might result in a stable peace if his master King Henry of England were to wed King Charles's niece Margaret. Her mother had already brought her from Lorraine; having been approved by Suffolk and his following, she was betrothed to him as proxy for King Henry, on a day in May when she had not long entered her fifteenth year. At the ceremonial banquet, she was seated by Queen Marie and treated as her equal in tacit acknowledgment of the Treaty of Troyes by which Henry was King of France. Appearances were kept up before the English embassage, but the inner workings went heavily. England asked for Anjou and Maine as dowry, but René resisted as he had done ten years earlier when Burgundy bargained for Bar. For nearly a year the affair hung fire; Margaret's was not a patient nature and her gouvernante may have had difficulty with her, for the Luxembourg suit persisted, having been renewed on Nevers's discomfiture.

At last a settlement was made, the islands of Majorca and Minorca on which René had a claim through his mother being named as dowry. France might wonder if England who controlled the Biscay coast was making a bid for the Mediterranean too. But like many of his other possessions René's right to the islands was titular; his daughter went to her husband with empty hands.

She was married to the Earl of Suffolk as proxy for King Henry in Nanci cathedral; at the same time and place her sister became the wife of Ferry de Vaudemont. As at child-marriages in India to-day, everything was done to distract the victims from looking forward fearfully into the future—feasting and pageants, King René excelling himself in his favourite pastime—the ordering of a tournament. The Luxembourg suitor, his blazon the daisy, was the conqueror and received the prize from Margaret's hands. The Earl of Suffolk was not the only deputy for King Henry that day.

The sisters who were brides together were really strangers to each other. After events indicate that the elder had a jealous nature that would grudge the fuss made about the other. But the husband of Yolande of Anjou was by her side an ardent lover with whom she would dwell among her own people, while her sister's for all the pomp and circumstance was as yet a bloodless shadow in a far and barbarous land. Some sense of the contrast may have come to Margaret herself like a cold wind of foreboding out of the North whither she was travelling, for, when taking leave of King Charles who rode with her two leagues out of Nanci, the high-hearted girl fell suddenly into a passion of weeping. It is not likely she was moved mainly by grief at parting from one who was using her to further his own purposes, but who mingled his tears with hers, made her a facile compliment and rode away. When she and her father parted at Bar-le-Duc it was without any words; so may Jephthah and his daughter have looked on each other.

In Paris she was carried in state to Nôtre Dame with "the grete apparyll of chayres and other costious ordinance" brought by the English embassage for such occasions. Duke Charles of Orleans, a man who in many ways resembled her father, was there, released from captivity in England by one of the conditions of her marriage treaty. As he rode with her towards

Normandy what did he tell her of the land where he had lived not unhappily for nearly thirty years? In him, at the English frontier, she bade farewell to her own near kindred and was enveloped by her husband's. Richard, Duke of York, the Governor of Normandy, took her to Rouen where it was said she had an attack of illness and her place in the state entry was filled by Lady Suffolk. But ill or well she was able to perform what was probably the first independent action of her life; she bought some pieces of silver plate bearing the arms of the house of Luxembourg and St Pol, had these erased and replaced by her own complicated coat. This venture in finance must have emptied her purse for her next was the pledging of two articles "of mock silver" to the Duchess of Somerset, wife to one of the Beauforts, a family that often came to the financial rescue of the sovereign.

At Harfleur she waited it was said for a fair wind; but there were those in England who did not favour the marriage and Parliament was dilatory about granting supplies. Only through much tribulation was Margaret to enter the kingdom of her husband, for when at last she reached Portchester she was "sick of the labour and indisposition of the sea by the occasion of which the pox had brokken out upon her". More likely because she, though the King's bride, was poorly lodged at Southampton in a hostel for pilgrims of all degrees and from all parts. Whatever the nature of the complaint it was not small-pox for she recovered in a week with the help of a trousseau of new clothes, the gift of King Henry and the work of an English dressmaker.

Thus at last was Margaret equipped for her real bridegroom. He is described "of stature goodly of body slender, to which proportion all other members were correspondent; his face beautiful in which continually was resident the bountie of mind with which he was inwardly endued". He was then twenty-five, she just seventeen; they were married by Bishop Ayscough in Titchfield Abbey on St George's Day. The wedding-ring set with a glowing ruby was that given by Cardinal Beaufort to the King on his crowning in Paris.

Duke Humphrey of Gloucester who had opposed his nephew's marriage behaved, when once it was accomplished, like the gentleman he was. With five hundred men-at-arms in his livery of white and scarlet he met the King and Queen on their entry into London, when they were abundantly welcomed by the people who loved the Duke and took their cue from him.

A month later in Westminster Abbey there was set on Margaret's head the glorious crown King René had had made for her by his goldsmith, a noted artist of the time, Clement Peak of Vézelai.

II

The political condition of her husband's kingdom was on the surface much like what Margaret had left at home. In the royal exchequer shortage of money and shifts to raise it; around the King a ring of relations, semi-royal and noble, all outdoing each other in intrigue. The difference was in the central figure: Charles of Valois self-absorbed and self-indulgent but determined at last to keep his crown by blending the feverish elements round him into one force for the expulsion of the common enemy. In England, his sister's son, gentle, peaceable, easily intreated with so devout a belief in his coronation as a sacrament that he never dreamed it could be undone, concerned for the true welfare of his people "with thoughts whose very sweetness yieldeth proof that they were born for immor-

tality". Already the College Roial of Our Lady and St Nico-
las was rising over against Clare Hall in Cambridge; when he
looked out from his house of Windsor, there, in the valley, lay
Eton College, the apple of his eye.

Now into his serene, contemplative existence burst an
urgent, impetuous being full of fresh interests and points of
view. He had a large tolerance for the pleasures and desires of
others, and delighted in her zest for life; but, except for a
hearty desire to be of use in the world and a complete innocence of its ways, they had little in common. She was the
child of her age and its conventions; he was as one born out of
due time, and went his own way. She loved hunting, and
understood "the manage of hawks and the making of dogs".

> "Trampling heard I all around
> Of hounds, of horses and of men.
> Much talk was there of hunting then
> How they had gone to slay the hart.
> The Master of the Hunt blew three
> Notes on a grete horne lustily
> At the uncoupling of the hounds;
> And soon they stir the hart that bounds
> Away hallooed and followed fast",

sang Chaucer in the days when the Duchess Blanche went
hunting; but the notes of the great horn had no message for her
descendant Henry of Windsor. He loved

> "The oakis grete streight as a line
> With branches broad laden with leaves new
> That spongen out against the sonne sheen,
> Some golden red and some a glad, bright green";

but though trained by Richard Beauchamp himself to "all manly exercises", the chase to him "was misplaced pleasure, vain satisfaction. He did not care to see the creature when taken cruelly defiled with slaughter nor would he ever take part in the killing of an innocent beast", says John Blacman, his confessor and friend. His wife was quick to resent and slow to forget an injury while he was of those who when smitten turn the other cheek. "Take it away," he said when told that a ghastly object on the Cripplegate was part of one who had been traitor to the King's Majesty, "I will not have any Christian man so cruelly mishandled for my sake." Margaret came from a Court where, in spite of poverty, all was ordered exquisitely, even sumptuously, the artist in her father requiring that he and those about him should go beautifully clothed and furnished. The artist in her husband would have seemliness in dress but no more to distinguish him unduly from his fellows. At a time when the dress and appointments of people of rank abounded in colour and fancy—

> "Ye prowd galontes hertlesse
> With your high cappes witlesse
> And your short gowns thriftlesse
> And youre longe peaked shoon—",

the King "always wore round-toed shoes and boots like a farmer's and a long gown with a rolled hood like a townsman and a full coat reaching below the knee with foot gear wholly black, rejecting expressly all curious fashion of clothing". In some ways an exasperating husband; but there is no doubt there was a real affection between them; "neither when they lived together did he use his wife unseemly but with all honesty and gravity"; while "his humility, his pitifulness, his patience" called up in her that impulse of championship which a good woman feels for a husband who takes no thought for himself. It irked her that he was not nor tried to be master in his own house. When those who had ruled his youth now strove with each other as to which should rule his kingdom, he withdrew himself as into a pavilion from the provoking of men and went on with what he knew he could do. She came from a country and a family whose women took part in affairs; she felt herself to the manner born and in panoply. But as yet she showed only the defects of her qualities; and in that she was very young "it behoves us pardon nature". By thoughtlessness in the choice of her friends she seemed to encourage the factions that honeycombed the Court; and, like many good people, she was officious. Did a dependant or one of his friends seek preferment in the Church or in government service or licence to hunt in a royal preserve or the love of a lady? Impulsive, friendly, recking nought of like or dislike, worth or the want of it, the Queen rushed to the rescue, wrote a letter with her own hand and the man was made, the banns were cried—or so she supposed. But the rich widow (a stranger to the Queen and double her age) who was ordered by her to marry Thomas Barnby "sewer of our mouth" mated elsewhere; and "The Quene came into this town. . . and she sent after my cousin Elizabeth Clere to come to her, and she durst not disobey her commandement and came to her; and when she came into the Queene's presence the Queene made right much of her and desired her to have an husband the which ye shall know of hereafter; but as to that", adds Dame Margaret Paston acidly, "he is never nearer than he was before".

This rôle of ministering angel was noted by a wise man who had the better opportunity for observing the Queen because he was a canon of "the free Chapel of St Stephen within the palace of Westminster". His name was Andrew Dokett and he was also the incumbent of St Botolph's Church in Cambridge and the Principal of St Bernard's Hostel in the University. By successive inspirations he had increased its revenues and importance; the King had endowed it and given a charter. Now the Principal bespoke the Queen's interest in a scheme to move it from the North side of his church to a site nearer the river beside the Carmelite Friary and the King's College. Before long the King had a petition from his "humble wyf Margaret who meekly beseecheth the foundacion and determination of the College of St Bernard to be called the Queenes College of Sainte Margaret vergine and martir and Saint Bernard Confessour".

After the usual conventional preamble about "the conservacion of our faith and augmentation of pure clergie namely the imparesse of able sciences and faculties theologic", there is a clause which occurs in no other document of the sort: "and to laude and honoure of the sexe feminine like as two noble and devout Countesses of Pembroke and of Clare founded two Colleges in the same University". Here is the gist of the matter and thus does this emulous woman appear the first self-confessed feminist in our history. The motive she imputes to the two noble and devout ladies would have puzzled them and may well have startled President Dokett. But they had passed to where beyond such problems there is peace, and he had got what he wanted from the Queen, one of whose lovable qualities was a capacity for enthusiasm and the power of communicating it. The Marquess of Suffolk, Edmund Beaufort Marquis of Dorset and Richard the Duke of York were witnesses of the charter of the College and were very likely benefactors also. The King gave another donation which was exceeded by Bishop Lumley's; he was Treasurer of the Kingdom and in a better position than anyone to know how straitened were the royal finances. Some of her household were swept into the vortex of the Queen's new charity; her steward Lord Bardolf, her chamberlain Sir John Wenlock and two of her gentlewomen the Lady Margaret Roos and Mistress Elizabeth Wydville. "Indirectly the College owes Queen Margaret considerable pecuniary assistance" says its historian, a statement for caution almost worthy of President Dokett. When she had money she was generous with it as when she had anything to do it must be done at once. In the end of July 1447 were the buildings begun; the first Court and the great gateway were finished within the year and another contract made for "the syde next the freres to be done in as hasty wise as they may be goodly". Here it may be remarked that King Henry's and Queen Margaret's foundations were the first in the University to have buildings designed from the beginning for the purposes of a college.

It was the Queen's College "to laude and honoure of the sexe feminine", but it was the King's building, work that instinctively he understood and this was his flowering time. The first court of his College Roial built partly of stones from the ruined Castle of Cambridge, is hid now from most of us by the old University Library of which it is a part. But the first court of the Queen's College and its gateway in whose vaulting are the figures of St Margaret and St Bernard have changed not at all in purpose and very little in appearance since the day when the Queen first looked on them and recalled in the rosy brick with facings of white stone some of the castles of her own home. It is easy to believe that this court had the same architect—whether the King "of his own avyse" or another who is nameless—as the contemporary buildings at Eton, for besides fineness of workmanship and outward resemblance both have a secret appeal to the sense of home "felt in the blood and felt along the heart with tranquil restoration".

The King chose William Millington the first Provost of his College to frame the statutes for the Queen's College. He had been educated over the way at Clare Hall to whose shelter he peacefully returned when the Fellows of King's ejected him from his office because he did not hold with the statute which exempted the members of the College Roial from the discipline of the University authorities; also he doubted the wisdom of the rule that all the scholars should come from Eton. Apparently this gave no offence to the tolerant founder "who grieved at his dismissal" and straightway trusted him with the statutes of the Queen's College; if he ever drew them up they did not weather the storms of later years. But the record of Queen Margaret's founding is writ in stone; her coat of arms is in the first court, and on the foundation stone of the Chapel are the words "The power of our Lady Margaret shall be our refuge and this stone laid in her name the sign of her protection".

She had meant to lay that stone herself when the Parliament met in Cambridge to discuss the vexed question of the possession of Anjou and Maine with the two kings of France real and titular. But instead of such high guests the town had a visitation of the plague which gave King Charles an excuse to stay away. It was to St Edmundsbury that "all the Commons were summoned in their most fencible array" to attend King Henry, who, as he went serenely to the shrine of one of his favourite saints, was probably the only man without an uneasy sense of gathering clouds.

Feb. 1447

Humphrey of Gloucester the heir to the throne dragged himself from a sick-bed to attend a Parliament packed as he knew well with his enemies. It is thought he meant to plead with the King and Queen for the release of his wife Eleanor Cobham, imprisoned these seven years for the sin of witchcraft by which it was said she had sought to compass the King's death. The poor, beautiful creature confessed at her trial that she had used magical devices but only to gain and keep her husband's love, a practice common enough at the time and for long after. Before the Duke could come to speech with the King at Bury, he was arrested by the Cardinal's orders on a charge of high treason and imprisoned in his lodgings where he died from natural causes and grief of heart, as is now thought. The candid, affectionate King was overcome by grief; he had a long memory for kindness and between him and his uncle was that gracious bond—the love of letters. But "the sickness how God knoweth", muttered the Londoners to whom the Duke was both hero and good comrade. His death took place in Suffolk's country for whom as for Cardinal Beaufort it meant the end of a long quarrel; and unfortunately the Queen who seldom thought twice made haste to claim a payment from the Duke's estate due to her revenues on the death of the heir to the throne. Often when she was only needy she has been called greedy, but now her motive was given an uglier name. "After this day the fortunes of the world began to fall from the King so that he lost his friends in England and his revenues in France for shortly after all was ruled by the Queene and her counsayll to the grete disprofyte of the King and his realm and to the grete maugre and obliquy of the Queene which syn that tym hath been well proved hath had many a wrong and false report made of her."

Then there was as yet no child of the marriage. Since the days of Queen Philippa, now made into a standard of perfection by the people, there had not been a really satisfactory royal family so that England could hold up her head before her enemies. The heir to the throne was now Richard, Duke of York, descended from Edward III through his granddaughter Philippa of Clarence who married one of the Mortimers. For the best part of a hundred years this persistent family had couched in the shadow of the throne yet ever "like a lion creeping nigher". Childless Richard II named one of them heir to the throne which cost his son Edmund years of attainder and imprisonment by Henry IV. On Edmund Mortimer's death his nephew Richard inherited his many titles to which he joined the name of Plantagenet the knightly cognisance of their ancestor Geoffrey of Anjou. Though it has long been the custom to give that name to Geoffrey's descendants from Henry II to Henry VI, they never so called themselves. It was Richard Duke of York who with a fine sense of advertisement revived Plantagenet after three hundred years and used it as his family name—a great advance on Mortimer. An alert, ambitious man of ready and persuasive speech, in determination of character ably seconded by Cecily Neville his wife, who bore him four sons. Beautiful, vulgar, pretentious and scheming (nowadays she would be called "a climber"), making no secret of her own and her husband's aims, parading her wealth and her charms and her fine, large family, she might seem more than a match for the childless young Queen. But Margaret bore herself towards her with an admirable dignity and managed never to fall out with her.

Ireland was the place wherein honourably to bestow a troublesome friend; thither was Richard Plantagenet sent as the

King's lieutenant, but his wife's nephew Richard Earl of Warwick remained on the watch in England; he had the gift of divining and directing the trend of public opinion which we find expressed in the popular songs and ballads passed from mouth to mouth in street and tavern and sometimes posted on the church doors. They might be called the forerunners of the newspapers of our day, and at this time they were nearly all in favour of the house of York. "This Richard (of Warwick) was not only a man of marvellous qualities...but also from his youth by a certain practice and natural inclination so set them forward with witte and gentle demeanour to all persons of high and of lowe degree that among alle sortes of people he obtained grete love, much favour and more credence which things were daily increased by his abundant liberality and plentiful housekeeping that the common people judged him able to do alle thynges and without him nothing to be well done." The same could not be said of the Duke of Suffolk now April since Cardinal Beaufort's death the King's (or the Queen's) 1447 chief minister. Before that, he had lived almost constantly in France which he loved and the English had been taught to distrust him.

> "For fear or for favour of any fals name
> Lose not the love of the commonalte."

Not many among the King's party had that. There was Talbot "our good dogge", the terror of the French, who was fighting for Bordeaux; but the people would have none of Edmund Beaufort the governor of Normandy. Others who held by the King were his half-brothers the young Tudors, who as yet did not count for much, Cardinal Kemp, Chief Justice Fortescu, the families of Ormond and Roos besides some who like Wenlock shuttlecocked between the parties. Though both had their share of brains the balance of character may be said to have been on the King's party; but "the children of this world are in their generation wiser than the children of light".

Among them all the King was a waif "governed by them whom he should have ruled and bridled of such as sharply he should have spurred. But on the other part the Queene was a woman of grete witte yet of no greter witte than of high stomach desirous of glory and covetous of honour, and of reason, policy, counsaill and other gifts and talents of nature belonging to a man full and flowing...but yet she had one point of a very woman for oftentime when she was vehement and fully bent in a matter, she was sodenly like a weather-cocke mutable and turnynge"—as when a bride, she wept on the road from Nanci. "Capable of fears, a woman naturally born to fears" which now were crowding thick upon her.

1449 The end of treaties, embassies and conferences was that France held Anjou and Maine, "called the keys of Normandy"; a year later the marriage truce was broken and the conquest completed of that principality. There were dark rumours that in spite of great Talbot Guienne and the rich wine lands were slipping away too—a judgment on the King for breaking troth with the daughter of Armagnac, said the people. And they murmured against the man who had brought about the profitless alliance with Anjou.

> "God kepe our Kynge and gide him by grace
> Save him from Southfolkes and frome his foos alle."

Though the Duke of York was in Ireland "The wind of his breth was in every corner of the land". The Duke of Suffolk was impeached by Parliament for treason and condemned to death, but the King had the sentence changed to one of banishment, and the Duke made for France, leaving a letter for his son, brief, simple, dignified, which gives his memory a certain nobility. In the channel a swifter ship than his overtook him and he was murdered "by persons unknown" but first granted May 2 the grace of shrift by his own chaplain from whom came the 1450 tale of the beheading with a rusty sword on the side of a small boat in the dark while they jeered at him "Ye shall die like a knight". The next day his body was cast up by the waves on Dover sands.

Lawlessness prevailed on land also. Already the sins and negligences of the Church had been visited on two of her bishops, Moleyns at Portsmouth and Ayscough whose own people dragged him from the altar of Salisbury Cathedral and brutally hacked him to death. In Kent the commons had risen and taken as their leader one who called himself Mortimer and claimed the succession to the throne by descent from Lionel of Clarence. He was really Jack Cade, an Irish adventurer and outlaw, only trying like his betters to get something for himself out of the welter of politics for "so inveigled were the brains of the noblemen that the honor of the realm was clerely forgotten and nothing yerthly but their private phantasies looked on". Cade's so-called "rebellion" was quelled in a few weeks and was not of importance except as a sign of the times and the cause of the return from Ireland of the real Mortimer. The King, as did Richard II in like case, prepared to meet Cade and his rabble on Blackheath, bearing arms in a serious cause for the first time in his life. The Londoners were overjoyed, as they told him, to live or die with him but the Queen would not have it and took him away to Kenilworth.

It may be that already she had cause to fear the untoward effect on him of strife and tumult and was wise in what she did; but it rendered his father's son contemptible in his people's eyes and deepened their suspicion of herself. Later he was allowed to make a progress through Kent and Sussex for the judgment of malefactors; "in his justice and compassion he considered how they with perverse people were seduced and deceived, and so punished the stubborn heddes and delivered the ignorant and miserable people". But "the same yere stood at ones thirteen heddes on London Bridge".

He could flee for relief to Cambridge and watch the growth of his chapel on a site to the south of the College and near the Salthythe, one of the wharfs on the river. The townspeople doubted of this gradual absorption of their trading grounds by the University, not foreseeing it was to be the chief source of their prosperity and the King's Chapel their crown of glory. He usually lodged in King's Hall (the foundation of Edward II), now part of Trinity College; though his statue has disappeared from its gateway he is still commemorated there by the shields which quarter the French lilies with the English leopards.

Why did he thus take Cambridge to his heart when Oxford was his father's university and also Duke Humphrey's who had fathered his intellectual life? Cardinal Beaufort was at Peterhouse for a year; but it is more likely to have been John Langton, one of the Royal chaplains, Master of Pembroke Hall, and Chancellor of Cambridge University at the time when the King was seeking an object to benefit, who suggested he should do for Cambridge what William of Wykeham had recently done for Oxford.

And neither Henry nor Margaret can have been ignorant of

the fact that it was the poor scholars of Cambridge whom their ancestress Queen Eleanor had chosen to benefit. Two years after her death (in 1290) another lady called Matilda atte Woulde granted "to the Chancellor and Masters of the University the advowson of the church of St Michael in Cambridge, in part for the maintenance of suffrages for the souls of the Kings and Queens of England, their children and others the benefactors of the University... and in part for the sustenance of poor scholars". About the time of the final foundation of Clare College (in 1347), Nigel Thornton the physician (whose house was bought by Badew for the beginnings of the College) "is said to have given certain houses in Shoemakers' Row for the support of the chaplain of the University whose special office it was to recite the names of the benefactors to the University and to pray for them". In the sixteenth year of King Henry VI, he received a petition from the Chancellor John Langton, the Masters and Scholars "for a common library for the use of students especially poor scholars with a certain chapel of surpassing beauty for the celebration of divine service for the souls of their benefactors". Thus it is evident that for the past hundred and fifty years the University had been used to remember them and their gifts before God.

The Queen's College was prospering quietly under provident President Dokett, when Margaret's energy found a new vent in an effort to establish in London a guild of silk-spinners all of "the sexe feminine", at which the citizens grumbled, fearing, quite without cause, for the wool trade. It was her lot to have her good evil spoken of, though she took trouble to conciliate the people, going about the country for this purpose like a modern M.P. nursing a constituency, only the whole of England was her affair. It was during one of these progresses that she interested herself in the marrying of Mistress Elizabeth Clere and gave audience to that critical lady Dame Margaret Paston who wrote to Sir John in London "I pray you that you will do your cost on me against Whitsuntide that I may have something for my neck. When the Queen was here I borrowed my cousin Elizabeth Clere's device for I durst not for shame go with my bedes amongst so many fresh gentlewomen as here were at that time." The possibility that the Queen who had her family's eye for gawds might mark the appearance on another of Mistress Clere's device did not occur to the country lady, shrewd though she was. It is not likely that Sir John took her hint; he was a careful soul.

One of the "many fresh gentlewomen" was Mistress Elizabeth Wydville whom the Queen dowered handsomely on her marriage about this time to Sir John Grey. Another marriage which the King and Queen had at heart was between two of his wards—his half-brother Edmund Tudor Earl of Richmond and solemn little Margaret Beaufort. She was a visionary like Henry himself; that she was also a considerable heiress was nothing to him who thought little of ways and means. When Cardinal Beaufort's executors offered him £2000 from the residue of the estate: "my uncle was very dear to me and did me much kindness while he lived; do with his goods as ye are bound to do, I will not have them", said the King. But he was troubled when the payments from his Duchy of Lancaster to the College Roial were unpunctual and insufficient, which was not seldom; and he made an addition to the salary of Sir John Fortescu "for his life to enable him to keep up his state more becomingly and meet his expenditure while in his office of Chief Justice, and also that expenditure which it will be fitting he should make when he shall

have ceased to hold that office". Yet, to quote a song of the day,
"So pore a Kynge was never seen
Nor richer lordes alle bydinge",

an unhealthy state of things which was not unnoticed by that same Chief Justice: "For certainly there may be no greter perill growe to a Prince than to have a subjett equipolent to himself. How necessary is it that the Kynge have grete lyvehoods in the which it needeth that he exceed gretely every man of his land which lyvehood undoubtedly he hath not at this day" said Sir John Fortescu later for the edification of the King's son. "The King borroweth his expenses for Christmas" wrote one of the prying Pastons to another with that pleasure in the discomforts of their betters that tartly flavours their correspondence; and "the King and Queen could get no dinner Twelfth Night for they had neither money nor credit". Yet the clutch of poverty never hampered their freedom of spirit nor impaired their personal dignity.

III

Now, far away on the Bosphorus "the faire citie of Constantine the Noble" was conquered by the Turks and an alien religion established in Europe. A black year for England for besides "the grete hindrance and shame to all Christendom" she had to face the loss of her French possessions and, consequently, her status as a European power. Of all that her king had inherited from France, there remained only the town of Calais and—a malady of the mind that showed itself in him at this time. Though the bells of Windsor and Eton answered each other and all the king's scholars shouted for joy because a

1453

Oct. 13 son was born to him, he sat "quiet as a stone" nor made any sign, even when the child was put into his arms.

A Parliament called in his name appointed the Duke of York Protector of the realm; the new-born child was proclaimed Prince of Wales, his rights as heir to the throne secured and an allowance granted for his maintenance and education. A yearly income was allotted to the Queen and special provision made for medical attendance on the King; the Protector ordered all things well but Margaret was not deceived. When Edmund Beaufort Duke of Somerset lost Normandy and was sent as a traitor to the Tower, she saw in it only the detachment of her chief ally. The Earl of Warwick was made Governor of Calais in his stead, which gave him control of the country's naval power, such as it was. An ugly rumour rose and spread and was believed that the child the Queen had borne was not the King's else he would have acknowledged him; Margaret was persuaded that the lie originated with Warwick. London was like a darkened room full of whisperings and hidden terrors "where no man may know his friend from foe". Freaks and monstrous happenings of nature were magnified into "prognostications of warre and trouble to ensue, such as the three wonderful fishes—a sword-fish and two whales so grete that they brake the nets of the Thames fishers"; Cardinal Kemp the Chancellor who might be thought to be a man of peace had his servants armed; certain gentlemen of the guard at Windsor asked "to have a garrison kept there for the safe-guard of the King and the lorde prince" but really for their own.

1454 When Cardinal Kemp died the Chancellorship was given— not to Bishop Waynflete whom the King would have chosen— but to the Earl of Salisbury Warwick's father and the brother-in-law of the Protector who, fate helping him, drew his meshes closer about the Queen. In the negotiations between France and England that had been constant since her marriage, she had never betrayed her adopted country, but had placed its interests first; yet, with all her intelligence she does not seem to have begun to understand the manner of its government nor wherein it differed from that of France. Now, in a violent effort after freedom and the control of affairs she asked from Parliament no less than absolute powers to act as regent for the King, and so put a weapon against herself into her enemies' hands.

> "It is right a grete abusion
> A woman of a land to be regent
> Queen Margaret, I mene, that ever hath ment
> To govern all England with might and poure.
> Now hath the devill alle his devys
> Now groweth the grete fleur-de-lys
> Wymonis wyttes are fulle of wynde
> For here the blynde ledis the blynde."

For her past loyalties she had no credit with the hasty people; to them she remained an alien and everything she did was read awry—except her treatment of the King. The degraded state to which his neglected grandfather Charles VI was allowed to sink was never his; but he was cherished gently and his malady studied with all the skill the times could furnish and an admirable resourcefulness which gave him the ministry of music —next to religion most wont to comfort his soul. At last he came to himself, weak in body but clear in mind, to rejoice 1455 over his son and give thanks for his name of Edward. Margaret had given the child an English name for the saint and king in whose city and on whose day he was born, knowing that it would be after her husband's heart.

The Duke of York now stood aside while Somerset was re-called and the King's friend Waynflete made Chancellor, in room of Salisbury. But the nerves of the country inasmuch as they were centred in the capital were set on edge. Men wakened in the night thinking fearfully that the prisoners were broken out of Newgate or else the dead were risen and roaming the dark streets when carts full of armour and weapons rumbled and clanked over the cobble-stones. Three noble kinsmen, York, Warwick and Salisbury, were gathering their forces "for the grete deliberation that shall at the last spill all together".

They had their reason ready; the King had need of them for protection against Somerset, "so each part taketh the other for traytours". The strife they brought upon their country was "in a manner unnatural for in it the son fought against the father, the brother against the brother, the tenant against his lord". Yet it has been decorated with a flowery name; but roses are said to thrive upon blood. "What about the getting of the garland, keeping it, losing and winning it again, it hath cost more English blood than hath twice the winning of France." It poisoned some of the rivers of the land—its peaceful commercial highways; "the great river Wharfe" that was used to carry the stones from the Yorkshire quarries for the King's Chapel at Cambridge ran red after Towton field from the slaughter of thousands of his subjects, "alle talle Englisshmen of one nacioun". In spite of all the loyalty and heroic en-durance, there is about it no sense of glory; only a fulfilment of the poet's vision:

> "Treason and greed are rulers in these days,
> Envy and poison and duplicity
> And shameful murder done in devious ways."

At the beginning of the troubles Margaret was twenty-four years old and, having just borne a child, might reasonably expect to rest and be cherished. But that was never her way and no one at the time was reasonable. She saw herself now the sole champion of two helpless creatures between whom lay the hopes of the kingdom. "To assure to us the possession of our Kingdom... with a generous heart and the force of a man, you threw yourself into all manner of danger and knew no fear" was King René's tribute to his wife after his Naples campaign; it may be claimed for their daughter Margaret that she entered into that inheritance and loyally fulfilled its demands even when the baited, bewildered King named the Duke of York next heir to the throne and her son was disinherited. Though at this time aspects of her character emerge that are not at all "to laude and honoure of the sexe feminine"—such as her treatment of Borvil and Kyriel after the second battle of St Albans, or after Wakefield when, Herodias-like, she looked on the severed head of her enemy Richard of York and laughed "long and violently"—yet neither was it woman's work that she had to do. If the unlovely human qualities slumbering in most of us are so readily roused by the fret of ordinary existence, how much the more by the ordeal of such a life as hers was for those seven years. But she was never the wanton of Warwick's invention nor the shrew she is made to appear in the plays of a later age where almost the only truth told of her is the line which stands at the head of this chapter.

Even an unsympathetic observer of her career must acknowledge that she had no luck; the blind forces of nature fought against her, especially the sea. But once in the thick of trouble, she did not waste her mind on morbid misgivings. With a buoyancy of nature which ignored the checks and warnings of the past, nor questioned what her powers might be, she bartered Calais to King Louis and Berwick to the Scots. After flying from a stricken field, she was enough herself to take in hand some of that efficient nation and teach them a bit of their own business.

> "God bless Margaret of Anjou
> For she taught our Dunfermline websters to sew",

says an old, unsponsored rhyme (doubtless rejected by the experts who weave the fabric of accredited history but perhaps worth treasuring as an early specimen of Scots humour). With clear eye and steady aim she brought down a buck in Alnwick park during the siege of the Castle; out of sufferings and indignities she could make a vivid story for her cousins of Burgundy in a poor one-room lodging at Bruges. For it was the former foes of her house who came when she called to France for help. Her father was overborne by his own difficulties, her prosperous sister was wondering only how little she could do for her, and King Louis, her first cousin, how much he could get out of her. But Duke Philip and his son Charles, though they were quarrelling with each other at the time, agreed in giving practical aid as well as much real kindness to her and her ragged retinue who served her and shared her miseries for little more reward than love; she had her family's gift of attracting and attaching faithful service.

So she rode the storm like the mother-eagle, "her nest on her wings". Except for one brief period she never parted from her child; but for him it is a question whether she could have endured. Like herself he was born and nurtured amidst the rumours and the traffic of war; at the age of seven he was knighted on a battle-field. Yet he grew up a happy, natural boy, taking for granted as children will the chances and changes of a homeless, disordered childhood. The French, apt to notice such matters, approved the grace and accomplishment of his manners which yet were not affected, but, like those of all the Edwards of his line before and since, modest, frank and friendly. They availed to soften the roughness of the rudest prince in Europe—his cousin Charles of Burgundy who was yet perhaps the truest gentleman of them all. "A goodly, feminine and well-featured young gentleman" was this Edward; and whoso notes this description of him and recalls his father's face can have little doubt about his being indeed the King's son.

The studies of good learning secured by his father for other men's sons were not denied to him in spite of the restless conditions of his life; at one time he had the best brain in England for his tutor, Sir John Fortescu Chief Justice of the King's Bench, who never enjoyed the pension his master set apart for him "when he shall have ceased to hold that office". He put on his armour instead and adventured his aged person in more than one pitched battle. When Warwick set the crown of England on the head of Edward Plantagenet and a price on that of everyone who would not acclaim him King, Sir John left the wife and children he loved and followed his rightful sovereign into exile in Scotland and France. The castle of St Mihiel on the Debatable Land between France and Burgundy, from which Countess Sophie ruled Bar in the eleventh century, sheltered her exiled descendants in the fifteenth and was still on debatable land and pregnant with the meaning of war for us in the twentieth. Sir John with the title of Chancellor to the King in Scotland was Henry's accredited ambassador to the French Court, adviser to Queen Margaret and supervisor of the Prince's education. He soon took the measure of King Louis. Writing to one of his colleagues he says "Touchynge the safe conduct which ye desire to have of the Kynge of France it were good that ye hadde it. Nathless I counsel you not to trust firmly thereupon for he hath made many appointments with our rebels by which it seemeth he hath not always intended to kepe the peace and truce which he hath made with us." From King to commons Sir John has a poor opinion of Frenchmen—"In all this contre is no man that will lend you any money have ye never so grete need"—and none at all of their institutions from the nature of their government to the state of their roads; of painful journeys, poorly horsed, to Paris and Rouen on the King's business he writes with gleams of rueful humour which disappear when he thinks of the salt tax. "It is cowardice and lack of harts and corage that kepith the French men from rising and not povertie which corage no Frenchman hath like to the English Man." Gallant Sir John, type of the real patriot to be found in all countries and times, who persists in the belief that righteousness and liberty are to be found only among his own people however desperate may be their plight. He never lost hope in the redemption of England but lived up to the meaning of his name Fort Escu—strong shield against despair for the exiles of St Mihiel. He used the leisure those seven years gave him to put forth his great work Concerning the Praises of the Laws of England—"that nervous treatise" as another great lawyer has called it. It is certainly copious, ranging wide through space and time from the creation of the world and man as set forth in Holy Writ, by way of Plato, Aristotle, Virgil and St Paul to the laws of England and the divine right of the House of Lancaster to administer them. It is written in Latin and in dialogue form, the Prince being the questioner, and would have been a heavy load of learning for the lad were it not for the nature of him who gave it: "a man truly just by the discernment of his fellows who venerate and obey him, trying to help everyone and to stand in no man's way; never would he injure any but would rather hinder those who do"—surely the ideal character of a lawyer and teacher. And there were forests for the boy's hunting (King Louis's niggardly new game-laws not as yet stretching to Bar), and trout leaping in the Meuse. The beginning and end of all so-called field sports, which is the larder, was a pressing consideration during those lean years. "We beth alle in grete povertie yet the Quene sustaineth us in mete and drink so as we beth not in extreme necessity. Her highness may do no more for us than she doth.

Item: the bearer had of us but eleven scutes for all his costs toward you by cause we had no more money. Item: my lord Prince sendeth to you now a letter written with his own hand."

So Sir John, pleased to display the progress of his eleven-year-old pupil, ends on a happier note enclosing a pleasant little letter "written at St Mychael in Bar with myn own hand that ye may see how gode a wrytare I am. Edward" to his "dear cousin" Lord Ormond who was nursing the family interests in Portugal. (Here the use of "cousin" is not a mere compliment; the Ormonds were the direct descendants of Elizabeth the Welshwoman fifth daughter of Edward I and his Queen Eleanor.)

It is evident that Queen Margaret and Sir John understood and trusted each other; the appeals for help with which at this time she was bombarding the courts and chancelleries of Europe show signs of his drafting and censoring though the passion that fuses them must be hers alone. But it was as well that some of his sentiments were hid from her (being in the Latin tongue) or she and he could not have lived so long under the same roof. "Neither can the fact that woman was made for the help of man call her to the performance of any great service. For women are kept from the brunt of war by timidity, from cares of state by tenderness of understanding, from the labour of tillage by tenderness of frame and from mercantile affairs by a certain kind of heedlessness." These were links in the chain of Sir John's argument that the House of Lancaster being of the male line of Edward III had a prior claim on the throne of England. He went so far as to look askance on the blameless birth of Philippa of Clarence ancestress of the House of York; but later, when Edward IV spared his life, he was wise enough to recant this and some other of his irrelevant heresies. Could he but have seen the day when his beloved country would be ruled by one, seventh in descent from Philippa of Clarence, one of whom it was said even by the Holy (c. 1586) Father himself: "She is certainly a great Queen, only a woman, mistress of only half an island, yet she makes herself feared by Spain, by France, by the Empire, by all."

Margaret's mother Isabelle of Lorraine died in the year of Prince Edward's birth; some years later Tiphaine the nurse went to her fine tomb in the church of Nantilly St Pierre at Saumur; when Margaret came home a fugitive with her son in her hand there were none of her own left to whom she might display him except her father, her brother and her sister— Yolande of Anjou now reigning with her husband in Lorraine and keeping a jealous eye on the reversion of Bar. With a fine mixed family of six of which one or two were about the age of her sister's son, she does not seem to have gone out of her way to make his mother and him welcome during the years they were her neighbours. The suspicion and distrust of which Sir John Fortescu complains may have had their beginnings with her. But more than once in the early years of the exile, King René came to his castle of St Mihiel where forty years earlier his marriage with Isabelle of Lorraine had been ratified. In his company Sir John could not but mend his opinion of Frenchmen while to young Edward his remarkable grandfather would be a rare companion. Not the least interesting thing about him was his spectacles; he was the first prince in Europe to use this invention lately come from the East.

It is a pity that he and his son-in-law Henry were fated never to meet. When his family fled to France the King remained in Scotland sometimes in Edinburgh with the Black Friars or in Linlithgow Palace where that thrifty Fleming the Queen-mother saw to it that her son's treasury was not the poorer by his entertainment. With the young King James a year older than his own son, Henry had more in common than an intricate kinship. James too was a child when the burden of a kingdom was thrust upon him in succession to an able, vigorous father; and he too was a lover of beauty especially in architecture and music. Here ends the likeness for he had neither Henry's religious genius nor mental instability. But the fair chapel in Linlithgow Palace and the Parliament hall of Stirling Castle (where also he founded a chapel with a fine service of music) show that as a builder James knew what he was about; and it may be that he owed some of his inspiration to the fact that his cousin Henry was his guest and intimate in the years that led him up to man.

The world looked upon King Henry as "an Innocent man neither a foole neither very wise whose study was more to excel other in Godly lyvynge and vertuous example than in worldly regiment or temporall dominion". But when the yoke was eased from off his shoulder and he had not to look upon the slaughter of his people he was sane enough and knew his own mind. He never put off the King, nor in captivity was he unhappy having long taken upon him that service in which is perfect freedom. So when one of those who judge of others by their own feeble lights asked him "about the time of the feast of Easter how his soul agreed at that most holy season with the troubles that pressed upon him and so sprouted that he could by no means avoid them: 'The Kingdom of Heaven to which I have devoted myself from a child do I call and cry for,' he said; 'for this Kingdom which is transitory and of the earth I do not greatly care. Our cousin of March thrusts himself into it as is his pleasure.' It is also said when the King was shut up in the Tower he saw a woman trying to drown a little child and warned her by a messenger not to commit such a crime and sin hateful to God, and she rebuked by this reproof desisted from the deed she had begun."

When he began to feel the effects of an alliance made by his cousin of March with his cousin of Scotland, Henry withdrew himself to the North of England; but there he was betrayed to his enemies and taken for the second time to the prison of the Tower of London. The ill news travelled fast to the little Lancastrian Court hundreds of miles away; Margaret and her ministers were never without "secret tidings of the likelihood of the world" in spite of the stringent penalties in force against those who were discovered to be corresponding with "the queen that was". She could not fail to know of Warwick's hunt round Europe to find for the usurper a wife who should strengthen and illustrate his position, for the sister of King Louis's queen was one of the ladies marked down, when

Edward upset everything by the announcement of his marriage five months previously to Elizabeth Wydville, the widow Grey, once a lady-in-waiting on Queen Margaret. Hence Warwick's rage at having been sent on "a sleeveless errand" and the beginnings of a rift in his relations with King Edward. And King Louis resented the insult to his sister-in-law which drove Edward into the arms of Louis's enemy Charles of Burgundy to whom Edward married his sister Margaret Plantagenet and then went on with the fatuous policy of promoting his wife's relations and ignoring his own. But Warwick too had a policy by which he detached Clarence the King's brother whom he married to Isabel Neville his daughter. Far different was this from the day of Ferrybridge when "the erle of War-wycke came blowing to King· Edward like a man desperate, mounted on his hackney...and lighted down and slewe his horse with his swourde saying 'Let him that wil flie for surely I wil tarry with him that wil tarry with me' and kissed the cross of his swourde". The see-saw was going again but with Warwick and Clarence on the Lancaster end. When that sank they fled with their families to France and asked help from King Louis. He now appears in the unusual rôle of peace-maker, which he played with some address, though his cousin Margaret was hardly to be persuaded to a reconciliation with the man who had slandered the birth of her son. But with the help of King René and Sir John Fortescu it was done, though Warwick had to bow the knee before her for nearly half an hour recanting the slander but gaining his end which was the betrothal of his daughter Ann to the Prince of Wales. For he dreamed of founding a dynasty and this was his second bid for it. And behind the puppets stood "sturdy and fell Lewes" working them all for his own ends.

March
1470

By September Warwick and Clarence had landed at Dartmouth and marched on London. "Upon the 12th day of October the Tower was given up by appointment and King Henry was taken from the lodgynge wher before he laye and was then lodged in the King's lodgynge while the Duke of Clarence drew nere unto the citye. And upon Saturday the next following the Duke of Warwick and the earle of Shrewsbury and the lord Stanley rode into the Tower and there with alle honoure and reverence set out King Henry and conveyed him to Paulys and there lodged him in the bysshoppe's palays and so then was admytted and taken for King through alle the lande."

Oct. 16
1470

It was now Edward Plantagenet's turn to fly; with his young brother Richard he cast himself upon their brother-in-law Charles of Burgundy who once had courteously entreated Lancaster and had now to shelter York. And as his enemy King Louis helped Warwick with men and supplies so did Charles equip Edward who returned to England to be joined by Clarence. "There was dayly waitynge upon the see syde for the landynge of Queen Margaret and prynce Edward her sone"; but they had first to fight the winds and waters which did not let them land till the middle of April, at Weymouth, only to hear of the triumph of York's forces and Warwick's death on Barnet field; little had Margaret ever thought to weep for that. With his wife and daughter, a mournful little company of women, she hastily took sanctuary in Beaulieu Abbey for King Edward was moving swiftly westward. The command of her forces was in the hands of the young Duke of Somerset who overruled her desire of pushing on into Wales to join Jasper Tudor, King Henry's brother. There was feverish debate and divided counsels resulting in the havoc of all her hopes at

Tewkesbury where her son now in his eighteenth year took   May 4
the field as a soldier for the first time and the last.   1471

When he was brought before his "cousin of March", there
was one there "gnawing his nether lip", as near to him in blood
and not three years older who had always hated him not only
for that he was Prince of Wales but for his shapely beauty, and
now he was the husband of Ann Neville. When the usurper's
arm felled Prince Edward to the earth, the dagger of Richard
of Gloucester was one of the first to pierce him. And Clarence
on whom he cried for help—Clarence too was consenting to
his death.

Margaret was now in the power of the man who is said to
have feared and hated her more than any other of his enemies.
She was carried in his train to London and lodged in the Tower
prison to which already her husband had been returned but it is
not likely that she was allowed to see him. A few days later he
"the victor victim" was murdered and by the same hand that   May 21
slew his son. For long he had been in that state of complete   1471
submission to the will of God which is the heritage of the
saints so it were presumption to pity him, but what of her upon
whom the ends of her world were come? Could King Edward
but have given her the mercy of death—but he took his re-
venge the rather by prolonging her agonies. These were
mitigated by his queen who remembering many kindnesses
procured her removal to Wallingford Castle on the upper
reaches of the Thames of which the châtelaine was Margaret's
first and constant friend in England Alice Chaucer the dowager
Duchess of Suffolk. After four years King Louis "less from
generosity than calculation" and her father King René effected
her ransom for fifty thousand crowns on condition that she
renounced all pretensions to the crown of England (which

must now have become to her a matter of indifference); also she was exempted from King Edward's authority and became again subject to that of King Louis—of which he meant to take every advantage.

He was gradually subduing the power of the nobles and absorbing their territories—Anjou among them—for the crown; "what he might not overcome with strength he would win with dyssimulation and trechery". Margaret now ceded to him her claims on Lorraine and Bar in return for her ransom. Two years earlier when making his will her father had assigned her a pension of two thousand crowns in gold and, "should she ever return to France", the castle of Kœurs in Bar for her residence. But Yolande kept her out of it, Yolande now a widow fighting fiercely for Lorraine against Burgundy as her mother had done. She knew her cause was lost if she put herself in Louis's power and could not suffer a dependant of his so near her as Bar though it were her destitute only sister.

Their father who always did what came natural had wisely turned his back on the ruins of his life. His son John of Calabria dead (and that mysteriously, it was believed by Louis's agency), his daughter Margaret un-queened and, like himself, beggared, he retired to the only part of his wide dominions that his nephew had left him and, with a second devoted wife, lived among the people who loved him sharing their gentle pleasures in the sunny, tuneful land of Provence. But neither here was any room for Margaret and her sorrows of which one of the bitterest must have been that now nobody wanted her; even politically she had lost her importance as her cousin Louis let her see when, on her father's death, she appealed to him for help. So, as was her way, she stretched a helping hand to another waif cast aside from the traffic of the world: George Chastellain a gentle old courtier magnified into a poet who had started life as a servant in the household of Philip of Burgundy and rose to be the herald and chronicler of The Golden Fleece, that order of Knighthood which Philip instituted. Chastellain spent his last years fashioning to Margaret's order, and after the manner of Boccaccio, the *Temple of Ruined Greatness* wherein all those within his memory and hers who had fallen from their high estate are commemorated and commiserated;

"For kingship intended
It might have been beautiful once
But now it is ended",

and sounds comfort dreary enough for the desolate woman. But she could conjure up other memories: the coming of her son, the day when his father's eyes first saw him with understanding, and he thanked God for the name she had given the child, how he looked when first he drew a bow and sped his arrow to a mark. If these were also but cobwebs of comfort, she had a more enduring substance in the first-born of her mind, the mate of the College Roial where "the power of the lady Margaret shall be our refuge and the stone laid in her name the sign of her protection".

When René gave up the castle of Angers and his thrifty nephew King Louis got rid of the beasts and birds kept in one of the great towers, it was left to humane René to provide for their gaolers. The keeper of the birds Bertrand de Gosmes and his Moorish wife Cresselle were given the Manor of Réculée where the Maine turned back upon itself, a pleasure house in a watered garden with delicate pictures of birds and flowers painted on its walls by René himself. Here his daughter

Aug. 25 tossed with trouble was taken in and comforted by his servants
1481   till she died and was carried across the river to lie beside her
        father and mother in Angers Cathedral.

> "Forget not yet the great assays,
>   The cruel wrongs, the scornful ways,
>   The painful patience and delays,
>   Forget not yet.
>
> Forget not oh! forget not this,
> How long ago hath been and is
> The love that never meant amiss,
>   Forget not yet."

CHAPTER V

ELIZABETH WYDVILLE

Queen Consort of King Edward IV of England

I

In the autumn of 1435 and in the forty-sixth year of his age, John Duke of Bedford died at Joyeux Repos, his villa above the town of Rouen where the Maid was burned who defied and outwitted him. His widow, Jacquetta of Luxembourg, a fine young woman of twenty, took her fortune into her own hands and staked it on handsome Richard Wydville, a gentleman in her service; it was a case of Joanna de Clare and her Monthermer over again only without the complication of a family. Richard is described as "an accomplished Knight"; he was the heir of his father who owned considerable property in Kent and Northamptonshire and was esquire of the body to King Henry V, seneschal of the Tower of London and then lieutenant of Calais. Nevertheless the Wydvilles were reckoned as of low degree, and on the discovery of Richard's marriage with a royal duchess, not only did her own family cast her off but that of her late husband brought a legal process against her for marrying again without the King's permission. Nothing abashed, she paid a large fine, gained her pardon, and kept her pension as widow of a royal duke with her title of Duchess of Bedford. Not for her the cowering attitude of her dispirited sister-in-law, Katherine, the King's mother, who lost herself in vain regrets and must have made a dull wife to Owen Tudor, her second husband. After her death and the departure to Normandy of the Duchess of York, Jacquetta was able to make good her position as the first lady in the land, and held on her conquering way without doubts or desertions to make the Wydville fortunes. Such as she are to be found in all ages and every station of life, from the nameless mother of Zebedee's children to certain among our own friends and relations. In their paths no stone is left unturned; dauntless, unashamed they go glancing, questing here, there, everywhere in the manner of the domestic hen. Jacquetta's brood numbered fifteen, of whom eleven grew up in the rule their mother taught them—the family before all.

1437   Elizabeth, the first fruit of her parents' love story and the cause of its discovery, was born in 1437 probably at her grandfather's castle of Grafton in Northamptonshire. Her parents, young, handsome, all the more interesting because of their romantic marriage, were not likely to be left long in the shade. Not only with matrons of her own rank but with those in the one below it who had social aspirations, Jacquetta established the reputation of her house as advantageous for the training of their daughters in manners and matrimony; Dame Margaret Paston had her eye on it. Far from losing his position at the Court of Normandy, Richard Wydville became more important there, and in time was chosen by the Duke of York as one of the escort who brought the King's bride to England. Jacquetta seized this opportunity to secure for her daughter the protection of the young Queen to whom she was related—if distantly—and who was thought to have a kindness for the family of Luxembourg.

When Elizabeth was little more than twelve years old she became one of Queen Margaret's household and, inevitably, a partaker in the intrigues of the Court which would, however, come natural to Jacquetta's daughter.

When, after the fall of Suffolk, the division between Lancaster and York began to show itself, the Duchess of Bedford was able to keep friends with both parties and even make them useful to her. In due course her husband was made Baron Rivers and a Knight of the Order of the Garter, by which time her attractive if poorly dowered daughter Elizabeth was contracted to an eligible young man of Lancastrian sympathies—Sir John Grey son and heir of Lord Ferrers of Groby, who could show a clear descent from King Edward I through Isabel Lady Ferrers daughter of the Lady of Clare.

Sir John Grey may have been twenty-one and Elizabeth sixteen when they were married; the Queen gave her a generous present of two hundred pounds and retained her services which looks as if the two were friends. If so it was by the attraction of opposites: the Queen frank, impulsive, heedless of consequences; Elizabeth full of common-sense, secretive, cautious, counting the cost, waiting on events, profitable qualities which were transmitted to the great-granddaughter who bore her name and successfully ruled the country. But she was gentle too, often soothing the frets and salving the wounds caused by her mistress's rash temper.

The second battle of St Albans, though claimed by the Lancastrians as their victory, was not so for long; four months later the Earl of March was crowned in London. Sir John Grey who had become Lord Ferrers was killed on the field; his title and property became forfeit to the Crown: there was nothing for his widow and children but the refuge of Grafton, her father's house. She was not of those who followed Queen Margaret into exile; the fields of Towton and Hexham meant a parting of the ways for many, and among them the Wydvilles.

Three years previously Lord Rivers and his son Anthony

had had a brush with the Yorkists when "my lord of Salisbury
rated Lord Rivers calling him Knave's son...and my lord of
Warwick rated him and said his father was but a little squire
brought up with King Henry V and since made himself by
marriage and also made a lord and it was not his part to have
held such language to those who were of King's blood. And
my lord of March rated him likewise." But Jacquetta was
much too clever to have a standing quarrel with any who were
in high places. It is remarkable that when the attainder and
forfeiture of King Edward's enemies was almost universal Lord
Rivers and his sons suffered not at all, nor did the pension of
the ex-Duchess of Bedford cease; indeed some of it was
advanced by King Edward's treasury and with a gracious
message.

Her next effort was for the removal of the attainder on
Lord Ferrers's widow and heirs. Times were bad and living
dear; no doubt two growing boys were a serious addition to her
already teeming family; their mother's presence, too, might
prejudice her sisters' prospects, and anyhow why should not
justice be done? She took the shortest way about it by encouraging Elizabeth to follow an old custom and plead her
cause with the King himself who happened to be hunting in
the neighbourhood.

He was now twenty-three, a bachelor but of large experience
in the ways of women; everywhere there was chatter about his
love affairs; it were good he should take a wife and settle down.
Warwick was searching for him abroad and not prospering;
let the King choose for himself at home and now in April, the
mating-time. "Thought is quick" and needs few words between two women like the Duchess and her daughter. So one
fair morning as the King rode free and careless through the

wood near the Castle, the Lady Grey and her children were taking the air; gentle, sorrowful, appealing in her widow's dress, she was a sight to give any man pause. Which the King did, lighting down to greet her and bidding his servants take the children apart that he might walk and talk alone with her.

She knew better than to weary him with complaining; it is likely that he wished the meeting longer for, having granted what she asked, he trysted her again and yet again under the budding trees. Then it was his turn to be suitor and to have the novel experience of refusal. She would have none of him except as husband in lawful wedlock for which she said she was not good enough. But all came about as Jacquetta had planned, though secretly. Very early in the morning of May 1464 Day they were married in the chapel of the castle "none present but the spouse, the spousesse, the Duchess of Bedford her mother, two gentlewomen, the priest and a young man who helped the priest to sing". Then the bridegroom went hunting as usual; but it was no longer in the greenwood that he trysted the bride.

When Lord Rivers returned some days later he found himself host to one of the men who had told him he was unfit to associate with the sons of kings. What were his thoughts when his wife revealed what she had done? The King was the King—young, handsome, everywhere popular; whatever was his company he was at ease in it, neither below nor above it so that all men felt at home with him; they called him the Rose of Rouen, though never since he attained manhood could he be said to have worn "the white flower of a blameless life". But Warwick was their sun, and there would be Warwick to reckon with.

The marriage has been called a romance and so at the time

it may have seemed to Edward; he thought it was of his own making and he was doing a fine, generous thing in taking a wife from a rank beneath his own; also, to him she was that novelty, a virtuous woman. As for her, five years older than he, she was not concerned with romance though like us all she might have her illusions. He was the King—earthly, sensual but very human; she believed she could manage him.

The two gentlewomen who witnessed the secret marriage could not be expected to keep silence long; all summer the story was whispered about "till nedely it must be discovered because of others which were offered unto the Kynge. When this maryage was first blowen abrode, forren Kynges and princes marvelled and mused at it, noble men detested and disdained it; the common people grudged and murmured at it." But one wise man who had bowed low before the blasts of the last nine years now saw his chance of bringing to the Queen's remembrance the jewel he was cherishing in the marshes beside the Cambridge river. President Dokett was already known to Queen Margaret's gentlewoman; he was probably one of the few single-minded persons of her acquaintance and he asked nothing for himself. Nor had she anything to gain by compliance; it was perhaps one of the few disinterested actions of her life. And close, calculating, worldly though she was, she had a certain constancy "to the things that grow not old", a sense of the value of continuity which is instinctive in women.

On Lady Day two months before her crowning she took the Quenes College under her protection; a new seal was made for it whereon the eagles of Lorraine representing the first foundress were replaced by the undistinguished Wydville coat quartered with the royal arms. Elizabeth is supposed to have allotted some of her income for the completion of the buildings but of this there is no documentary proof; if such ever existed it may have been destroyed by the careful President in the brief Lancastrian interregnum. Though she had little enough to give she had learned from her mistress to set others on to the good work, notably her friend and fellow in that mistress's service, the Lady Margery Roos who was descended from the Dispensers and did much to redeem the honour of their name, especially by her generosity to the College founded in "laude and honoure of the sexe feminine". Therefore when she died, the President and Fellows gave her the signal distinction of burial in their chapel. The King's mother, "the Quene that should have been" as Cecily Duchess of York was wont with characteristic lack of dignity to sign herself, patronised the College. But to the rival power behind the throne—the Queen's mother—the Quenes College owed nothing.

Jacquetta had other matters to occupy her. Thirty years had passed since her marriage to a squire of low degree had caused her family to cast her off; but she was never needlessly vindictive and now gave it the chance to recognise a kinswoman in the Queen Consort of England. Philip of Burgundy was the more inclined to be gracious because the marriage had alienated his enemy King Louis; so the Count of St Pol, head of the family of Luxembourg, came to his niece's coronation as 1465 Burgundy's representative on Whit-Sunday of the year 1465 in Westminster Abbey.

II

No one now openly called the Wydvilles upstarts; gradually, gracefully but surely they had arrived, though in the face of Warwick's "patient, deep disdain" and the violent outspoken remonstrances of the King's mother. The position had therefore to be strengthened, and there was an orgy of marriages; two of the Queen's brothers and three of her sisters were swiftly and eligibly if not all suitably mated. Katherine Wydville was nine and her bridegroom sixteen, while John aged twenty took to wife the King's aunt, the rich dowager duchess of Norfolk who already had worn out three husbands and was to outlast this one. Next year the Queen's son, Thomas Grey, was married to the King's niece, little Ann Holland, heiress of that Duke of Exeter who chose to follow Queen Margaret and went barefoot in Bruges begging food and shelter while his lands and goods were bestowed with his daughter on the stepson of the usurper. Meanwhile Lord Rivers was advanced from baron to earl, made a Privy Councillor, Treasurer of the Exchequer and then Lord High Constable; he had the Garter already from King Henry. So Jacquetta made the best of both worlds. But the Queen, though like her a ready mother, brought forth in six years three girls only, in spite of the King's traffic with soothsayers who were in and out of prison according as their prophecies suited his hopes of a son.

1468 On the death of Philip of Burgundy the friendship of his son and successor, Charles the Bold (of Lancastrian descent and sympathies), was secured by his marriage as a widower of thirty-seven to Edward's young sister, Margaret Plantagenet. "As for the Duke's court I heard never of none like to it save King Arthur's court. And by my troth I have no wit nor remembrance to write to you half the worship that is here; by my troth they are the goodliest fellowship that ever I came amongst and best can behave them and most like gentlemen" writes the younger John Paston, dazzled by the glories of the wedding festivities at Bruges. So in England too the Court was gay and went its reckless way in a racket of pageantry that aped the age of chivalry. Duchess Cecily loved display and it was bred in her children. "The King came through Cheap tho' it were out of his way else he would not be seen"— being the sort of king who is not born but made. Parliament there was none for three years; when Edward wanted money he plundered a people stupefied by want and ruled by fear. "In the midst of the city was mischief and sorrow"; it is at this time that we find the first record of the use of torture by the State.

Though Warwick stood godfather to Edward's first child and even proposed to marry her to his son, he was all the while laying his mines; with him were his brothers, George Neville whom Edward unwillingly made Archbishop of York, and the Marquis of Montagu, a less certain quantity. Clarence, the King's brother, was deftly detached from his allegiance and married to the elder daughter of Warwick who now began to call the Wydvilles "seducious persons". When their property in Kent was raided and despoiled, his connivance if not his direct agency was suspected though "the wyttes of Kentysh-men be ever moveable at the change of princes". Jacquetta herself "was brought into a common noise of slander and witchcraft for that an image of lead made like a man-at-arms of the length of a man's finger was made by her to use with sorcery".

Then "in the wyde rumour and styrrynge the lord Rivers and Sir John his son. . . were beheaded", and at Kenilworth in Warwick's country. Not that this was taken as a national calamity; Rivers had made an incapable Treasurer; some thought him barely honest. His other office of High Constable was given to Tiptoft, Earl of Worcester, a scholar and a man of parts but whose studies in the new learning had not preserved *his* "humanities" for it was he "that for his cruelnesse was called the butcher of England".

So "led by blynd avarice and devilish ambicion forgetting scruple of conscience and the ende of all honestie" two men of the same blood who had once been friends and brothers-in-arms struggled for the mastery. Warwick was the first to feign withdrawal, taking his family (in which Clarence was now included) to France and allying himself openly with King Louis and Queen Margaret. Six months later he landed at Dartmouth with an army; then Edward's nerve failed and he fled to the Low Countries with his young brother Richard and Anthony Wydville.

The Queen was in the palace of the Tower awaiting the birth of a fourth child; on the rumour of Warwick's approach on the City, she removed to the Precincts of Westminster Abbey where she registered herself, her three children, her mother and one of her ladies as "Sanctuary Persons". "In that place which men reckoned as a prison what a rabble of Thieves, murderers and malicious heinous traytours there be." But it was her only way of safety. Soon the trumpets were sounding the restoration of gentle Henry from whom she could have nothing to fear; but Warwick was behind him and in the Parliament that met not many steps from her refuge she and her children were denounced as traitors "along with all or any who should aid and abet them".

Yet such there were who secretly sent food and comforts into the dismal place for pity of the child unborn. Elizabeth had the services of her own doctor and a friendly mid-wife (besides her mother who had borne fifteen) when just after All Saints another Edward was born at Westminster

Nov. 3
1470

though not this time in the Queen's fair ordered chamber, nor acclaimed by the shouts of the people and the sound of bells. Fearfully and in secret he was cradled, and christened, though in the Abbey Church, "like any pore man's sonne", without the pomp that had attended his sisters' baptisms but probably with more religious significance. The three little girls, Elizabeth, Mary and Cicely, were at this time too young to be affected by the unholy nature of their lodging, Sanctuary though it was called. It might weigh on their mother through the dark winter days but she could endure for she had borne a son. With the spring her lord came again bringing deliverance and the beginning of a new world where Warwick was not. By order of the man who owed him the kingdom his dead body lay "naked and open" for two days in the City that all men might see their sun had fallen from heaven. The end of the house of Lancaster was as nothing in comparison; for the people, King Henry and his son had long since passed into the world of shadows.

Queen Margaret was lodged in the prison of the Tower for a time, but was sent later to the stronghold of Wallingford on the upper reaches of the Thames of which the châtelaine was her oldest friend in England, Duchess Alice of Suffolk who lived nearby at her manor of Ewelm. This was arranged by Elizabeth, and was a kind as well as ingenious way of dealing with an irksome situation.

Those who had secretly helped the Queen when she was in the Sanctuary were now suitably recognised and rewarded, from the Abbot who was made a bishop to Mother Cobb the midwife. The King took pains also to entertain one who befriended him when he was a fugitive in Flanders, Louis de Bruges Sieur de Grauthuys. "When the sayd lord came to

Sept. Canterbury he was presented with wyne, capons, Fezantes,
1472 Partryches and other presents suche as they had in those religious places. . . .The mayre and his Brethren presented him
also with such deyntes as they had." His progress through the
land was marked by a succession of rich meals "with fruit and
swete wyne"; but he survived and reached Windsor where he
was received by the King and Queen. She who had just recovered from the birth of a second son was with her ladies "at
the marteaux, some playing at closheys of ivory and some at
divers other games the which sight was full pleasant. Also King
Edward danced with my lady Elizabeth his eldest daughter."
A pretty domestic scene calculated to impress the visitor from
Europe where Edward's reputation was anything but that of
a model family man. The next morning "my lord prince also,
borne by his chamberlain called Master Vaughan bade the lord
Grauthuys welcome" before he went hunting with the King in
the little park. In the evening a banquet in the Queen's apartments after which, at the discreet hour of nine, she and the
King and the Court generally seem to have accompanied their
guest to "three chambers of plesaunce all hanged with whyte
Sylke and lynnen clothe and all the Floures covered with
Carpettes. There was ordeined a bedde of good doune as could
be gotten the sheetes of Rennes also fyne Fustyans the Counter-
pointe Cloth of Gold furred with armyn. . .as for his hed Sute
and pillows they were of the Quenes own ordonance." But
the greatest glory was in the third chamber "where was
ordeined a Bayne or Two covered with tentes of white clothe".
Having displayed these the King and Queen and the Court
withdrew leaving the guest to "my lorde chamberlain who de-
spoyled him of his garments and went together to the Bayne
and when they had been in their Baynes as long as was their

pleasour, they had green Ginger, divers Cryppes, Comfyttes and Ipocras and then they went to bedde".

The next solemn function chronicled by the secretary of the Sieur de Grauthuys was on St Edward's Day when "William Alynton the speker of the Commons Parlemente declared before the King and his noble and sadde counsell the entente and desyre of his Comyns especially in the Comendacioun of the womanly behaviour and grete constancy of the Quene he being beyond the See". Then Louis de Bruges was created Earl of Winchester and so departed his hands full of gifts. Oct. 13

The choicest of these to him who was collecting a library would be the works of Christine de Pisan which enlightened persons of the time considered necessary to their intellectual equipment. It was the gift of Anthony Wydville (who had translated Christine's *Morale Proverbes* into English); as the frontispiece testifies, it was presented by Christine herself to the notorious Isabelle of Bavaria, Queen of France, who certainly can have made no use of it. It then passed into the possession of Duchess Jacquetta when her first husband was the Governor of Normandy; as he considered his nephew Henry VI was King of France, he may have helped himself to the book from the Royal Library to which it was restored after the death of Louis de Bruges. It contains what is believed to be the autograph of the Duchess: Jacquette fair and clear with an effect of grace and finish in elegant contrast to the sprawling, uncertain signatures of some of her famous descendants. Whether by intention or a trick of coincidence it was traced over the partial erasure of three words still decipherable as Sur Tous Autres—Above All Others—surely the expression of her whole life's persistence.

She did not live to welcome her countryman Louis de

Bruges to England; but she had seen the end of Warwick and triumphantly vindicated her reputation from the charge of witchcraft when she died on the edge of sixty, a year after May the return of her son-in-law the King, and when, such is human 1472 perversity, it is possible that he and her nine surviving children experienced a strange sense of freedom.

In the days of her first husband, John Duke of Bedford, his country ranked as a European power and largely by his efforts. In the course of forty years, during which she brought her second husband to glory and honour and seated their daughter on the throne, the realm of England had shrunk to a petty province given over to domestic feuds, with no financial credit, of little account in European politics.

Originally and entirely this was not Edward's fault, but neither was he the man to set it right. He was not concerned with the country's honour; his only title to kingship—besides good manners—was his ability as a soldier and now he was without the sinews of war. Though he devoured widows' houses and from one of the infrequent parliaments had secured the grant of an income for life, it all fell short of his needs. So, backed by the blessing of the Church, he went on tour about the country, a royal beggar "gently speaking to all men and especially to such as were aldermen whom he called worshipful and by their proper names saluted", making pilgrimages when convenient "and this way of levying money was after named a benyvolence". What the people thought of the tasks or taxes is told with no uncertain sound by the Paston family: "There shall be a convocation of the clergy in all haste which men deem will avail the King a dyme (a tenth) and a half" and "I beseech God send you good health and greater joy in one year than you have had these seven" writes Sir John from London to his mother in Norfolk. "Money is very scarce," replies Dame Margaret, "the King goeth so near us in this country both to poor and rich. I wit not how we shall live but if the world amend. I can sell neither corn nor cattle to no good prove." Later William, a young gentleman of Eton, light-heartedly advises her about the fitting reception of the King in their home county: "The King will be at Norwich on Palm Sunday even, to tarry there till Easter then to Walsingham wherefore ye had need to warn William Gregory and his fellows to convey them of wine enough, for every man beareth me in hand that the town shall be drunk as dry as York when the King was there. It were well for you to purvey you of some gentlemanly things against the King's coming for sure he will bring you guests enough. . . . My sister with all other goodly folks hereabout should accompany with Dame Eliza-beth Calthrop. . . for my lord hath made great boast of the fair and good gentlewomen of the country so the King said he would see them sure."

"Men look after they know not what but men buy harness (body-armour) fast; the King's menial men and the duke of Clarence's are many in this town; the Lord Rivers came to-day to purvey in like wise." So Sir John, and his mother answers him with the awful, inevitable understanding of her who has lived through years of war: "If your brethern go over the sea advise them as ye think best for their safe-guard for some of them be but young soldiers and wot full little what it is to be a soldier nor for to endure as a soldier should do."

But neither of her nor of her sons was this required at that time. King Edward indeed landed at Calais in July with an 1475 army gloriously arrayed for battle, but he was met by King Louis with the kiss of peace and his hands full of gifts. His miserliness might be a byword in Europe, but none knew better when it was worth while to scatter as now he did royally throughout the English host. It was not only "the archer's son" (as he persisted in calling the Duchess Cecily's eldest born) who returned home his pensioner bound over for seven years to keep a peace which Charles of Burgundy, baffled and furious, called "bothe as honourable and profittable as a Peascode and not so wholesome as a Pomegranite". As the French lords merrily expressed it, "the force of England hath and doth surmount the force of France, but the ingenious wittes of the Frenchmen excel the dull braynes of the English-men".

The usual inevitable betrothal sealed this treaty of Pec-1475 quigny; the Dauphin was contracted to the lady Elizabeth who was thenceforth treated with exaggerated state in her father's court. That questing parent then arranged the marriage of his son Richard with Ann Mowbray, orphan heiress of the Duke of Norfolk and a ward of the Crown. The children, both about six years old, were actually married in St Stephen's Chapel when the small bridegroom was invested with the late Duke's titles and revenues. Not that these meant much for all his life John Mowbray was kept a poor man by his rapacious mother, eighty-year-old Katherine Neville, the King's aunt and the Queen's sister-in-law. But such was his tact that she resigned a large part of her jointure as dowager of Norfolk to this very young couple.

III

"Pass banners pass and bugles cease
And leave our desert to its peace"

was all the universities asked at this time that by their poverty they might escape depredation. But the President of the Quenes College in Cambridge never missed a chance of securing its position or adding to its revenues. After the return of the house of York the College received a second pardon for its relations with the house of Lancaster; a certain Lady Joan Burgh was permitted to bestow a manor and two Fellowships were founded by citizens of London. Then "Elizabeth the 1475 Queen wife of the most illustrious King Edward IV as the true foundress by right of succession brought to completion what her predecessor had commenced but had not finished and put forth statutes". She had visited Oxford when her brother Lionel was Chancellor of that University; but he does not seem to have reminded her of the Queen's College there with the wistful appeal of its motto: Queens shall be thy nursing mothers.

Later, "by direction of our lord the King, of the most excellent princess the queen and of the most illustrious and potent prince Edward" the mayor and bailiffs of Cambridge sold to the College for forty marks the island between the river and Queen's Piece which to-day is called the Grove. "At the same time the College undertook to lengthen the small bridge (belonging to the town) next the College by twelve feet and also to widen the river on the East side of the island to fifty-one feet and had leave to build a bridge across it the arches of which should be as wide as the arches of King's College bridge." So should York be even with Lancaster.

"The most illustrious and potent prince" was at this time a delicate, shrinking creature of about five years old. His uncle Anthony Rivers, perhaps the most interesting of Jacquetta's children, was one of his governors; another was John Alcock, Bishop of Rochester, a man of God and a good physician for the evil humours that were poisoning church and state. In a later reign, as Bishop of Ely, he renewed the face of his university by rebuilding "the church of blessed Mary near the Market", endowing Peterhouse and founding Jesus College.

There is no doubt the Queen was a conscientious mother who took thought for her children. Conceived and born as they were in times "savage, extreme, rude, cruel, not to trust", inheriting neither her phlegm nor their father's coarse fibre, they might be "ill-fitted to sustain unkindly shocks", but were strong in their love for each other and for the things that are more excellent. Mercifully these are never left without witness which may be found at this time in some of the poems of John Lydgate (who died about 1451), and especially in the rhymes for Lytel John. Though primarily a manual of table manners, they set a standard of universal good breeding which five centuries have not bettered. The root of the matter is in honesty, humility, unselfishness and cheerful contentment "rememberynge that manners maketh man". Boasting is excluded along with pride, greed and especially cruelty: "Caste ye no stycke nor stone at foule or beest." That Lytel John may be intelligent in his prayers, the poet translated into English the *Salve Regina* or *Hail Mary*; and for Her sake

> "One thing I warn you specially
> To Womanhede take awe alway
> And them to serve loke ye have an eye

And theire commandements that ye obeye
Plesant wordes I avyse you them saye
And in all wyse do ye your diligence
To do them plesure and reverence."

"Playne in sentence (meaning), playner in language", there
is nothing here to insult a child's intelligence as in some of the
books for the young of our days though "children must be
of childly governance And also they muste entreated be with
esy thing and not with subtlety". Therefore

"Avyse ye well when ye take your dysporte
Honest games that ye should haunt
It is to a goode childe well sytting
To use dysporte of myrthe and plesaunce
To harpe or lute or lustily to synge
Or in the press ryght manerly to daunce.
Exercise yourself also in redynge
Of bokes enorned with eloquence
And revyse the laude of them that were
Famous in our langage these faders dere
That lysten so our langage to enhance
So my chylde these faders auncyent
Repen the feldes fresshe of fulsomeness
The floure fresshe they gathered up and bent
Of sylver langage the grete ryches
Who will it have my chylde doubtless
Must of them begge ther is no more to saye
For of our tongue they were the lock and keye."

From these words we may see that English as the mother
tongue had come into her own. They were among the earliest
to be printed in England by the man who above all others

magnified the reign of Edward IV and made it honourable,

1422 William Caxton, born about the same time as Henry VI, but of humble parents in the Weald of Kent where were the sheep whose wool made the people's clothing. Therefore it was natural to apprentice him to a mercer or cloth-maker of London, a man Large by name as by nature who left the boy a sum of money with which at twenty he crossed the sea to seek and find his fortune. He lived in the Low Countries for thirty years, chiefly at Bruges, prospered in business and developed a talent for affairs; at one time he was governor of the Company of Merchant Adventurers who looked after the interests of English trade in foreign parts. Thus he gained experience of men and manners as well in the courts of princes as in the markets of the world; his countrywoman Margaret the Duchess of Burgundy took note of him and persuaded him to give up business and be her mayor of the palace. But such a life could not content him long; he began to employ himself with letters "as a preventive against idleness", gratefully remembering that his parents had given him a good education. His translation from French into English of *The Histories of Troye* was soon in such demand that he was led to consider "an invention which began in a city of Almaine named Mayounce" twenty years before. When he was over fifty, a time of life which has been called the youth of old age and is not without its own intuitions and aspirations, he set himself to master the "craft and emprynting of bokys"; then, forsaking the Duchess and her household, he returned to his own country for the greatest adventure of his life. A hundred or even fifty years earlier he might have been persecuted as a wizard; but men's eyes were now opening on wider horizons and their thoughts were saner. Neither did he come as a stranger; he had never lost touch with London, being indeed a freeman of the Mercers' Guild. Also the fame of his book went before him and he had powerful protectors; it is likely he was known to the King whose sister he had served. So the Merchant Adventurer set up his press at Westminster in the Court neighbourhood and peacefully practised his hobby amidst the prancings of its mighty ones.

Foremost of those who came about him to see the marvel was the Queen's brother Anthony, Lord Rivers, though to him a printed book was not the novelty it might be to some. While he was journeying to Compostela for the Jubilee of St James, a fellow-pilgrim put one into his hands "which book I had never seen before and it is called the Sayenges and Dictes of the philosophers...because of the holsom and swete sayenges of the paynims a glorious fayre mirrour to all good Cristen people". Finding on his return that he had been appointed one of the Governors to the Prince of Wales, Lord Rivers made his second venture in letters by the translation of the great work into English "thinking also full necessary to my said lord the understanding thereof". As "a recreation and passynge of Tyme" for either uncle or nephew the book now seems stale and unprofitable, and only remarkable because it actually was the first to be printed in England. Some of the Dictes and Sayenges were omitted by the translator whether out of a regard for the reputation of the philosophers or for the tender age of the child for whose sake he undertook the work. When he brought it to his friend Caxton as to a mentor "to correcte and amende where as I sholde fynde faults and other fynde I none sauf that he hath left out those dictes and sayenges of his audtour Socrates touchynge women", the editor, printer and publisher obligingly added a chapter of his own prefaced by the remark "that ther is none so grete empedement unto a man as Ignorance and Women". Then, suddenly taking thought, "Socrates was a Greke living in a farre contre from hens which contre is alle of other conditions than this And men and Women of other nature than they ben here in this contre. For I wote wel of whatsoever condition Women ben in Grece the Women of this contre ben right Good, Wyse, playsant, humble, discrete, sobre, chaste, obedient to theyre husbandis, trewe, secrete, stedfaste, ever busy, never Ydle, Attemperat in speking and Vertuous in alle theyre Workes, or atte lest sholde be so."

Of all "the Women of this contre" the one who had the most need of this panoply of the virtues was its Queen. She had married the King with her eyes open to the fact that it was not in him to be a faithful husband; but she was true to her part of the bargain and besides had the sense to avoid boring him by playing the part of the injured wife. Thus she kept a certain hold over him though not over his family who always suspected and resisted her. Upstarts all—Plantagenets, Nevilles, Wydvilles—despising and distrusting each other, scrambling and elbowing for money and place and power while the people perished. Now it was Clarence who stirred up strife, bringing against both the King and Queen accusations that were a tangle of truth and fancy. He was judged a traitor and sent to the Tower prison, where soon after he died "as a 1478 fool dieth". Some thought that the manner of his death (by which he has become one of the buffoons of history) was arranged by his brother the King in order to avoid a public execution, though Edward made a great show of mourning. Then, that obstacle removed, he went on his way to feast and flatter the rich City merchants for their money, of which there was more need than ever, for the Duke of Gloucester's campaign in Scotland. After this came a thunderclap: King Louis stopped payment of what the English called the "tribute" and broke the marriage contract between the Dauphin and the lady Elizabeth—a grave affront. Edward replied by a declaration of war; but before he could follow it up, "this noble Kynge deceased in that tyme in whyche his lyfe was most desyred". April 9 1483

Thus, about thirty years later, wrote Sir Thomas More in an edifying account of the deathbed scene which it is to be remembered would meet the jealous eye of Edward's grandson, More's sovereign and friend. "But this wote I well," so the dying man is supposed to have addressed his own and his wife's relations, "Ye never had so grete a cause of hatred as ye have of love. That we be all men, that we be christen men this shal I leve for preachers to tel you—and yet wote I nere whither any preachers wordes ought more to move you than his that is by and by gooyne to the place that thei all preche of." Though we in our simplicity may ask which place, we may be sure Edward had no doubt about it any more than the grandson in whom he lived again.

Immediately after the King's death a Council was called which summoned his eldest son to Westminster to take the kingdom. The boy, now thirteen years old, was at Ludlow on the Welsh border with his first friend Sir Thomas Vaughan, Lord Richard Grey his half-brother, Bishop Alcock and Lord Rivers his governors. His mother knew he was safe and in good hands, nevertheless she asked the Council to order that a strong force of the loyal Marchmen should escort him to the Capital; but she was overruled and while silently she mused on what this might mean the fire of suspicion burned higher and hotter within her. A letter of sympathy from her brother-in-law Richard—after her sons the heir to the throne—did little to

quench it though he told her he had had King Edward V proclaimed at York and was himself about to escort him to London. Then she heard of their meeting at Stony Stratford, of
the Duke of Gloucester picking a quarrel with her brother
Rivers and sending him and Vaughan and her son Grey
prisoners to Pontefract. At this, in terror, she fled into Sanctuary, on the other side of the palace wall, with Richard,
Duke of York, and his five sisters—Elizabeth and Cecily
(who had been there before), Ann, Katherine and Bridget
aged three. Next morning when she looked forth, behold
the river as well as the Precincts thick with men-at-arms
in the livery of the Lord Protector as it seemed the Duke
of Gloucester should now be called. She could remember
when his father Richard held that office and how deadly
possessive he made it.

This was now the Fourth of May, the day on which she had
planned her son should be crowned at Westminster; and here
was she virtually a prisoner while he entered his capital in charge
of another. All she knew (or was ever to know) of his kingship was the noise faint and far off which the people made
acclaiming him. The procession did not touch Westminster
but turned off to the City where the boy visited his grandmother in her town house by the river, Baynard's Castle, long
a centre for the plots that quickened at the death of kings, when
up from Fotheringay would come Duchess Cecily on the
watch like some old spider with her great, brilliant eyes—all of
her beauty that was left. How much was her work in the web
that was now weaving? She who had had more than her share
of health and beauty is said to have had a weakness for the one
ugly, ill-shaped child of the nine she bore. And he was married
to one of her own stock; their son was descended fairly from

old John of Gaunt—not a slip of the Wydvilles like the dejected lad now before her. If he were to reign there was no knowing how far the Wydvilles might go.

After Baynard's Castle, he was taken to the Bishop's house by St Paul's to wait his uncle's pleasure and told that his mother had taken his brother and sisters into Westminster Sanctuary where even though it might be his birthplace it was not meet for the King to go. It seemed that no sooner was he King, than everyone he loved and was used to fell away from him; "Gone are they all the old, familiar faces."

Elizabeth could not better have served her enemies' ends than by her blind flight into Sanctuary though she thought only to ensure the safety of both her young sons. "Each of these children is others defense while they be asunder and eche of their lives lieth in the others body", she told those who came to take the Duke of York from her and put him in the care of "his loving uncle" as Buckingham, his chief henchman, called the Lord Protector—Buckingham "neither unlearned and of nature marvellously well spoken", the husband of Katherine Wydville yet busier than any about working up a case against her sister. In that hour, though her brother Lionel, the bishop, and her eldest son Dorset, deserting his post at the Tower, had fled with her into Sanctuary, Elizabeth might truly have said "There was no man with me". Alone, but for the boy in her hand, she faced those lords spiritual and temporal who a month ago had wept by her husband's death-bed and sworn to protect his children; she made a brave resistance, but "Therewithal she said unto the child Farewel my owne swete sonne God send you good Keeping let me Kis you ones yet ere you go for God knoweth when we shal Kis togither agayne. And therewith she kissed him and blessed him, turned her back and wept and went her way leaving the child weeping as fast."

Then the days went by in a twilight of rumour shot with agonies of conjecture. Out of the neighbouring palace came sounds of preparation for a coronation—whose? the kitchens smoked as for a banquet, then the fires went out, the food went bad and was thrown into the river. The princes were moved from St Paul's to the Tower, their own servants discharged and only one rough fellow appointed for their service. It was said that they pined: "the prince never tyed his points nor ought rought of himself but with that young babe his brother lingered in thought and heaviness. . . . Alas he sayd I wolde my uncle wolde let me have my lyf yet though I lose my Kingdom." That uncle lay at Crosby Hall between which and Baynard's Castle was continual coming and going for the Duke of Buckingham and the Mayor of London "toke it upon them to frame the Citye to their appetite. Of spiritual men they toke such as had wytte and were in aucthority amongst the people for opinion of their learnynge and had no scrupulous conscience." Such an one, the Mayor's brother Dr Shaa, was retained to preach at Paul's Cross a so-called "sermon" wherein not only the children "Elizabeth Dame Grey calling herself Queen" bore to the King but he himself were declared to be illegitimate, and Richard of Gloucester announced as the only lawful issue of his father Richard of York. The people might murmur and chafe, but there was no open protest. "These matters be Kings' Games," they said, "as it were stage plaies for the most part played on scaffoldes in whiche poore men be but lookers on and they that be wise will meddle no ferther."

1483   Midsummer came and the next day the Kingdom was

"offered" to Richard of the withered arm, who took it and was crowned with Warwick's daughter Ann Neville than whom no woman more unwilling was ever called Queen. It was his hour and the power of darkness into which passed two childish figures never to be seen on earth again by any that loved them. His son Edward fondly named by poor Ann after the husband of her youth (that ended on Tewkesbury field) was proclaimed Prince of Wales, when hope must have died in the heart of Elizabeth. During those fearful days she heard of the end of another of her children, Richard Grey, and of her brother, Anthony Lord Rivers, perhaps the only man that in all her life as queen she ever really trusted. About three weeks after the young King was taken from them, they were beheaded along with Vaughan at Pontefract Castle of murderous memories, and without even the pretence of a trial. While at Westminster, he by whose order this was done "streightly commanded the judges of the realm to execute the lawe without favour or delaie with many good exhortations not one of which he followed". Then to the Abbey Church to receive the sceptre of St Edward while the monks sang the Te Deum "though with faint courage".

Anthony Wydville had more reason than most to desire length of days. He had a quick, enquiring mind; marriage had brought him material wealth and family interest preferment. Though childless, he possessed the love and observance of the child who was heir to the throne; it was not in him to abuse such a trust; he would have been indeed a king-maker. But he died as he had lived, a philosopher, and with a knightly salute to Fortune who had thrown him in the lists. This we know from the "Ballet of Earl Rivers" made in prison while he waited for death.

"Somewhat musing and more mournyng
In remembering the unstedfastness
This world being of such wheeling
Me contrareing what may I guess?

I fere doutless remedeeless
Is now to see my wofull chaunce
For unkindness withouten less
And no redress me doth avaunce

With displeasure to my grievance
And no durance of remedy
So in this traunce now in substance
Such is my daunce willing to die.

Methynkes truly bounden am I
And that gretely to be content
Seeing plainly Fortune doth wry
All contrary from mine entent.

My life was lent me to one entent
It is nye spent. Welcome Fortune
But tho I ne'er went thus to be spent
So it is meant. Such is her won."

Something of his courage was in his sister Elizabeth. Grief
might take its toll of her body but her restless spirit nourished
itself and took action on the "secret tidings of the likliehood
of the world" brought to her by the doctor from outside who
attended her as she lay sick in the Sanctuary: the King had done
with Hastings the chamberlain, arraigned and beheaded between dawn and noon, "the King not being able to take his
dinner in comfort till he knew that head was off"; he would
like so to serve Sir Thomas Stanley the steward but that he feared

Stanley's son Lord Strange, a power in the Midlands. Morton also, the Bishop of Ely, might have been haled to the scaffold but that he was a churchman and the people were growing restive, misliking so many beheadings; so he was banished to Wales and put in custody of the Duke of Buckingham, though that cousin and henchman seemed not holding so fast to the King as he had done. At the time of the coronation he feigned sickness and was for staying away, "but the King sent him word to rise and ride or he would make him be carried". Then he came, a figure of such magnificence as brought all eyes upon him; but he withdrew himself from the feast afterwards so that men marvelled what it might mean. It meant, and that soon, a rising in Wales to put down King Richard and bring Henry Tudor, Earl of Richmond, to the throne. Then Dorset escaped out of the Sanctuary, surrounded though it was by the King's Guards, and joined his uncle Edward Wydville in support of the last hope of Lancaster.

Buckingham's rebellion seemed to fade out as quickly as it started. Henry Tudor got no farther than Plymouth whence he returned to Brittany where Bishop Morton, the Wydvilles and Dorset joined him; Buckingham was captured and beheaded at Salisbury. His widow Katherine Wydville afterwards married Jasper Tudor uncle and protector of Henry. In love as in war the Wydvilles were an accommodating family.

But "under white ashes may be coals of fire". The soft-footed doctor stealing in and out of the Sanctuary, curing the ex-queen, and not by drugs alone, was in the service also of the Lady Margaret Beaufort, the mother by her first husband of Henry Tudor. She was now, as the wife of Sir Thomas Stanley steward of the Household, holding her own at Richard's perilous Court in attendance on his queen, which did not prevent her from making, through the medium of the doctor, an alliance with the ex-queen for the betrothal of her daughter Elizabeth of York to Henry Tudor. Nor would it trouble the elder Elizabeth that the legitimacy of his father's birth was questioned, or that that father was but the half-brother of King Henry VI, any more than that she, the widow of the Yorkist King, should be helping to set the crown on the head of the Lancastrian claimant.

But King Richard who "never hadde quiet in his mind nor thought himself sure...when he went abrode his eyen whirled about, his body privily fenced, his hand ever on his dagger like one alway ready to strike again"—King Richard had his doubts of his cousin Margaret Beaufort. Her liberty was curtailed and the Steward was warned that his wife should from thenceforth send no message either "to her sonne nor to any of her other friends whereby any hurte might be wrought against the King which commandment was accomplished".

IV

1484 This year in the autumn died Andrew Dokett, founder and first President of the Quenes College, where for thirty-seven years while his country was one of the dark places of the earth he kept the lamp of life alight. Each of the three queens who reigned during his life as President had adopted the College—though the great rents with which "the most serene Consort of the most renowned Prince Richard the Third" (as they called poor unhappy Ann Neville) "augmented and endowed the College" were to its discomfort, being those that King Edward had stolen from her mother the Countess of Warwick. Like many of their ancestors and successors, he and his brother practised the art of vicarious generosity and had besides a value for what the wit of a later age has called fire insurance. When Elizabeth visited the College with her husband and son 1477 Edward, Richard then Duke of Gloucester also took upon himself to endow it "out of certayn funds late belonging to Elizabeth Countess of Oxford", whose husband, a loyal Lancastrian, was attainted and imprisoned while she was in hiding, earning a wretched living by sewing. The fellows of the Quenes College, who were of the Duke's foundation, were required "to pray satisfactorie for the prosperuse astates of the sayd duke, dame Ann his wife and Edward erle of Salisbury their first begotten son...also for our soverayne lorde King Edward IV, our soverayne ladye Elizabeth, fundaresse, the prince and all the King's childer. And when the president and fellows shall kepe a solemn Dirige in ther chapelle for ther fundaryse, there being the Universitee, then the sayd Richard Duke of Gloucester to have a speciall collett joyntly with the fundaresse."

But by an act of the first Parliament of Henry VII the Countess of Warwick and the Earl of Oxford were reinstated in all their honours and properties, the taint of King Richard's benefactions being thus removed for ever from the Quenes College, "which no whit grieved thereat as sensible that no endowment can be comfortable which consists not with equity and honour".

The Fellows of the Quenes College may well have been half-hearted in their prayers for Richard Duke of Gloucester, at least they did not avail him much. In the spring he lost his 1484 only child, the third Prince of Wales in thirteen years to die untimely. About this time Richard's sister-in-law, Elizabeth, and her family came out of the place where she had borne a son and lost a son and tasted the sharpness of death. Now she had to come to terms with the King, for she was at the end of her resources with four portionless girls dependent on her. The eldest, Elizabeth, beautiful in mind and body, with a tenderness for all unhappy, helpless creatures, renewed her friendship with Ann, the Queen whose boy she had petted and played with; the two were perhaps the only human beings who brought 1485 any natural happiness into Ann's life as Queen. She died a year later, leaving Richard free to find another wife and begin again to found a family.

There was not much choice; abroad he had lost caste, at home people were beginning to wake up from the spell his crooked will had cast upon them. When he proposed to marry his niece Elizabeth the only support he received was from her mother. Soothsayers who were as the priests of his religion to King Edward had promised him that not in his sons but in his eldest daughter should his dynasty be established. And better is an enemy at hand than a friend afar off. Elizabeth may have cheated herself into the belief that she was fulfilling her duty to the dead when undeterred by her own chequered experience of a queen's life she sought to force her daughter into it and with the man she had cursed and called her worst enemy. But she had not reckoned with the victim herself; not for nothing was she her mother's daughter. Though portionless she had her share of the serpent's wisdom that was the dower of the Luxembourg family. When her mother broke faith with the Lady Margaret Beaufort she held to it; and making her own interpretation of the soothsayers' promises, she contrived to communicate secretly with Henry Tudor across the sea through his step-father Sir Thomas Stanley, "that wiley fox", who cheated the devil, and who, though he could not read or write,

ruled Richard's household, kept his confidence and in the end Aug. 22
betrayed him on Bosworth field. 1485

After Henry of Richmond had reaped his harvest there and
been crowned King in London, he sent for his cousin Elizabeth
to the North whither Richard had banished her in his rage at
her repulsing him. Within six months she was married to King
Henry; a year later, having justified her existence by becoming
the mother of his son, she too was crowned in Westminster
Abbey. The glory of that ceremony she had all to herself; even
her mother did not share it. As if to mark before all men his
recognition of the fact that she was the lawful heir of the king
her father, Henry was not openly present but watched with his
mother from a secret place in the church.

The same discretion and nice sense of justice showed in his
treatment of his mother-in-law to whom he gave a suitable
pension, a choice of residences and all the consideration due to
her as queen-dowager. Her daughters Cecily and Ann were in
due time provided with husbands and dowered suitably; the
youngest, Bridget, being, as her name behoved, the bride of
Christ in a close order of nuns at Dartford. The King arranged
a marriage for Elizabeth herself, now a personable widow of
fifty, with the widowed King of Scots, James III, who was
about the age of her son Dorset. But his murder by his rebellious subjects put a stop to what might have proved a new
source of trouble for Henry. Her talent for intrigue cannot
have helped her, near or far, to be a comfortable member of
his family, especially when pretenders to the throne were
starting up. Dorset, a poor creature who took his cue from
her, was imprisoned for a time under suspicion of supporting
Lambert Simnel. Before long, after receiving an annuity from
the King, she made a dignified retirement to a convent of

Cluniac monks at Bermondsey, whose guest-house was endowed by her husband's ancestor Richard de Clare (grandfather of Elizabeth de Burgh). There as "founder's kin" she claimed and received hospitality till her death eighteen months
1492 later at the age of fifty-five, when she was laid "beside the body of my lord at Windsor without pompous interring or costly expenses thereabout". Herein she was obeyed to the scandal of such (they are ever with us) as are offended at simplicity. On Whitsunday—the twenty-seventh anniversary of her crowning —"the queen dowager's corpse was conveyed by water to Windsor and there privily through the little park conducted into the castle without any ringing of bells or receiving of the dean but only accompanied by the prior of the Charter-house, Dr Brett, Mr Haute and Mistress Grace and no other gentlewoman; and as it was told to me, so privily about eleven of the clock she was buried without any solemn dirige done for her obit. . . . Also a hearse such as they use for the common people with wooden candlesticks about it and a black cloth of gold, on it four candlesticks of silver gilt everyone having a taper of no great weight."

Was it because of some kindness from the dead woman that Mistress Grace, a natural daughter of King Edward, followed the coffin to Windsor? On Tuesday came Elizabeth's surviving children, all except the Queen who was sick, and Mistress Grace stole away. "That night began the dirge. But neither were the twelve old men clad in black but in divers garments and they held old torches and torches' ends."

> "God bless all our gains, say we;
> But, May God bless all our losses
> Better suits with our degree."

So Elizabeth Wydville died, poor, obscure, almost for-gotten like Queen Margaret her mistress. Nevertheless for that which they did in the morning of their days "shall mercy and truth preserve them; their lives are prolonged and their years as many generations so that they abide before God for ever".

CHAPTER VI

AN INTERLUDE AND A PORTRAIT

In the reign of King Henry VI there lived in Cheapside, London, a mercer "of a good figure and reputation", called Thomas Wanstead, with his wife and only child Jane. As became her father's position she was "honestly brought up"; that is, she could read and write, spin and sew, and had very likely been trained in the higher arts and graces by residence in the family of some lady of rank. She was worth teaching for she had wits and could use them; moreover she was beautiful. Therefore her father, good man, was minded to get her early settled in marriage and gave her to William Shore, a goldsmith "of a very fair character both for religion and morals". He sounds a dull husband for one who was little more than a child when she was married to him. But gentlemen of the Court who came about the house in Lombard Street to do business with him stayed to be entertained by her for she was "mery in company, redy and quick of answer, neither mute nor full of babble, sometimes taunting without displeasure and not without dysporte"; like Nicolette of old "sweet was the mirth of her answering word". Her fame went through the Court; lord chamberlain Hastings tried to carry her off but failed; she was on higher thoughts intent. When Edward IV returned in 1470 and took the kingdom, he took her also as his mistress. What her husband did about it is not clear except that he never denied her the use of his name; as "Shore's wife" she was known till the day of her death and after.

Edward, when first he usurped Henry's throne, laid jealous hands on his foundation of Eton College and diverted many of its revenues and possessions to the use of St George's, Windsor, the foundation of their ancestor Edward III; King's College, Cambridge, suffered also, though in a lesser degree, from these depredations. Though they were checked to some extent by the manful resistance of Westbury, the Provost of Eton, and restitution was grudgingly made from time to time, King Edward continued his cat-and-mouse game with the College which was in a state of great poverty and uncertainty as to its future. Then in the autumn of 1476 the Archbishop of Canterbury ordered the Chapter of Windsor to abstain from molesting the College under pain of "the greater excommunication" and to restore its property. This was done before the death of Westbury in the following year when he was succeeded by Henry Bost, Provost of the Queen's College at Oxford and Master of the King's Hall at Cambridge. He seems to have been able to hold one or both of these offices, for a time at least, along with the provostship of Eton for which he was the King's nominee. Yet another charge he had—perhaps the gravest of all—the soul of Mistress Shore whose confessor he was.

His epitaph records that by his influence the wife of King Edward IV largely benefited the College; certainly her brother, Anthony Lord Rivers, did so and perhaps at her suggestion. They and their fathers before them had served the house of Lancaster for which the Queen had the regard that comes of ancient kindness; if she combated the King's jealousy of its greater glories, it would be quite in character for her to do so— like Provost Bost—obliquely. Tradition, which often defies and outlasts chapter and verse, has it that the final reinstatement of Eton College in all its possessions and privileges was due to the mediation of the King's gay companion, Jane Shore. For this reason a portrait of her hangs in a place of honour in each of the colleges of King Henry VI's foundation. As works of art they are negligible and it is to be supposed they are not good likenesses, for "Proper she was and faire, nothing in her body that you would have changed but if you would have wished her higher; thus say they that knew her in her youth. The King's favour to sai the truth (for sin it were to belie the devil) she never abused to any man's hurt but to many a man's comfort and relief. Where the King took displeasure she would mitigate and appease his mind; where men were out of favour she would bring them to his grace."

In this portrait by one who served as a youth in the hall of a great churchman where they talked of her (though her day was done) as of one who could not be forgotten, there is more than mercy. See that ye despise not, He said, who shall judge us all. She was neither king's daughter nor honourable woman, yet wise men continue to do her the justice of grateful remembrance.

CHAPTER VII

MARGARET BEAUFORT

*Countess of Richmond and of Derby, mother of King Henry VII
of England*

I

Among the Flemings who came to England with the Hainault
family early in the fourteenth century was Sir Payne Roelt versed
in knightly lore and courtly usage to whom was given by King
Edward III the office of Guienne Herald. He had two daughters:
Philippa, the elder, entered the service of the Queen whose
name she bore and is believed to have married Geoffrey
Chaucer. Katherine, the younger, married Sir Hugh Swynford, a knight of Kent, and, when in France with him, attracted
the notice of the King's son John of Gaunt, Duke of Lancaster
and Guienne, who gave her the post of gouvernante in his
household and declared himself entirely satisfied with "the
good and agreeable service our very dear and beloved Dame
Katherine Swynford has done for our beloved daughters
Philippe and Elizabeth". Her contemporary Christine de
Pisan, who has laid down the law for such as she, would not
have commended her so highly, for she bore the Duke four
children, if not in her husband's life-time, certainly in that of
the Duchess Constance of Lancaster. Two years after that
lady's death, the Duke married the widow Swynford and made
his nephew King Richard II give a patent of legitimacy to her
children who were called Beaufort after the place of their birth,
that castle in France which Blanche of Navarre had as part of

her dowry when she married Edmund of England, brother of Edward I; they took their badge of the portcullis from it.

By the time their half-brother Henry IV had usurped the throne of England, their mother had seen her "valorous offspring" well on the way to be one of its ruling families, foreigners though they were, both by blood and upbringing. But they were descended from a king of England and made it their business to serve it in the whole-hearted, thrusting manner of "time-honoured Lancaster" which Shakespeare has transmuted into something very like patriotism. The three sons were soldiers, for Henry Beaufort though a clerk in holy orders took the field more than once in the French wars. His brother John, Earl and then Marquis of Somerset, reinforced his royal blood by marriage with Margaret Holand of whose legitimate descent from Edward I there could be no question; their daughter Joan married for love James Stewart, the poet, and King of Scots. Thomas, the third son, was Duke of Exeter (the title of Duke being as yet reserved for those of royal descent) and Admiral of the high seas. From the daughter Jane who married Richard Neville, Earl of Westmorland, descended Edward IV, Richard III and the Earl of Warwick called the king-maker. These are they who, honestly believing that it is by them the world goes round, sometimes manage to make it think so too.

But not John Beaufort of the second generation. A captivity in France devoured his youth and may have given a twist to his nature which was close and suspicious; as counsellor or leader of men he was a failure. Though promoted from Earl to Duke of Somerset and given as to father and grandfather before him the government of Guienne, he thought he should have had Normandy. When that went to

his rival Richard of York he was a man with a grievance, in-
tolerable to his fellows and at last to himself. When he died
at the age of forty-two, it was supposed that he took his own
life which his uncle, Henry the Cardinal, would count not only
sinful but poor-spirited.

As the Beauforts used, he had married prosperously the
heiress of the Beauchamps of Bletsoe in Bedfordshire, a younger
branch of the Beauchamps of Warwick. At the time of her
husband's death the Duchess of Somerset must have just returned from France whither she went with other "honourable
personages women as well as men" to bring home King
Henry's bride; indeed it was she who came to that young
woman's rescue at Rouen when her purse was empty. John
Beaufort was Margaret Beauchamp's second husband; their
only child was Margaret who was born at Bletsoe on May 31,
1441.

By her father's death three years later the child became a   1444
ward of the King, who deputed the Earl of Suffolk her guardian
as a return for his services in the matter of Henry's marriage.
But she was brought up with her mother's children by a former
marriage at Bletsoe a peaceful corner of England instead of at
the petty court of a restless, foreign capital which would have
been her fate had her father had his way about Normandy.
Her mother "ryght noble in manners as in blode", herself left
an heiress when very young, early gave her to realise the
responsibilities of an owner of property as well as the graces
desirable in such a position. And there might be before her a
yet greater future.

In the Beauforts' patent of legitimacy they were allowed "to
assume all honours, dignities, pre-eminences, estates, degrees,
and offices public and private whatsoever as well as perpetual,

temporal and feodel and noble by whatsoever name they may be called". When Henry IV confirmed this he added what he thought was a saving clause: "except the royal dignity". But his "dear brother" Henry Beaufort the clerk versed as well in civil as in canon law knew the clause to be inoperative, as it was inserted after the patent had received the sanction of Parliament. By the time he was Chancellor of England, his great-niece Margaret representing in her generation the elder male line of Beauforts had a place in the succession to the crown by right of that patent. The Duke of Suffolk her guardian was also aware of this; and when her mother married again he put his ward in charge of his wife Alice Chaucer her kinswoman, so that Margaret might make their son's better acquaintance.

Three years later when Suffolk was accused of treason and brought to trial, it was alleged that he "intended to make John de la Pole his son King of this realme marrying him to Margaret sole heir to John Beaufort Duke of Somerset pretending her to be nexte heire inheritable to the crowne for lacke of the issue of the Kynge's body lawfully begotten".

The King showed he feared neither of them as supplanters by removing the attainder on John de la Pole to whom he restored his murdered father's titles and property; also he revealed a plan of his own for the marriage of Margaret Beaufort of whom he resumed the wardship.

Not twenty years previously, "without counsel of her friends, regarding more her private affection than her open honour", Queen Katherine the King's mother had married a gentleman of her household. Sold at seventeen by her mother for a kingdom, at twenty-nine she made a bid for the happiness that is the birthright of every one of us, and in spite of her timid, despondent nature she may have a little succeeded. For

Owen Tudor was "a goodly gentleman and a beautiful person garnished with many goodly giftes both of nature and grace" —or so says the chronicler for the benefit of that king who was Owen's great-grandson. He was certainly a contrast to his wife in lightness of heart, a good dancer, a brave soldier and, the Tudors being the second of the five royal tribes of Wales, counted himself worthy to mate with a Daughter of France; for him Cadwallader was as good as Charlemagne.

But the King's uncles, at this time the virtual rulers of the land, thought otherwise and put in force a vexatious law against any "who shall marry a queen-dowager or any lady who holds lands of the Crown, without consent of the King and his Council". This sent Owen Tudor to Newgate and other places of bondage from which he escaped time and again till he got speech of his step-son and persuaded him of the folly of imprisoning one who asked only to be fighting for the King. He got his freedom which was all he wanted; that he and his four children were otherwise ignored by the Government did not trouble him any more than the problem of their maintenance and that of their mother.

She died in the Guest house of Bermondsey Abbey where by a foundation of the Earls of Clare she as the widow of a king of England had received the hospitality accorded to founders' kin. Three years later her two surviving children Edmund and Jasper Tudor were brought to the King by her friend Abbess Catherine de la Pole who argued that as they had a share with him of the blood royal of a country of which he was called king, it was fitting they should be made known to him. The boys, it was guessed, might be about eleven and ten years old.

By this time the King was of age and free to take his own 1441

175

way, at least about his private affairs. "For certain causes him moving" he not only made his step-father an annual grant of £40 "out of his privy purse by special grace" but he shouldered Owen's responsibilities. The boys were taken from a furtive waif and stray existence into the King's house and treated in all things as members of his family. "Also he provided for them in their boyhood and youth the most straight and safe guardianship putting them under the care of the most virtuous and worthy priests both for teaching and for right conversation." Then, in a good hour, came their cousin the young Queen— the same age as Edmund—to show them the joys that go with hawk and hound and horn.

Within as many years the three men died who had ruled the kingdom and the King; so he could in the warmth of his heart do much more for his brothers. Their birth was declared legitimate by Parliament; Edmund was created premier earl of the kingdom with the title of Richmond (hitherto reserved for a member of the king's family). Jasper was given the palatinate earldom of Pembroke; to the brothers jointly was deputed the wardship of Margaret Beaufort which meant the arrangement of a marriage for her.

Strangely enough and perhaps at the King's instance the child herself seems to have been consulted about this. Though Suffolk's plans for her had never reached the irrevocable stage, she had her scruples as to whether she were not in honour bound to his son. For "she which was not fully nine years old, doubtful in her mind what she were best to do asked counsel of an olde gentylwoman whom she moche loved and trusted which dyd advyse her to commend herself to St Nicholas, the Patron and helper of all true maidens, and to beseech hym to put her in mynde what she were best to do. The whyche in a dream dyd appeare unto her and naming unto her Edmund bade take him unto her as an husband."

Sure her kind saint (who was also the King's) took pity on her and gave her in her innocence her heart's desire.

And what of John de la Pole whose fortunes were diverted all unwitting by his cousin Abbess Catherine? Notwithstanding King Henry's generosity towards him he went his own way in the end to the other camp, and, not to be baulked of a royal union, took to wife Elizabeth Mortimer or Plantagenet, a sister of Edward IV. Long afterwards their son John Earl of Lincoln fell on the field of Stoke fighting for the Crown against the son of Margaret Beaufort.

II

During the five years that must pass before her marriage could be accomplished, Margaret was in charge of her mother whose husband Lord Welles held by King Henry. Then that was fulfilled which is written: Woe to the nation whose king is a child. Long since had his governor Richard Beauchamp—"Old Warwick"—despaired of "the Kynge's simplesse" whence came intrigues and divisions. "For it is an old said saw: There is an hard battle whereas kin and friendship do battle either against other; there may be no mercy but mortal war."

Those were uneasy years that forecast Margaret's future and hurried her out of childhood. Suffolk her Governor was murdered in darkness on the sea and none brought to judgment afterwards; the people raged furiously, two bishops were foully done to death, one of them at God's altar. From far away came a frightful rumour that Constantine's fair Christian 1453 city was taken and sacked by unbelievers; though the Holy Father called for a crusade, the princes of the world held aloof. Time was when a Beaufort followed the Cross to Barbary and kept the heathen out of Christendom; now his son had all he could do to keep England's hold on France. Had Edmund Beaufort died like great Talbot in that struggle it had been more glorious than to return as he did, a beaten man, all gone but Calais.

And the King, loyal friend, generous brother, lover of godliness and the studies of good learning by which he thought to cure the troubles of his people—the King was becoming more and more unfit for his supreme office. One day he was stricken senseless knowing no one and nothing, not even that he was the father of a fair son.

Again in the kingdom there was a rule of three; but instead of Henry Beaufort, Humphrey of Gloucester and William de la Pole who, whatever might be their privy feuds, had the country's honour at heart, a family party took command: Richard Duke of York, the Earl of Salisbury and his son Richard Neville, Earl of Warwick, whose ends were their own. On the surface all was ordered fairly: Parliament was summoned and named the Duke of York Protector; provision was made for the care of the sick King and the Queen's maintenance; the child whose birth had undone the Protector's plans was proclaimed Prince of Wales. But underneath, slander like a snake was busy; the loyalty of even the King's brothers was blown upon; none trusted his neighbour. It was put about among the people who would take anything from Warwick that the Prince was not the King's child. The Queen in fury only hurt her cause by demanding the regency and absolute control; her chief supporter was Margaret's uncle Edmund

Beaufort who was sent to the Tower as a traitor, but his house beside the Blackfriars remained a centre for the Queen's party.

Then suddenly the King recovered and his friends were gathered to him. Somerset's head which was still on his shoulders was lifted up out of prison, and soon afterwards the marriage of his niece Margaret was celebrated with her guardian the Earl of Richmond.

III

When he joined the two side issues of his family King Henry did better than perhaps he knew, though Edmund Tudor, "father and brother of Kings", compared by a Welsh bard of the time to Hercules, Hector and Caesar, is after all but a shadowy figure. When other men of his age and rank were making them ready to battle he seems to have stayed at home and died in his bed a few months after the first battle of St Albans at which he was not present. But he was the husband of Margaret Beaufort's vision; and though later she made two other men entirely happy in matrimony, he seems to have remained so.

It was at Caermarthen on the morrow of All Souls' that she 1455 became a widow, not fifteen years old, and with the prospect of motherhood. Her uncle Somerset had fallen in battle; it was for Jasper Tudor her brother-in-law and now sole guardian to decide and that quickly what was to be done with her. Richmond Castle in the far north, nothing but a barrack within, stands by Teasdale Gap, a thoroughfare for the marauding Scots, and in the neighbourhood of Middleham, a Yorkist castle; winter was drawing in to make bad roads worse. So

Jasper took her to the gentle West Country and to the part they called "Little England beyond Wales" where "Pembroke Castel standeth upon an arme of Milford on a hard rokke and is veri large and strong being doble warded". Three hundred years before this, Richard de Clare called Strongbow made it so that he might hold the Irish sea and land; succeeding generations of the rich Earls of Pembroke had used it as a home and furnished it with what comfort they might. Some of the rooms in the Outer Ward had hearths and chimneys and were soundly roofed with timber and lead. In one of them, on the eve of St Agnes, four months after her husband's death, Margaret bore a son and called him after Henry her King and Governor who had guided her to this hour.

Feb.
1456

It is not likely that she ever saw the King again. Sceptre and crown were tumbling down; the world they knew was being torn in pieces by their kin. Mercifully she had the child, sound in mind and body and of quick understanding. For the first three years of his life they lived in Pembroke Castle "which is more wonderful than any other. There is the Wogan Hole that mervelous grete vault" under the hall, cut out of the rock none knew how or when and opening on to the creek by which all manner of secret persons—lovers, smugglers, traitors flying from the King's justice—used to come and go. The castle had a long history of the troublesome traffic between England and the Irish land, that cloud the size of a man's hand over in the West, that you could mark if you climbed "the grete round tower gathered on the toppe with a roof of stone almost in coneum and Reverid with a flat millestone". Earl Jasper, a builder like his brother the King, appreciated the glories of his Castle and had begun to make his mark upon it by refashioning the Oriel and the Chancery room and making fire-places with

180

raised hearths for the fuel they called sea-cole, though they picked it out of the earth in the neighbourhood of the castle.

But now Jasper's business was the King's and Queen's; he came and went from the Castle with news of doings and un-doings. The King had been sick again but recovered enough to meet his loving cousins in Paul's Church on Lady Day when it 1458 seemed each was paired with his particular foe except the King who owned to none and walked alone while the Queen gave her hand to the Lord Protector, Somerset had Salisbury and Exeter had Warwick. It was all planned by the King and the Archbishop and Bulleyn the Lord Mayor; they called it a Loveday and the people rejoiced and made rhymes about it. But soon enough the Queen was falling out with my lord of Warwick; at another time Dame Grey her gentlewoman and Mayor Bulleyn were at pains to compose her quarrels with the citizens. The King had spent Easter in retreat at St Alban's Abbey, where, having no money, he left his best robe of state as offering; it was said his Treasurer had much ado to redeem it. The Queen was going here and there about the country raising money and friends, sometimes carrying the King with her but the Prince always—a gracious, fair child; to see him go about among the people giving them his badge of the silver swan none could doubt but that he was indeed the King's son.

Sir Owen Tudor would come to the Castle and take stock of his grandson and teach him to dance. And another there was who came to court the Countess, her second cousin Sir Henry Stafford, son of the first Duke of Buckingham and the Lady Ann Neville. It was Margaret's duty to marry again but even at that time when early marriages and untimely deaths were neither rare nor extraordinary, few women attained to two husbands and a son before the age of twenty. Though the younger son of a Lancastrian family Sir Henry was rich and managed to remain so; thus he and his well-dowered wife were the better able to steer an even course through the storms of the ten years following their marriage. King Edward valued his rich relations, like the lady who kept on good terms with her neighbours because you never know when you may want to borrow something.

When everything but his title was taken from her son, a special clause in the act of attainder exempted the property held by Margaret Beaufort, both as her father's heiress and as Countess of Richmond. Her place, if she chose to take it, was assured at Edward's Court; she was a friend of his Queen and intimate in her nursery. She would be an agreeable presence anywhere for "she had in maner all that is praysable in a woman; of singular esyness to be spoken unto; full curtayse answere she would make unto all that came unto her. Of mervylous gentleness she was unto all folks."

Though her husband was not a fighting man she had losses 1461 and alarms during the war years. Lord Welles her second father died of wounds after Towton field; Owen Tudor, gallant, reckless, absurd, the child of a subject race through whom all unwitting was to come the redemption of England —was ingloriously beheaded in Hereford market-place because he would not run away after the defeat of Lancaster at Mortimer's Cross. His son Jasper had more sense and escaped with his life though with little else; when Edward was proclaimed King, Jasper was attainted of treason and all he had was forfeited to the Crown. Pembroke Castle and town and later the earldom, with its perquisites including the wardship of Henry of Richmond, were given to Sir William Thomas, a Welshman, one of King Henry's knights but who deserted to the banner of York, and was rewarded by the English barony and name of Herbert.

For a time Earl Jasper was in France, his mother's land, helping Sir John Fortescu with the embassies and bargainings between Queen Margaret and King Louis—less than kind to needy kin. In spite of that, it was perhaps a job that suited Jasper better than manœuvring troops on a battle-field.

Not only gratitude and loyalty to King Henry moved his half-brother to this activity. The astute man had long foreseen what the future might hold for his nephew Henry of Richmond and made capital for him out of his exile while the boy was in the land of his fathers, a very different upbringing to that of his fugitive and homeless cousin the Prince of Wales. Meanwhile Henry's mother was on the watch and kept friends with the Herberts who were not likely to hold such a worshipful lady at a distance; besides Lord Herbert had fought under her uncle's banner in France.

Moreover she had a way of domesticating herself wherever she happened to be living, sometimes by joining a religious confraternity as lay persons are permitted to do or by the purchase of a bit of property such as the advowson of the church of Manorbere in the neighbourhood of Pembroke, by which she secured a stake in the place. And the tomb of her boy's father was at that time in the church of the Grey Friars at Caermarthen.

That Henry was never left very long in one place was all to the good for it meant the increase of his friends amongst a warm-hearted, imaginative people who knew all about him and were if anything more inclined to Lancaster than York. Especially was this so in Little England beyond Wales where, hundreds of years before Queen Philippa thought of it, a colony of Flemish weavers had settled whose successors prospered in trade protected by successive Earls of Pembroke —Clares, Marshalls and Valences. When Jasper Tudor's turn came he rebuilt and fortified the walls of Tenby, their fair haven.

1456-7

In the fourth year of Edward IV's reign, Jasper returned to try to hold Harlech Castle for Lancaster, but was overcome and captured by his supplanter William Herbert and his brother Richard who, however, extorted an unwilling pardon for Jasper from the King. (From this merciful Richard were descended in the fourth generation George Herbert the poet and his brother Edward of Cherbury the philosopher.)

Back went Jasper to St Mihiel to tell Queen Margaret that King Henry was betrayed and in the Tower prison, that the widow Grey who had brought two boys to her first husband had now given Edward only a girl for heir, that Warwick was making cause against her family who were devouring everything before them like the plague of locusts in Holy Writ; also, Warwick and Herbert had fallen out over an heiress whom each desired as the wife of his infant son.

Lord Herbert had turned his coat once and was not going to do so again for Warwick, which was unwise; three years later he and brother Richard were taken and beheaded in the Lancastrian rebellion that was secretly provoked by Warwick. As in the frequent absences of her warrior lord, Dame Herbert continued to rule Pembroke Castle and Henry of Richmond to whom she was a good step-dame though she did not see herself as his mother-in-law. Another of Lord Herbert's matrimonial schemes had been the betrothal of Henry to their daughter Maude.

March
1470

After a second Lancastrian rising in which the Lady Margaret's half-brother Sir Richard Welles figured as leader and

184

suffered for it, Warwick withdrew to France, a country once held in fee by England, but now taken by her discredited rulers as a refuge. Having married one daughter to King Edward's brother Clarence, Warwick to the amazement of all now contracted another to King Henry's son. Commines, that seasoned worldling, above being surprised at anything a human being may do, even Commines wondered at him. But he was bent on founding a dynasty; so also would he be a king-maker. With an army supplied by King Louis he returned to England in September and, there being none to hinder (for Edward ran away), brought King Henry out of prison, "in the streets the people on the right hand and on the lefte rejoysing and crying God save the Kynge as though all thyng had succeeded as they would have it" is the dry comment of a chronicler.

Jasper Tudor who was one of Warwick's generals naturally resumed the charge of his nephew, now fourteen years of age, whom he presented to the King at Westminster. Kind and vague, Henry blessed and encouraged the boy but nothing was said or done about restoring his estates. For Clarence on whom King Edward had bestowed them was standing by; already he was wavering and must be humoured. His brother had only to return to whistle him back, which came to pass in six months' time at the battle of Barnet when Edward again proving the better soldier made an end of Warwick. King Henry was re- April turned to store and his cousin of March thrust himself anew into 1471 the Kingdom.

After the all too tardy landing of Queen Margaret and her son, King Edward, vowing to make an end of them also, moved swiftly to his own country of the Marches where he forced her with exhausted troops to give him battle. Jasper Tudor who had gone to Wales for reinforcements hurried back to join her, but was met at Chepstow with the news of her defeat at Tewkesbury and the death of the Prince of Wales. Having on his mind another mother and her son now the only hope of Lancaster, he returned to Wales followed by a spy of King Edward "whose person the Erle shortened by the length of his hede. Then the Erle in good haste departed thence to Pembroke whom incontinent Morgan Thomas by King Edward's commandement so strongly besieged and environed his Castel with a ditch and a trench that he could not lightly escape thence. But he was after eight days delivered by his trusty friend David ap Thomas brother of Morgan."

It is thought that it was by way of the Wogan Hole that the Tudors, uncle and nephew, escaped to the Creek whence they were conveyed to Tenby, grateful and friendly. The Mayor Thomas White, who was King Henry's man and too rich for King Edward to quarrel with, concealed the fugitives in his house which had dry roomy cellars for his wool-packs and wine casks, giving on to the haven, till a day in May when heavy at heart for news of King Henry murdered and Queen Margaret a captive, they put to sea, in one of the Mayor's ships and "by fortune's leading landed in Brittany".

Like most of the course of his life hitherto this flight was planned and the means provided by Henry's mother who had intended France as the journey's end; but the wind for once doing Lancaster a good turn drove him to Brittany where the omens were favourable. Its Dukes had in the past been also Earls of Richmond in England; Francis the reigning Duke was nearly related to the Tudors by his descent from Jeanne as theirs from her sister Katherine, the daughters of Charles VI of France. The coast was strangely like that of Henry's native Pembroke, deeply indented by the sea; and inland, though mountains there were none, you might think you were still among "the sweet, green fields of Wales". The country people, toiling for the harvests of sea and land, came of the same stock as Henry's Welsh followers and could make shift to understand their speech as could the Duke the French of his younger cousin.

At the moment Duke Francis was struggling like a fly to keep out of the web called the League for the Public Good which King Louis was spinning about the peers of France, and was glad of any outside support even from landless and homeless kin. "He received bothe the Erles with all benignitie and shewed to them no less honor, favor and humanities with suche entertainment as if they had been his naturall brethern giving to them his faith that being with him they should sustain no manner of wrong." This as Jasper well understood was far better than the uneasy hospitality or rather disguised captivity they would have got from King Louis at Plessis-les-Tours just over the border.

Before long King Edward requested the return to England of the Earl of Richmond, ward of the Crown, to which the Duke replied that to do so would not accord with his honour; and there the matter rested for four years. When Edward tried again, a holy man was his ambassador with a proposal to 1475 marry Henry—now nearly twenty—to one of Edward's daughters. By this time the spider had caught the fly; the honest Duke had succumbed to King Louis and also to a visitation of that malady which like King Henry VI he inherited from Charles VI.

Earl Jasper was absent on one of his questing expeditions when the Englishmen came and went having secured young Henry who was "in a nervous fever deeming he was going to his death. But one John Chevelet revealed their treachery to the Duke who incontinent sent Peter Landois, his treasurer, he not slugging nor dreamynge his business came to St Malo where the English were abyding the wind", and occupied them with fair words and meat and drink the while he had Henry conveyed into sanctuary. "So the Kynge of England purchased the keepynge of his enemye by the space of three dayes and no more"—and again as at Pecquigny, the ingenious wits of the French outdid the dull English brains.

IV

"The way is long and hard...
     But whoso creeps from cradle on to grave
     Unskilled save in the velvet course of fortune
     Hath missed the discipline of noble hearts."

These alarms and excursions were not hid from the Lady Margaret, who would have agreed with Commines that "it is not a shame to be suspicious and keep your eye upon them that come and go; but to be too suspicious is not good". That was her father's mistake, of whom it was said that he would burn the shirt off his back if he thought it knew his secrets. She inherited his quality of closeness but without its defects, and went about her business with an admirable composure though the treasure of her heart was far away in the midst of so many and great dangers.

Who were the great ladies of her childhood to whom she had looked as ensamples of honour? Margaret the Queen, Cecily Neville "she who should have been so", and her sister Katherine of Norfolk?—all terrible as an army with banners.

Or Duchess Jacquetta and her daughters prevailing by the serpent's wisdom with the similitude of the dove? Rather Alice Chaucer or Margaret's own mother whose strength was in quietness and their confidence in other than themselves.

She was now thirty, a good deal younger than her husband, who left to her the personal supervision of their estates, seeing she had the Beauforts' ability for affairs and the management of money, which they knew how to use as a good servant; it certainly never either mastered or hardened her. "Readily bespoke of every poure person", she made an individual of each, which is the secret of sympathy, and divined not only their troubles but the limitations and deprivations of their lives. Active in mind and body, she went hither and thither amongst all kinds of people seeing for herself how it was ignorance that pulled the country down.

In spite of the attainder on the Beauforts, King Edward permitted her the use of one of their favourite manors, Woking in Surrey, which her ancestors the Holands held of the Crown "for the service of paying one clove gilly-flower a year". It was here that Lord Henry Stafford died—a retiring gentleman 1480 who, unlike most of his family, refrained from meddling in public affairs. Perhaps the most valuable of his many legacies to his widow was his steward Reginald Bray, "sober, secrete and well-witted", who remained in her service when she married again shortly before King Edward's death. 1483

Her third husband was likewise her third cousin; it would have been difficult to find anyone who was not related to her of sufficient consequence as to family and fortune to mate with her. He was Thomas the second Lord Stanley and came of a family that, like the flowers, had turned ever to the rising sun. His first wife was Warwick's sister. When Clarence—another turncoat—took King Henry out of prison, Thomas Stanley rode at his right hand; when Edward reigned again who but Stanley was chosen Steward of the Household. He and Hastings the Chamberlain were to King Richard as his chief butler and chief baker were to Pharaoh; when Hastings's head rolled on Tower Hill, Stanley after but a brief sojourn in prison was continued in his office. His wife took the opportunity to obtain from the King the grant of a valuable piece of land for John White of Tenby, son of that Thomas who helped her son out of the country ere yet he had come to be called "the King's rebel and enemy"; she contrived also to win a "general pardon" for her servant Reginald Bray, presumably for his Lancastrian sympathies; his father is thought to have been one of King Henry's physicians. When Ann the Queen was crowned, her heavy train "of purpille cloth of gold upon damask" was borne by her cousin the little Lady Margaret.

For "she was both jimp and small", with fine, slender hands and feet about which she had a pleasing vanity. "I thanke you hertilye" she once wrote to her cousin Ormond, about a commission he undertook for her in Paris "that ye liste soo soone to remember me with my gloves the whyche wer ryght goode save they wer too muche for my hande. I thynke the ladyes in that partes be gret ladyes all according to theyr gret estates they have gret personages."

Nous avons changé tout cela; nowadays it is the ladies of France who take the smaller sizes in gloves.

So, as in the last reign, "her ways were ways of pleasantness and all her paths were peace". Later, the King made a gesture which must have brought comfort to her faithful heart: the body of King Henry VI was removed from Chertsey Abbey to the "new chapel in the quire" of St George's, Windsor. But in spite of this and his complaisance about her petitions, she could not bring herself to speak to King Richard of what was nearest her heart. She and her son—now a man of twenty-eight—had been parted for fourteen years; she pondered long as to how he could be given back to her in honour and peace.

At King Richard's coronation an office equal in consequence to her own had been filled by the Duke of Buckingham, the nephew of her second husband and her own near relation. It was said that the King could do nothing without him; how could she know how far his heart was now from the man whom his quick wits and ready tongue had helped to stand where he did? It was the story of the king-maker over again who asks himself "when the tumult and the shouting die", what is my profit in it all?

Chewing the cud of his bitter thoughts the Duke was riding home after the coronation when behold the Lady Margaret on her way to Worcester to lay her troubles before the shrine of the Mother of the Redeemer: "She was clene out of my mind as tho I had never seen her"—(neither unusual nor unnatural in a young man suddenly faced with an unfamiliar and elderly kinswoman). "But she praied me first for kindred sake, secondarily for the love I bore Duke Humphrey my grand-father which was sworn brother to her father to move the Kynge to be goode to her soune Henry of Richmonde and to licence him with his favour to return agen into England and if it were his plesure so to do she promised that the erle her soune should marry one of King Edwarde's daughters at the appointment of the Kynge without anything to be taken or demanded for the said espousalls which request I soone over-past and gave her faire words and so departed she to Our Ladie of Worcester and I towarde Shrewsburie"—and so on to

Brecon where he held Morton Bishop of Ely "in a kind of liberall captivitie".

Three Kings in thirty years had this Bishop seen on the throne of England; to them all he was a faithful counsellor for "he was a man of grete naturall witte very well lerned and of honourable behaviour lackynge no wise ways to winne favour". He had followed Queen Margaret to St Mihiel and been a father in God to her little Court there, taking his part with Sir John Fortescu in the education of King Henry's son, in spite of which King Edward spared the Bishop's life after Tewkesbury and "had him in secret trust and special favour whom he nothing deceived". When Richard, not so wise as his brother, banished him from the Council the good man—now nearly sixty—took it as a sign from God that he should concern himself henceforth only with his beads and his books.

But now to him in Brecon Castle comes his host with a tale of grievance and frustration mixed up with his meeting the Lady Margaret on the highway and her prayer to him for her son. And here amid the welter the Bishop began to see light and hope for his country.

It happened that with each of her marriages Margaret had acquired a valuable servant: the doctor Edward Lewis whom she found in Wales, Reginald Bray with whom Lord Henry Stafford provided her, and Christopher Urswick "an honest and wise priest" (which sounds as if such were rare in the land) who came from the neighbourhood of her third home in Lancashire; these three were her intelligence department. What Lewis "a physician out of all suspicion and mysdemeanynge" did for her has been told already; Urswick went abroad (which a priest could do with less suspicion) and kept her in touch with her son and Jasper Tudor; Bray, her messenger in England, was now summoned by the Bishop to Brecon. Lionel and Edward Wydville, brothers of the ex-queen, and her son Thomas Grey Marquis of Dorset "did secretly move and sollicit the people to rise and make insurrection, and others by privy letters and cloked messengers did strive and incite to this new conjuracion".

Thus from a chance wayside meeting and the appeal in all innocence of an agonised mother came the Buckingham Rebellion wherein the Duke himself was the chief sufferer. Betrayed by a servant, he was beheaded at Salisbury where was the King who, however, did him the compliment of "a newe scaffold". The rest of the leaders escaped over the water —the Bishop to Flanders, Dorset to Paris, while the Wydvilles, Brandons and others of the fighting men joined Henry Tudor 1483 in Brittany. On Christmas Day in Rennes Cathedral he took an oath to marry Elizabeth of York; "then all the company did him homage and swore to him fealtie as though he had been at that time crowned Kyng and annoynted prince".

But outlaw and attainted rebel in his native land where the hunt was up; his mother was included in the act of attainder, and forbidden to communicate with him, told to keep her distance from Court and some of her servants who were among the "cloked messengers" were put to death. She submitted with a disarming meekness that confirmed the King in his belief "it was to small purpose that women could do". With his badge of the boar Richard had surely absorbed some of its stupidity or else he had a blind spot for Stanley the Steward who on the attainder of his wife contrived to secure her property to himself for his life. When the ex-queen Elizabeth and her daughters reappeared at Court he was their friend—instituting with the girls that safest of all relations, the avuncular

—and was able to arrange a secret correspondence between the young Elizabeth and Henry of Richmond whereby they plighted their troth.

Jan.
1484/5   It was about this time that the King opposed the institution of Richard Fox as Vicar of Hackney "because he is with the grete rebel Henry ap Tudor". Fox had been at both the English universities—it was he who "thought it sacrilege for a man to tarry longer at Oxford than he had a desire to profit" —now, though he did obtain the living of Hackney, he found it better for his health to continue his studies in Paris.

Put away privily though she might be at her husband's house of Knowsley in the North, the Lady Margaret was not

1483   ignorant of all this nor of the death of the Prince of Wales and the proclamation of John de la Pole as heir to the throne— he who might have been her son. Soon afterwards her cousin Ann the Queen died; then followed a disquieting rumour that the King was in league with the ex-queen who favoured his suit for her daughter's hand; and, because the girl resisted, she was banished to Middleham Castle where Clarence's son, the rightful heir to the throne, was a prisoner also. Would either of these young creatures ever come out alive?

By the time this news reached Henry Tudor he had left Brittany, Pierre de Landois who saved him from King Edward's wiles having fallen for King Richard's bribes and joined Dorset in a plot to kidnap Henry and deliver him to the King. But, timely warned by Urswick, Henry escaped over the border though with but an hour to spare—and joined his uncle at Angers; then to Langeais to beg for help from Charles the young king and his sister Madame the Regent. Jasper, a universal uncle, had taken trouble to make friends with these two children of King Louis. Charles, though ignorant and stupid, was not

without a sense of kindred and some generous instincts; ugly
and awkward in his own person, he could yet wholeheartedly
admire his cousin Henry for "his noble manners, the grace and
beauty of his expression and his kingly bearing". Charles prevailed with his powerful sister, who was still acting regent, to
provide the English beggars with a certain amount of money
and some two thousand "soldiers" so-called, though Commines
says they were the refuse of the Paris jails and lazar-houses.
Herein did Madame appear the true child of her father who
said of her: "Though the women of this world are none
of them wise, my daughter Anne is the least foolish among
them."

It was as well that Henry could already count on "the manly
Bretons and forty well furnished shippes" given him by Duke
Francis who as long as he kept sane was a sound friend. And
at Paris whither Henry followed the Court he found Bishop
Morton and Richard Fox "who could see through the present
to the future" and who "pursued his negociacions at the French
Court with such dexterity and success as gave great satisfaction
to the Earl of Richmond". When Dorset's perfidy and consequent flight to Flanders were discovered, it was Fox who
had him pursued and secured from making more mischief
with Margaret, the dowager of Burgundy, King Richard's
sister. Meanwhile Henry moved to Rouen, where was John
de Vere the Earl of Oxford, not a whit abashed by nearly
fifteen years' captivity in Hammes Castle, from whence he had
escaped bringing with him its Governor Blount and Fortescue
the Captain of Calais.

But tarrying at Harfleur for that fair wind that was ever
slow to serve the cause of Lancaster gave time for an anxious
mind—inherited from grandmother Katherine or from grand-

father Beaufort—to weigh chances and count the cost and wonder whether it was all worth while.

> "Come o'er the bourne, Bessy
> Come o'er the bourne, Bessy
> Come o'er the bourne, Bessy to me.
> Her boat it hath a leak
> And she will not speak
> Why she may not come over to thee."

She to whom he was plighted was forsaking him it seemed for crooked Richard Plantagenet; and the lady Cecile her sister who was to have taken her place "was preferred to a man founde in a cloude of an unknown lignage and familie". Let them go; he had never beheld either of them; he would stay where he was and wed where he pleased. Of Maude Herbert he might no longer think; she was married these ten years to another Henry—Percy of Northumberland—and the mother of little Hotspurs, but there was her fair younger sister "of age to be coupled in matrimony" who also had been his playmate. Or he would return to Brittany where he felt at home, marry Anne the Duke's daughter and join the province with Richmond as in the past. As for crown and kingdom, he thought on the Kings he had known and what they had made of these: Henry his uncle, lover of his people but neither their guide nor leader, his mind wholly in another world while this one that was his business went to waste about him; Louis "in wanton and disguised apparell more like a minstrel than a prince royall" feared and hated by all, making a show of piety while practising his motto: "he who knows not how to deceive knows not how to reign"; Charles his son, loutish, unkingly, ruled by a woman. Henry had never met either of the brothers who in his lifetime had taken the government of England on themselves; but he knew to his cost how they had abused that fair trust. It were better for him to keep out of it all and his head on his shoulders.

"He was indeed full of apprehensions and suspicions but as he did easily take them so he did easily check and master them; his thoughts were so many they could not well always stand together." Now he put doubts and desertions behind him, helped by kindly Jasper to whom his moods were familiar, and the strong natural sense of his confessor, Urswick, son of the people, who held a watching brief for the mother far away. Also those others, priests and soldiers "all tall Englishmen" with a stake in the country, eager to get back to it and renew their Lancastrian allegiance—he must not fail them. And "though the waies were narrowly watched, a message came from Morgan Kidwelly learned in the temporall lawe which declared that Ryce ap Thomas a man of no lesse valiantness than activitie and John Savage an approved captaine would with all their power be partners of his quarrell. And that R. Braye had gotten together no small money for the payment of the wages of the souldiers." There was hope too that once Henry should show himself in the country his friend Sir Walter Herbert, Maude's brother, would rally to him with her husband Henry Percy, a power in the North.

So, the wind at last playing fair, they took ship and landed on August 7th at Milford Haven where the ravens of Rhys ap 1485 Thomas with many other pennons fluttered in greeting.

> "All the country is the King's
> Save where the Rhys doth spread his wings"

ran the rhyme. While Henry was scrambling up the rocks he

stumbled and fell as did William the Conqueror on a like occasion, and, like him, recovered himself with a jest. Then to his knees again to recommend himself to God in reciting the forty-second Psalm (of which doubtless Cousin Richard also would make use). Afterwards he stood up "fair and slender, pale-faced but comely, active and well-formed" before his fellow-men and told them he was come home. "He had no sooner finished his oration but all flocked unto him in a con-fused manner mingle, mangle without all order as being trans-ported with his eloquence and ravished with his presence, some kissing his hands, some his feet, some adoring the ground he trod on as if he were some angelical creature... then beating their drums, winding their cornets to express their inward joy and contentment they fell to shouts and acclama-tions, clapping their hands and crying up to heaven. 'King Henry, King Henry, down with the bragging white boar.'" There were also those who cried out "Welcome Jasper, thou hast taken good care of thy nephew". "And when they had for a little while in these loud plauses and sweetest jubilees penetrated the air and echoed forth their most loving affection in the most pleasing manner of expression, Rhys ap Thomas when he saw his time drew them back commanding every man to his colours whereby the Earl might see in what order and obedience he held them to their places of service."

Then again speeches and pageantry such as is still the delight of that lovable and self-unconscious people, an entertainment natural and refreshing (if somewhat protracted) for the batta-lion of French gaol-birds shuddering with fever and sea-sickness. To Earl Jasper a justification of the policy which arranged that his nephew should be born and bred a Welsh-man, and, in truth, it was the end of the long quarrel between

Wales and the crown of England. "A better people to govern than the Welsh, Europe holdeth not" said Sir Henry Sidney not a hundred years later.

It was then decided at a council of war to divide forces and approach England by different routes. For some distance they all rode together when suddenly there was a halt and a cry of Treason: Rhys and his ravens were gone, here was his horse riderless—when up he came from beneath a bridge shaking his shoulders as if freed from a burden, caught his horse, and took his place again at Richmond's right hand. It seemed the good man had been touched in conscience about the oath of his allegiance to King Richard that only over his body should any other man take the kingdom. The Bishop of St David's to whom he confessed himself came to the rescue with the bright notion that Rhys should hide beneath a bridge over which Henry ap Tudor should ride—an old joke but it bore repetition by several others among those men of war with the hearts of children as they rode merrily into Haverford. There the ways parted, Earl Jasper taking one division to find Sir Walter Herbert, the other under Richmond and Rhys going to join Sir William Stanley the justiciar for North Wales.

His brother Thomas had retired to his house of Knowsley near Liverpool when King Richard called him to join his forces; but Thomas pleaded sickness. To the King the excuse had a sinister sound; Buckingham had sent him just such another when summoned to the coronation. This time the King announced that he would hold Stanley's eldest son Lord Strange a hostage for his father's good faith. So Zimri, well assured that his brother the justiciar was busy, abode in his tents till the hour of his master's defeat when he was at hand to pluck Richard's crown out of a thorn-bush on Bosworth field and set it on Henry's head. And if, as some say, this is mere legend, it was taken for truth by Henry's son who caused a green bush to be set on high between the red rose and the white in the windows of the King's Chapel at Cambridge.

Then departed Richard "without being desired; howbeit they buried him but not in the sepulchres of the Kings". A naked corpse flung from the back of a galloping horse on to a street in Leicester was retrieved by pitiful nuns, recognised and given a grave in the church of the Grey Friars while the son of Margaret Beaufort was acclaimed in London by the voices of the people and Te Deums in the high church of St Paul. There he offered three banners made ready "for a fitting occasion", showing the lions of England, the dragon of Wales and "the dun cow"—whose appearance is thus simply stated but never explained by any herald or chronicler. But as Henry and his mother, who numbered a herald among their ancestors, were learned in the gentle science and particular in its employment, it may be that it was for the sake of her traffic with Guy of Warwick from whom their Beauchamp ancestors were descended that they gave the homely animal a share in the triumph of the King.

V

"And as the fervent smith of yore
        Beat out the glowing blade
Nor wielded in the front of war
        The weapons that he made,
But in the tower at home still plied his ringing trade;

So like a sword the son shall roam
 On nobler missions sent;
And as the smith remains at home
 In peaceful turret pent,
So sits the while at home the mother well content."

These are brave words in which a poet with more than a touch of his nation's self-complacency acclaims his mother; but mothers like Margaret Beaufort know better who have listened to Simeon the seer. "When the Kyng her son was crowned in alle that grete tryumphe and glorye, she wept mervaylously." Though her son was King he was a stranger; after the first outburst of welcome the people seemed to hold aloof in a certain fearful looking forward.

They were the more daunted by a strange epidemic they called "the sweating sickness", something like what we call influenza and for which they blamed the Frenchmen who came over with the King. Whether or no, the infection had every chance of success in London where, in spite of repeated legislation, all manner of loathly refuse was cast on the open streets and alleys which were never cleansed unless for the passage of royalty or such public occasions. The tidal river and its tributary brooks were trustfully used as sewers; when sickness came, due to the laziness and ignorance of man, it was piously accepted as the will of God.

Nor were there wanting busybodies in the town to make the most of its distresses for the edification of country correspondents: "There be many enemies on the see and dyvers shippes taken, and there bee many of the Kynge's house taken for thieves. Also they begin to dye in London; there is but few paritches free; in summer they dye faster."

The King, who kept his health and his nerve, insisted on the coronation going forward to provide the people with some distraction, then summoned Parliament and had the crown entailed on himself and his heirs. "Also it was publisshed the same day that the King's guid grace shall wed my lady Elizabeth (so she is taken as quene) and that at the maryage ther shall be grete joustyngs. Divers lords, knights and esquires were summoned, among them Lord Lovell, Sir Robert Brackenbury and William Catesby and John Ratte."

> "They rule all England under the Hogge
> The Cat, the Rat and Lovell the dogge"

ran the rhyme in King Richard's time. The three were his familiars and catspaws (Brackenbury, an honest man, had kept himself clear). For a time Henry held his hand from the attainder of these his three predecessors to the surprise of the wiseacres who, as is their way, had their theories about what he would do. But, in spite of his own avowed unhappy memories of captivity, he deemed it expedient to continue the imprisonment of Edward Plantagenet, son of Clarence and rightful heir to the throne. And after the fashion of his cousin of France he instituted the King's body-guard as a precaution against assassination, being the first sovereign of England to do so. "Also the King hath resumed by the Parlemett into his hands all manner of patents offices...also it is in actte in the Parlemett that all maner huntynge in parks, chases and forests belonging to the Kyng is felony and all maner profytynges"— these last also echoes of King Louis's policy and not likely to make for popularity.

On the other hand, the rich London merchants, used for many years to the sovereign's depredations, found the old order changed with this young man who, though long starved of the pleasures of princes, was chaste, sober-minded and just, stole neither their money nor their wives, and repaid their loans with interest and punctuality. After he had established his throne, in honour, his next care was for the country's trade "in whiche" as the Mayor of Bristol said "his Grace should so helpe them by dyvers means like as he shewed unto them that they harde not within this hundred years of no King so good a comfort". Then he turned to the rewarding of his friends.

His step-father Thomas Stanley was created Earl of Derby, chief steward of the Duchy of Lancaster North of Trent— where was most of his property—and continued in his office of High Constable of the kingdom. Uncle Jasper became Duke of Bedford; Rhys ap Thomas and the other Welshmen were ennobled and given honourable positions in the King's household. Philibert de Chaundé, commander of the Frenchmen, was created Earl of Bath. Bishop Morton became Primate of all England; Fox was made Bishop of Exeter, principal Secretary of State and Lord Privy Seal. Christopher Urswick refused the burden of a bishopric and, having a sympathy with learning, was content for a time to be Master of the King's Hall at Cambridge. Reginald Bray was made a Knight of the Garter and Privy Councillor. The doctor, Edward Lewis, seems to have been already promoted to the service of the Court of Heaven.

As for the King's mother, she was reinstated in all her possessions with full powers "to make her will thereof from tyme to tyme at her plesure in as large a forme as ainie woman may doe in this roialme". A quick reaction to this was the erection of an almshouse for poor women by the old chapel of

St Ann in Westminster, the neighbourhood of her friend Caxton the printer. Some of the Beaufort estates were secured to her for life, notably Woking Manor afterwards a favourite abode of her descendants, Henry and Elizabeth Tudor. The King gave her as a town-house one that in its time had seen life, "the hostel, mansions or tenement called Coldhareburgh situate in Thames Street in the parish of All Hallows-the-less within the City of London". Edward the Black Prince had lived in it, also Prince Hal (afterwards Henry V) from whom it passed to John Holand Duke of Exeter. When Henry VII took it over, it was the place of the Heralds to whom, after many vicissitudes, the site at least has been restored for their College. The name Coldharbour has nothing to do with either ships or cold storage, the house being in fact by the Hay Wharf and Ropery so that the King's mother when in town dwelt amongst one of its few agreeable activities.

1486   The King's wedding was followed by others; Lord Welles, the Lady Margaret's half-brother released from prison and attainder, was rewarded for his Lancastrian loyalty by the hand of Cecily of York, the Queen's sister. Jasper Tudor, a bachelor of fifty, made Buckingham's widow, Katherine Wydville, Duchess of Bedford—the title her mother Jacquetta had borne triumphantly for forty years. The government of her infant sons Edward and Henry Stafford was given to the King's mother; two Percys also, the children of Maude Herbert and the Earl of Northumberland, were brought up in the Lady's family. (It may be noted that Alan Percy was, later, Master of St John's College, Cambridge for two years.) Both Staffords and Percys being descended from Edward III were related to her; as their governor she received from Crown and parents comfortable augmentations of her income by which the children profited. One of her letters is to the Chancellor and Regents of Oxford University asking them "to dispense with the presence of Maurice Westbury of that University as he was retained by her for the purpose of instructing certain young gentlemen at her finding". But it was not only the well-born and wealthy among her kin over whom she spread her wing; remembering the uneasy childhood of Edmund Tudor her first husband she had a care for waifs and strays; in one of her letters to the King she asks his consideration for a bastard son of Edward IV.

Hers was a household ordered surely in all things where the comfort as well as the duties of each, even the meanest member, was considered; thereto would the King himself resort "to recreate his spirits and console himself with his mother". Besides the minstrels usual in a great house there was for a time a poet of sorts in her service; and, whatever her own secret austerities, religion in her house was a practice "not harsh and crabbed" but beneficent, natural and necessary as daily bread. Hence her wisdom peaceable and easy to be entreated. "Gently, gently", she said once when she saw one in authority in the College of her foundation dealing over harshly as she thought with a young scholar. For she was not one of those who readily forgot their own youth with its needs and short-comings. And "as it is not good to occupy the eyen and study overmuch in bokes of contemplacion", she caused Master Caxton to translate from the French "The Historye of Kynge Blanchardyne and Queene Eglantyne his wyfe for gentyll yonge ladies and damosellys for to learne to be stedfaste and constaunte in their parte to them that may have put their lives often in jeopardy for to playse them to stand in grace".

Before long, an expectant grandmother of forty-five, she was ordaining "what preparation is to be made against the deliverance of a queen as also of the christening of the child of whom she shall be delivered".

For six weeks before the child's birth the queen was to be confined (in the literal sense) to her own apartments which were to be "hung and ceiled with blue cloth of Arras enriched with gold fleur-de-lys" instead of tapestries showing "figures gloomily glaring" whence might come scares and nightmares. Every breath of the eating air was to be excluded and almost all the daylight except from one window which might be left uncurtained should the Queen so desire. Except for the King and the priest and the doctor none but those of her own sex were to visit or to serve her. What wonder that before the birth of one of her seven children the victim rebelled, broke prison and outraged the oracles by taking the air in her barge on the river with minstrelsy and the company of her friends of both sexes.

> "Company with honesty
> I love and shall until I die.
> Then who shall say
> But pass the day
> Is best of all."

So years afterwards sang her son Henry, who had her light heart.

But she must bring forth her first-born according to formula the rigours of which, however, he thoughtfully took it upon him to mitigate by appearing "in the eighth month which the physicians do prejudge, but the child was strong and able". This he must have been to survive christening and confirmation at the age of five days "and the weyther full foule and rayny" when he and his gossips, of whom his mother was one,

Sept. 20
1486

206

waited in Winchester Cathedral for another of them, John de
Vere, the Earl of Oxford, who was three hours late. But the
grandmother who devised the seemly ordering of the ceremony, being a comfortable lady, had "a faire panne of live
coles sett within the chirche and a fine cloth of Rennes" to line
the great gilt christening bowl brought from Canterbury for
the occasion; so that the child wrapped warm in furs and velvet
in the arms of Aunt Cecily took no harm; "howbeit the Queen
suffered of an agu" for days after. But "overall Te Deums
songen with Ryng of Belles, and in the most Partes Fiers made in
the Praysing of God and Rejoysing of every true Englishman".

Not long since Thomas Mallory had with Caxton's aid 1485
revealed to his countrymen the glory of him

> "who sent a thousand men
> To till the wastes and moving everywhere
> Cleared the dark places and let in the law
> And broke the bandit hordes and cleansed the land",

"in whose acts there is truth enough to make him famous besides that which is fabulous". So when the King's son was
born at "Winchester which is Camelot" he was christened in
the name of Arthur, whereby Henry saluted an ideal long
cherished and also made a wise departure from the succession
of Edwards and Henrys—names which however men regarded
them might have given a sinister forecast.

It was at this moving time of her life, on the appearance of
the third generation, that the King's mother began the use of
the signature Margaret R. (for Richmond).

"As arrows in the hand of the mighty so are the young
children." No sooner did the King begin to fill his quiver than
his enemies came out into the open. First "Lovel the dogge"

then John de la Pole whom Richard III had proclaimed heir to the throne. It may be said for him that he was not now so much seeking to make good his own claim as that of Simnel, a pretender personating Clarence's luckless—some said witless—son. The conspiracy was the more troublesome in that it was secretly abetted by the Queen's mother and her son Dorset; but it ended on Stoke field where Henry appeared anything but the "Welsh mylksoppe lacking in courage and experience" that his cousin Richard had called him. Not only was he an able commander in action, but he took forethought for the comfort and the good conduct of his soldiers, who were forbidden to bully or offend the country people or impound their goods without honest payment. "In especiall there were imprisoned grete nombre of common women and vagabonds wherfore ther was more reste in the Kyng's Hoste and the better rule."

1487   The battle of Stoke is taken as the end of the so-called Wars of the Roses. John de la Pole fell on the field and his estates were given to her who might have been his mother but became instead the mother of the King. Simnel who survived was pardoned by the King and given a menial office in the Royal household.

The Queen was crowned on St Katherine's Day in Westminster Abbey and the Court went to Greenwich for Christmas when "ther was a goodly Disguysing and many and dyvers Plays. And the King went to Evensong on Twelfth Night in his Surcote outward with Tabert Sleeves the Cappe of Astate on his hede and the Hode aboute his Shoulders in Doctors wyse. And on the morrow at Matens tyme al other Astats and Barons had their Surcots outward with their hodys. And my ladye the Kynge's mother wore like mantell and surcott as the quene with a rich crownall on her hede."

By the King's desire she was preparing "ordinances and reformations of apparylle for princes and estates with other ladies and gentlewomen". One of the survivors of the world before the Wars, she could be trusted to recollect and transmit its worthiest traditions; and from Guienne King-at-Arms, whose cognisance of a Katherine wheel for Roelt appears in her coat-of-arms, she inherited also a sense of the value of "that noble usage which mounts guard over the memories of a great people". For such were the English becoming under the rule of her son the first King of the country since Edward I to be also a man of intellect.

With the self-respect which he was restoring to his country came the increase of its prestige abroad. Spain at this time, by the union of the crowns of Castile and Aragon, the most powerful nation in Europe, was willing to consider an alliance with England and by the usual method of matrimony. Prince Arthur was still in his "littel cradell of Tree faire set forthe by Painters crafte" when a marriage was proposed for him with Catharine, a year older, the second daughter of Ferdinand and Isabella. The intricate business of settlements required the presence in England of several Spaniards both cleric and lay whose voluminous correspondence with their sovereigns illuminates these years for us also.

After the feast of All Hallows the King received a sword and 1488 Cap of Maintenance from Pope Innocent VIII by the hands of his Legate in St Paul's Church "the Mayor and Aldermen being present in their formalities and alle the Craftes in their clothings". Such recognition by the Holy Father would raise Henry in the estimation of his kinswoman Isabella the Catholic. And at such a season it would be the more readily remembered that the last king of England to be so distinguished was

Henry VI who received the Golden Rose from His Holiness Eugenio IV.

1489   Next year Prince Arthur, not yet four years old, was brought to Westminster to be knighted by his father. "At that season were all thos of the King's Chappell redyng the Sauter for the goode spede of the Quene which then traveled. And anon upon nine of the clock that same nyght she was delivered of a Princesse whiche was christened on St Andrewe's Day in Westminster Chirche in the riche font of Canterbury by Bishop Alcocke of Ely", father in God to the Queen's family. The baby received the name of Margaret from her grandmother and godmother who gave her also a chest of silver gilt full of gold. "At that season ther wer the Meazellis soo strong wherfor on St John's Day the Quene was privily chirched or purified."

Two years later the succession was established by the birth of a second son who was called Henry.

Thus fortified the King set out for fresh combats. A new pretender had appeared out of Flanders, Perkin Warbeck, personating Richard of York brother and heir of Edward V. He may very well have been a son of Edward IV; the time of his birth coincided with that of that king's residence in Flanders in 1470. The Queen dowager was not alive or confusion had been worse confounded; but other pseudo-relations rallied to Warbeck such as Margaret the dowager of Burgundy who received him as the nephew she had never previously beheld and furnished him with money. Also King James of Scotland besides supporting him in a raid on England helped him to a beautiful wife Katherine Gordon called the White Rose, a slip of Beaufort stock.

More serious was the defection of Sir William Stanley the

justiciar; but, not as skilful as heretofore in calculating chances, he was taken and beheaded as a traitor; this did the King no good with the people who remembered what he owed to Sir William. Already they were alienated by a levy they sourly called Morton's Fork because devised by the Archbishop and Chancellor and announced by him as a "benevolence". It was one of Edward IV's ways of raising money but had since been declared illegal; and Henry had not the natural charm nor would he use the tricks of manner by which that other had commended his extortions. Thus the Warbeck conspiracy was more stubborn than Simnel's and ended only after seven years with Warbeck's execution and the judicial murder of Clarence's son, innocent victim of the warring ambitions of his kindred.

Yet there were among them some as blameless as he to mourn him: his sister Margaret Pole, now the last of Warwick's descendants, and the young Queen who had shared and cheered his captivity in Middleham Castle during the Reign of Terror. At this time also she received and befriended Warbeck's widow, her cousin and the King's. Elizabeth's early experiences in Westminster Sanctuary, refuge of the hunted and homeless, seems to have intensified her natural tenderness for wronged and helpless creatures. She had queer friendships which may have dated from those days with certain humble people who had easy access to her presence when she became Queen, and brought her homely offerings such as fresh eggs and vegetables, never themselves going empty away. Some she employed to their spiritual benefit in pilgrimages which, from frequent ill-health, she could not herself undertake; thus she would commemorate "our uncle King Henry of blessed memory"— whom her father had twice ousted from the throne—and Prince Edward the child of her unhappy friend Queen Ann.

Among her pensioners were the nurse of her brother Edward V, and a man who had attended her uncle Anthony Rivers in his last days at Pontefract.

The Quenes College refounded by her mother in the year of her birth did not interest her at all though it possesses her signature "Elysabeth" to a mandate recommending for a fellowship one "Billington scoler" of whom nothing more seems to have been heard in connection with either the College or the University.

Her charity began at home with Cecily, Ann and Katherine her sisters who even after they married continued to live at Court on her bounty; the baby sister Bridget, a close nun and faithful to the rule of her Order, she comforted in various ways, not least by keeping her in touch with her family. With all these generosities and in spite of rigorous personal economies, Elizabeth could not but run into debt which would be pain and grief to the punctilious King; but he was generous in coming to her rescue.

The human race has been divided by a humorist into three classes: Improvers, Approvers and Disapprovers; most of us go from one class to the other; this queen among women was never found in the last one. "A low voice and a light heart is best, and not to judge" was her way. She covered and softened the personal faults of the King who must have been interesting to live with if difficult, for he was reserved, suspicious, moody, curiously and unreasonably jealous not as husband but as sovereign. He grudged her the success she had with the people who loved her first for her father's sake and then for her own; while he who was bringing their country back to unity, peace and honour remained to the end a stranger in their midst.

"The Queen is a very noble woman and much beloved.

She is kept in subjection by the mother of the King. It would be a good thing to write often to her to show her a little love" observed the Sub-Prior of Santa Cruz in a letter to Queen Isabella. Like many a half-truth, this generalisation is misleading and superficial. The Queen and her mother-in-law were both reasonable women who practised the virtue rare in man or woman of tolerance, and were besides attached by their common devotion to a man whom the rest of the world found hardly lovable. In the early years of her marriage, with the appraising eyes of both mother and mother-in-law upon her, Elizabeth may have had her difficult moments; but she went her way in largeness of heart where there was no room for the poison of self-pity to work.

Her third son was born at Greenwich and named Edmund 1496 after the King's father. The ceremonies of making him first a Christian and then a peer of the realm—as Duke of Somerset— "were such as though an heir to the throne had been born" said Don Pedro d'Ayala dryly in a letter to Queen Isabella. Nevertheless the chief godmother who was the Lady Margaret had leisure to remark a young man, one of the proctors in attendance on the Vice-Chancellor of Cambridge University; it may be that he was recommended to her by Bishop Alcock for he too came from Beverley in Yorkshire. He was John Fisher, son of Robert a mercer of substance and Agnes his wife, who like Hannah of old lent her son to the Lord; like Hannah's son he was to become a power in the land. At this time he was thirty-six and a Fellow of Michael House (now part of Trinity College, Cambridge) of which in the following year he was chosen Master. He was not a great scholar in the way his University has come to define the term but he had a large and liberal appreciation of the value of learning. It was remarked of him that it was not so much what he knew and said nor how he said it as what he was in himself that gave him his power over others; he had cast out the sin of self-love by which the light that is in us is darkened. Bishop Alcock who was purging his floor and gathering the wheat had soon discovered him. To these two as much as to the men of later generations specifically styled Reformers we owe it that truth and justice, religion and piety were established among us.

When he appeared at Court the King's mother distinguished him by an invitation to dine with her. As her hour was 10 a.m. (on fast days eleven) this might be thought to be of the nature of an ordeal; if it were he came through it successfully. As she told him some years later: "For the more meryte and quietness of my soule pertayning to the same I vowe to you to whom I am and have been since the first time I see you submitted verely determined (as to my chief and trusty councillor) to owe my obedience in all things concerning the weale and profytte of my soule."

But there was more in it than that. At the age of fifty-four she had the refreshing experience of a new friendship and with one of a younger generation which to the elderly is as the dew of Hermon and far more stimulating. They were both of them "ae-fauld", which being interpreted is single-minded, not "coloured with doubleness", he never seeking nor asking aught for himself, she eager to give nor hampered by the self-will that is often bred of the monied habit. Without impediment it was "a marriage of true minds" that was to bear fruit an hundredfold.

In the year 1446, one Thomas Collage, inspired perhaps by his name, had left £40 to preachers of the Universities of Oxford and Cambridge, viz.: "to everyone as long as the money lasted, six-and-eightpence at a time to the end that encouragement might be bestowed on divinity which now was at a low ebb". After fifty restless years the money was done and divinity had ebbed farther than ever from the source of its inspiration. None knew this better than Fisher, but now he knew also where to look for fresh encouragement.

The King's mother was no stranger to Cambridge, the University King Henry VI delighted to honour and to whose "poor scholars" her uncle Thomas Beaufort Duke of Exeter had been a benefactor. Bishop Alcock, soon after his appointment to Ely, had claimed her interest in his scheme of rebuilding and beautifying Great St Mary's Church, and then, later, for his new foundation of Jesus College. Into this the Lady drew Dame Bray, Sir Reginald's wife, a childless woman who gave largely to this College in recognition whereof she was allowed to nominate the master of the Grammar school then held within its walls.

Also, the Lady when endowing a Chantry at Wimborne in Dorset to commemorate her parents whose tomb is there, had ordained that its priest should "teach grammar freely to all theym that will come to him". She would have no idle singing priest who, once his masses were said, might sit about the alehouse. "Grammar with the silver key that unlocks the door to science everyway" was a necessary preparation for the Universities. According to a very old definition it meant "that the pupil should learn not only to write and read correctly but also to understand and prove"—surely the beginning and end of all true teaching. "Understandest thou what thou readest?" said Philip to the man who asked him for guidance.

The year after Fisher's introduction to her, the Lady Margaret asked the King for licences to found a perpetual

Readership in holy Theology in each University. Archbishop Morton, the Chancellor of Oxford, recommended Edward Wilsford, doctor of divinity and fellow of Oriel College, who during the next Trinity term, in the public divinity schools, "began to read solemply the quolibets of the subtile doctor" (the Franciscan Duns Scotus who died in 1308). It was some years before the Cambridge appointment was made or the Readers' duties clearly defined. Subtleties were not what Fisher wanted; he was aware and not afraid of the new learning. "That grete hindrance and shame to all Christendom"—the capture of Constantinople by the Turks in 1453—had issued as a revelation of the truth and beauty in the ancients' world, and the mind of man was born again, not as an infant but full-grown, into an incorruptible inheritance and the use of a new language which was to enrich his own and give him a better understanding of the Word of God.

The wise men of Christendom were being drawn into closer fellowship and a noble rivalry of wits. Mountjoy, a young Englishman who had tasted of the new learning and could not have enough of it, induced his teacher Erasmus, a Dutchman, to visit England at this time. Urswick, now Dean of Windsor, had met this scholar in the Low Countries where he gave him a horse "and a good horse too", for it twice carried him across Europe. Now Erasmus brought the Dean a New Testament "hoping to wheedle a new horse out of him" but without success, though Erasmus was generally a good beggar. He speedily found himself at home in London where there was a great company of scholars whom he made his friends: Colet the Dean of St Paul's, holy and humble of heart, clothed with simplicity—Erasmus notes that "he went in wool when other churchmen were ruffling in purple and fine linen"—the Grecians Lyly and Grocyn and Linacre with their pupil young Thomas More whose profession was the law, whose passion was religion, whose pastime was letters, of whom the others kindly said that "he made very promising verse in Latin and English". But the church of St Lawrence Jewry which Grocyn the curate lent him was crowded by his fellow-students from Lincoln's Inn to hear his lectures on St Augustine's City of God and Plato's dreams of the ideal State with which he joined the tales now in every man's mouth about the new world in the West "of unlaborious earth and oarless sea", where the people, gentle, chaste and fearless, knew not the use of money nor of weapons yet lived in peace and justice with every creature. So he began to show forth his own Utopia, that happy island shaped like the crescent moon where

> "Things are evermore sincere
> Candor here and lustre there,
> Delighting."

To these visions of the young men the dreams of their elders did hardly accord. King Ferdinand who had seen himself, like another Alexander, taking toll of the kings of Asia, was not interested to hear only of an island or two peopled by innocent savages. But for Queen Isabella who would pledge the Crown jewels of Castile to give Columbus the means to put forth again, Spain had missed the glory of discovering the new world. King Henry's reactions may be gathered from a letter of Pedro d'Ayala to his master and mistress:

"I think your Majesties have already heard that the King of England has equipped a fleet in order to discover certain islands and continents which he was informed some people from Bristol had found who manned a few ships for the purpose last year. I have seen the map which the discoverer has made who is another Genoese like Columbus. The people of Bristol have for the last seven years sent two or three or four caravels in search of the island of Brazil and the seven cities according to the fashion of this Genoese. . . .The year before they brought certain news that they had found land. I told the King that in my opinion the island was already in possession of your Majesties; but though I gave him my reasons, he did not like them."

The true begetter of all this exploring business was Henry of Portugal called the Navigator, a grandson of John of Gaunt; when the King's mother was a child, he was the Conqueror of Ceuta in the Barbary Crusade and thereafter came to England in a blaze of glory to receive the Garter from King Henry VI. But he has a more enduring fame by his charting of the Western Ocean and exploration of that coast of Africa. That he and his followers were the first Europeans to enslave the natives is a blot on his glory for us though not for the men of his time. Though he had been dead thirty years it was to Portugal that Columbus went at first for help as did also Giovanni Caboto "that other Genoese" commissioned by the King of England "to seek and find whatsoever isles, countries, regions and provinces of the heathen and infidels which before this time have been unknown to all Christians"—(after which concession to piety King Henry went on to secure for himself one-fifth of the net gains of the expedition). In Lisbon John Cabot sought out Fernandez the Lavrator (farmer) of the Azores who, inspired by the discoveries of Columbus, had once sailed to Iceland and Greenland seeking a route to Asia by the North-West. His reward was not with him then but when Cabot landed on that icy coast and named it—not for King Henry whose flag he set up, nor for himself but Lavrador for his friend.

Not much more than a week later yet another Italian, Amerigo of Florence, a minion of Columbus, landed on the same coast and claimed it as his own discovery whence it came about that the New World bears the name of a supplanter.

John Cabot sailed back to Bristol and was called to Court to be rewarded by the King for finding "the country of the Great Kam seven hundred leagues West of Ireland". And he died and his son Sebastian put forth in his stead.

The King's mother was concerned not so much with these tales of a brave New World as with the troubles vexing the old one where the Pope was calling for another Crusade to keep the Turks at bay, and again calling in vain. "If the Christian Princes would have warred for the enemyes of the fayth", she said, "I would be glad yett to go follow the host and helpe to washe theyre clothes for the love of Jhesu."

So this adventurous century died leaving a dim, uneasy consciousness in the minds of the children of men that Mother Earth was greater in soul and body than they had believed.

VI

With the new century came again a King's daughter out of Spain to be the bride of the Prince of Wales. Such was the violence of the autumn storms that "it was impossible not to be frightened"; as with admirable restraint, the child who had never before sailed on the sea wrote to her parents. But at Plymouth "she could not have been received with greater rejoicings than if she had been the Saviour of the world".

Two hundred and fifty years before this, when Eleanor of

Castile rode into London, a harassed and discontented people murmured at the outlandish men and beasts in her train. Now the reception of the Infanta Catharine was "by our Soverayne assigned as well for the increase and magnifying of the Princess's honour and estate as for the maintenance of the old and famous appetites that the English people ever have used in the welcoming of acceptable and well-beloved Strangers".

For at last the Spanish marriage, hindered long enough by Ferdinand's doubts and desertions, was within sight of accomplishment. Now, the only trouble—and that not of his contriving—was the rain driving against the bridegroom and his father as they rode "to meet and greet her on her way". When lo! in their path, Don Pedro d'Ayala to unfold at this eleventh hour yet another difficulty: according to the Spanish custom the Princess might not meet or speak with either the Prince or the King till the actual hour of the marriage ceremony.

Check to the King, that stickler for form and ceremony; besides, what might be behind this? It was well known that Joanna, Catharine's sister, was mad, which nevertheless had not prevented her marriage to the Emperor's heir. This girl might be like her or deaf and dumb, blind, halt, of sickly breath and complexion like poor Joan of France, or swarthy, with hair on her lips, a blemish from which King Henry was particularly averse. While he thought on these things and looked on his son, handsome and wholesome, the Council hastily summoned sat on their horses round him and the indifferent rain poured on all.

At last one of them—it sounds like Sir Reginald Bray "noted to have with the King the greatest freedom of any Counsellor, a freedom the better to set off flattery"—discovered the trouble for what it really was: the timid scruples of a Court-drilled duenna. But, as the writs of Spain could not run in England so neither could her customs prevail there where the King alone might order the manners of his Court. Before nightfall Arthur and Catharine had looked in each other's eyes, had even supped in company and plighted their troth in the presence of the King who duly informed her parents that "he and his son much admired the beauty of the Princess as well as her agreeable and dignified manners". But he so far spared their feelings and Donna Elvira's reputation as to delay this communication till after the wedding in St Paul's church on Nov. 14 St Erkenwald's Day when the bride was led to the altar by the 1501 bridegroom's brother Henry Duke of York. The banquet was in the Bishop's house adjoining; next day there was a tournament at the Palace of Westminster, part of the yard being railed off for the use of "the common people" who came in crowds to see the show. To rejoice with them that do rejoice is ever the Londoners' habit.

At the great party in Westminster Hall were pageants and shows full of emblem and fantasy; also some of the Court ladies "having instruments of music such as Claricords, Dulcimers, Claricimbals and such other played upon them all the way coming from the lower end of the Halle till they came before the King and Queen, so sweetly with such noyse that in my mind it was the first such plesant myrth and property that ever was held in England of long season". But dancing was the chief delight.

"Then came down the Lord Prince and his aunt the Ladaye Cecille and daunced two Bassdaunces and departed up agen, the Lord Prince to the King and the Ladaye to the Quene." She had carried him to his christening had Cecily and now, "less fortunate than fair", widowed these five years, was living at Court with her two little girls under her sister's wing, light-hearted as ever, the life and soul of every party.

"Eftsoones the Ladaye Princess and one of her ladies with her in apparell after the Spanish guise came down and daunced other two Bass Daunces and both departed up to the Quene agen." Here was neither the listless prowl nor graceless shuffling to be seen in our ballrooms to-day, but "Knights and ladies they also daunced together deliberate and pleasantly, and so in seemly sort disported and daunced many and divers Roundes and newe daunces full curiously and with the most wonderful countenance"—the spectators as much interested as the performers.

Nor was nature denied her due. "In the third and last place Prince Henry having with him the Ladaye Margaret his sister in his hand came down and daunced two Bass daunces. Afterwards perceiving himself to be accombred with his clothes the Duke sodainly cast off his gowne and daunced in his Jacket in so goodly and plesaunt a maner that it was to the King and Quene grete and singular plesure."

So, when her father was king and she a slim child of six did Elizabeth dance with him before the Court at Windsor for the entertainment of his friend Louis de Bruges. And well might her son Henry rejoice in the dance; it was the beginning of his family's fortunes. Surely somewhere out of the shades, great-grandfather Owen "who danced and danced till by good hap he danced himself into a Queen's lap", was watching them all, well pleased.

At such times the elders have a way of taking stock of their memories, though there were not many left who could barter these with the King's mother: Bishop Fox who the day before had joined the young couple, Derby her husband,

Urswick and Bray her friends, were still beside her. That handsome youth helping Prince Henry to his gown again was Charles Brandon son of Walter the Standard bearer who was killed on Bosworth field; the King took the boy to bring up as an elder brother to his own children who loved and followed him. Lord Welles her half-brother, husband of the Lady Cecily, had died about the same time as Jasper Tudor whose widow then took a third husband, but kept the title Jasper had given her, and now ruled the Queen's ladies. It was a pity Jasper left no one to bear his name honourably, though his daughter's child Stephen Gardiner was said to be a bright boy who might come on for the church. Gone was the Queen's mother who would have enjoyed herself these days; neither was old grandam Cecily any longer growling in the background. Margaret herself was perhaps tending thither.

Yet she had played her part in the entertainment of "the Spanish ladies and gentlemen at her lodging called the Cold-herber for whom that place was ryght ryall and plesantly beseen and addressed and enhaunged with riche clothes of Arras and in the halle a goodly cupboarde made and erecte with grete plentith of plate both silver and gilte and they were sette at the boarde encompanyed and couplid everyone of them as well the men as the women with his companion of England to make them chere and solass".

For all the skill of the hostess and the glory of the service that would be a silent banquet. As a means of communication between persons of high breeding the Spaniards were unaware of any language but their own; either from pride or laziness they could not even meet the English half-way in French. Tired of the cumbrous Latin in which her advances to her new daughter were entombed by secretaries, Elizabeth the Queen had dared to suggest that the Princess might practise the use of French when writing to her and to the King's mother, but in vain; nor could it be supposed that Catharine should learn the language of her new country. Even after she had lived there for five years she wrote to King Ferdinand: "I do not understand the English language nor know how to speak it." Yet she was both intelligent and conscientious.

The way the English dealt with such a situation was to call her Catharine who was Catalina to her own countrymen, while Don Pedro d'Ayala became Peter Elias; so might everyone feel at ease.

Catharine's first home in England was at Ludlow in the Welsh Marches; when the Mortimers turned themselves into Plantagenets they kept their hold on the country of their origin. The Governor of the Marches at this time was Sir Richard Pole nephew of the King's mother, being the son of her half-sister Edith St John; he held also a post of confidence in the Prince's household, and his wife was Margaret Plantagenet daughter of Clarence and Isabel of Warwick. She was a wholesome woman sound in heart and head who mothered the girl of fifteen and was her life-long friend even to a martyr's death for her sake. The studies of both the Prince and Princess were directed by Thomas Linacre the physician, not the least of whose gifts to his country was the light of the knowledge of the glory of Greek. "I should never be done were I to begin to tell how much is missed by him who has it not", said Thomas More, one of Linacre's pupils at Oxford, whose fine English prose shows what he gained from Greek.

1501   "This yere came a great ambassade out of Scotland by reason whereof conclusion of marriage was made between the King of Scottes and dame Margaret eldest daughter to our soverayne lord." Not for nothing was she born and christened in the octave of St Andrew.

Two friends of King Henry had been his ambassadors for this business: Bishop Fox, then reigning at Durham and Don Pedro d'Ayala—or Peter Elias—who while trying to detach King James from the cause of Warbeck and the influence of France, was able to discover to Henry something of the nature of what was to him as it still is to most of his country-men—a foreign land.

The observant Spaniard found the people of Scotland in-telligent with a surprising amount of education, living simply but comfortably and though thrifty, given to hospitality, the ladies being good housekeepers and agreeable hostesses. Chiefly, as was expected of him, did he illuminate the character and policy of the king of the land; it would give his cousin of England some secret satisfaction to hear that James was holding his own against the nobles who mastered his father, although his way of consorting with the common people like one of themselves might not so much commend itself to Henry as to Henry's mother. It was apparent that James was trying to unite the nation; one of his chief cares was for its trade; he was growing and felling timber to make ships for its protection and encouraging the sea-fisheries of the country whose patron saint was a fisherman. James Stewart's mother, Margaret of Denmark, was a sea-king's daughter; he had the sea in his blood.

But he was not eager to dance to his cousin's piping and the English Council had their doubts about the marriage till their long-headed chief persuaded them of the likelihood of union "when the lesser kingdom would follow the greater; England would gain all and lose nought".

Katherine Gordon, Warbeck's widow, who had to her comfort and advantage exchanged the Scots for the English Court, could nevertheless rehearse their cousin's graces and accomplishments in the ears of King Henry's family: he had all the languages of Europe—even the Spanish—on his tongue; he was a master of various forms of musical expression such as "speaking to the psaltery", a fashion of the old trouvairs which had come round again. The Queen who encouraged, if she did not also practise this pleasing art, straightway ordered new strings for her daughter's lute.

It was nobody's business to tell that Prince Charming, by nature shallow, conceited and showy, was a light o' love, promiscuous in his gallantries and too prodigal of his favours.

> "He is a man and men
> Have imperfections; it behoves
> Me pardon Nature, then",

especially in princes. The chief promoter of the marriage, Archbishop Elphinstone, could truthfully discourse to the King's mother of James's piety—as Christian in his generosity to the Church, as son for ever mourning a father murdered—and of the third Scots University (there being as yet but two in England) even now rising in Aberdeen upon whose walls he would be commemorated as Invinctissimus. To both these simple people the marriage meant the establishing of peace between their countries, so near and yet so far, and a happy settlement for the volatile prince.

So, like Joan Makepeace, was blue-eyed Margaret offered up, 1502 declaring on St Paul's Day in the palace of Shene that "wittingly and of deliberate mind, having twelve years complete in age, the month of November last past she did espouse the

King of Scottes" by his proxy the Earl of Bothwell. Henceforth she was given the style and title of Queen of Scots.

If this were a study of coincidence instead of a sober relation of facts it might be observed that King James's proxy was the ancestor of Bothwell, the third husband of Mary Stuart, while Margaret Tudor became the grandmother, not only of that poor, ill-guided woman, but also of her second husband Henry Darnley. This leaps to the memory at sight of Margaret's portrait by an Italian artist of her time in our National Portrait Gallery near one of her grandmother, Margaret, painted about 1505 by an unknown Englishman. The other portraits on the wall are as lifeless masks in comparison of these two; but they provoke wonder as to what sort of a life was before the one and behind the other. Each in her own way must have lived very close to Nature: Margaret Tudor "exquisitely wild" yet wistful too, and Margaret Beaufort whose face as God made it is serious, yet not sad like one who listens, a page of history, not a jumble of anachronisms.

"A hydeous thunderstorm on the night of December xxi., the name of the King's palays of Shene changed and called after that Rychmount", the escape across the sea from the King's justice of the last Yorkist plotter against the King's peace, two marriages in the King's family and how "about this time the Gray Fryeres were compelled to take their old habit russett as the sheep doth dye it"—thus in a breath the chronicler Fabyan tells what befell in the years 1501-2, then cuts off his tale to observe with laconic irrelevance: "In Apryll following died the noble Prince Arthur in the towne of Ludlowe."

It was not the first time the King and Queen had tasted as parents the sharpness of death; two children, Elizabeth and

Edmund, had already been taken from them. When the news reached them of the death of their first-born, it was the Queen who put it where alone sorrow and unhope may be absorbed and turned to fair uses. "God is where He was", she said, "and also other great, constant and comfortable words" whereby the King's head was lifted up and his courage renewed.

Feb, 11
1503

He needed it all when within a year she died also, on her birthday, a week after the birth in the Tower palace of their seventh child Katharine. The King like Edward I after Queen Eleanor's death "departed privily to a solitary place to pass his sorrow and would that no man should resort unto him", but sent two of his gentlemen "to afford the best comfort they could to the Queen's servants with good and kind words".

In the following July he accompanied his daughter Margaret on her way to Scotland as far as his mother's house of Colyweston in Northamptonshire. The prayer-book he gave her at their parting has two inscriptions in his writing, one after the commemoration of St George: "Remembre yr kynde and lovynge fadyr in yr good prayers"; and "Pray for your lovyng fadre that gave you this booke and I giv you at all tymes God's blessing and myne. Henry R." Here is an echo of the elder Margaret's motto: "Souvent me Souvient": Forget me not.

"There is no country in the world where Queens live with greater pomp than in England" as the Spanish marriage commissioners had heard from their English colleagues; "they have as many Court officers as the King." Two of these were lent by Henry to his daughter and conveyed her to Scotland: Sir Davy Owen the carver, and the Somerset Herald John Yonge who, for the comfort of the King and the King's mother kept a diary of the journey; it is, in effect, a Court Circular. "Veray noble was the convaying and the caryage and the sumpters with coverynge of whyte and grene and the armes of Scotlaunde and of Englaund helf-perted with Red Rosys and Portcullis Crowned." No wonder that dwellers on the route made holiday and crowded to see the pageant of knights and ladies the glory of whose jewellery and garments to a button is recorded by John Yonge with the precision and the passion of a Court dressmaker. Henry Percy, Earl of Northumberland, surnamed The Magnificent, who did the honours of the North Country, is specially commended for the bravery of his tinkling ornaments and the graceful gambades of his horse; but then he was educated in the family of the King's mother, and he was a son of Maude Herbert, Henry of Richmond's first love. She came to York to greet Henry's daughter, "the Queen kissing her in the wellcoming". In Earl Percy's park at Alnwick "the Queen shot a Buk from her Bowe", like another Queen Margaret before her. Certain of the more important towns such as Dunbar fired off cannon "for luff of her wych was a delight boath to here and to see", if you were far enough off for gunpowder was as yet an unchancy business; it was remembered that King James's grandfather was killed by the bursting of a great gun.

But John Yonge was not very sure about King James owing to his eccentric manner of presenting himself before his bride—once in the guise of a falconer "his Lure behinde hys Bak", again riding a mule, "though richly beseen as becomes a Kyng" and always "hys Beerde something long". And he had his own way of receiving the Church's blessing from the numerous bands of clerics who beset the couple as they drew slowly towards Edinburgh. Then there was but one faith, one baptism for both countries; as yet neither English nor Scots had to any great extent discovered religion as matter for politics.

But everything that does not conform to his conventions is indulgently condoned by Somerset Herald as "the custom of the country" with that kindly, humorous superiority which Englishmen still use towards foreigners.

But King James's largesse was all proper; after the ceremony, his wedding garments were given to Somerset Herald, those of the Queen going to the Scots Heralds. Next day, however, whether from sentiment or carefulness, she had them back again, sending money instead; what Lyon King or his lady had to say about this is fortunately not recorded.

Sir Edward Stanley, a son of Lord Derby and a kinsman of the Queen, was one of her knights "who played a Ballade and sang therwyth wych the King (James) commended right much. And incontynent hee called a gentleman of his that could sing well and mayde them synge togedder the whyche accorded varey well. Afterwards Sir Edward and two of hys servants sang a Ballade or two whereof the Kynge gave him good thauncke."

"The first and chief use of Musicke is for the Service and Praise of God whose gift it is. The second use is for the Solace of Man." Long before John Playford the first music publisher thus patronised his Maker and advertised his wares, his countrymen had discovered music for themselves as a natural and happy means of approach to God and of fellowship with each other. Not only King Henry VI and his cousin of Scotland with their choirs of singing men and boys in the royal chapels, but their subjects of all degrees were able to use music as a homely pastime to relieve the tedium of a journey or those domestic delays and crises from which none of us is exempt. And we know of one young gentleman of this time whose father kept him so short of money and so hard at work during

his scanty two years at Oxford that as he says quite contentedly,
"I could indulge in no amusements either guilty or dangerous",
who yet found time to perform agreeably on both the flute
and the violin.

VII

"Grow old along with me
The best is yet to be"

cried a poet of our day.

"Old age with lockes sere and hoare
Of our short life the last and beste parte"

said Thomas More who was not yet thirty years old when he
laid this flattering unction to our souls. The Lady Margaret
for whom the cares of this world began before she was fourteen was now sixty-two. Though it does not appear that like 1503
these inexperienced poets she either feared or welcomed old
age she was not forgetful of its warning, What thou doest do
quickly, and was setting her house in order. The Readerships in
holy Theology were this year established in the Universities:
John Fisher, D.D., Master of Michael House and the Lady's
spiritual director being appointed in Cambridge and John
Roper, D.D., in Oxford. The Abbot and Convent of Westminster had the administration of the revenues which came
from certain manors in Middlesex, among which were Pad-
dington, Westbourne, Drayton, Kensington and Willesden—
acquired by the Lady from Sir Reginald Bray. That "sage and
grave person, a very father of his country and a fervent lover
of justice" died about this time and was laid in the chantry he
himself had designed within St George's, Windsor.

The Lady Margaret's Readers were required to expound without fee or reward other than their salaries "such works in divinity as the Chancellor or Vice-Chancellor with the college of doctors should judge necessary" in the common schools of divinity to everyone resorting thither for one hour from seven to eight in the morning every accustomed day in each term (except in Lent) and in the Long Vacation. The lectures were in Latin as was all teaching in the Universities at this time; but in Lent both teachers and taught were to show forth the fruits of their labours by preaching to the people in their own tongue.

Preaching by academical persons of the time was concerned usually with "subtleties" and debates of the schoolmen or with the commendation of some political measure. In the parish churches the so-called sermons dealt with trivialities and were often only exhibitions of buffoonery; serious and simple exposition of the Scriptures was almost unknown. "The word of the Lord was precious in those days; there was no open vision" except it were with the Lady Margaret and her counsellor who knew that "where there is no vision the people perish".

1503   At the feast of All Souls she founded a Preachership in Cambridge University. The preacher was required to give in the English tongue six sermons annually—one in two years at St Paul's Cross in the City of London in turn with one at St Margaret's, Westminster; the rest were to be given in certain specified towns and villages in the Eastern Counties; Ware and Cheshunt in Herts., Bassingbourne, Orwell and Babraham in Cambs., Boston, Manea and some others in Lincolnshire. The sower went sowing far afield; his stipend of ten pounds a year was adequate at that time; but the sermons in the outlying places were dispensed with by King Charles II (who inherited the Lady's consideration for other people's financial limitations), on account of the heavy cost to the preacher of transit.

Her desire to bring the Bread of Life within reach of the simple was shown also by a translation of "Imitatio Christi", done at her instance by Dr Atkinson one of the first Fellows of Jesus College, Cambridge and printed for her by Pynson at Caxton's press. She herself translated from the French the fourth Book which treats particularly of the Holy Communion; so, as the manner of some is, she has been labelled "learned woman", than which nothing would have more amazed her. She would never have dreamed of evening herself with the like of Christine de Pisan, stern daughter of learning who, it may be remembered, did not recommend it for her own sex. But the ideal she set before it was realised by this Lady who had a mind of her own capable of being perpetually educated by life and its demands and upon which nothing was lost. Such as she have an inner fastness of the spirit whereunto they may always resort to be nourished by what really interests them; whatever it be it engenders a wisdom which being rooted in charity gives them to understand the manifold, unutterable needs of their fellow-creatures.

Thus her advice was sought by all manner of them for the composing of their quarrels, private and public. Of more particular interest to us are those between the University and the town of Cambridge about "claims to jurisdiction on the one side and complaints of extortion on the other". She did not rely upon herself alone for the settlement of such disputes but arranged for other arbiters who met, not on the scene of strife, but at her London house where they were hospitably entertained. "For the suitors it is not unknown how studyously she procured justice to be administered by a long season, so long as she was suffered and of her own charges provided men lerned for the same purpose evenly and indifferently to here all causes and administer ryght justyce to every party which were in no small nombre and yet mete and dryncke was denied to none of them."

Thus to spend money is easy; it is in the expense of spirit that true generosity lies.

Afterwards "the parties were said to have lived at better peace to the great benefitt of themselves and the whole realm beside".

She visited Cambridge frequently, coming either from her house of Colyweston about forty miles away or from Buckden Palace where she stayed in the great red brick tower called The King's Lodging, which the loyalty of three successive bishops of Lincoln had put at the disposal of the royal family. Her friendly relations with the town of Cambridge extended over many years and are recorded in its Annals: "In spices 6 lbs. of comfits given the mother of the Lord the King, 6/8 and in one flagon of Ipocras given to the same, 3/4d., and for roasting a Buck given by the mother of the Lord the King 2/-. For red wine given to the minstrels of the Lady 5d., and in three pike fish given to the same lady 12/-, and in monies paid to the steward of Master Reginald Bray Knight in wine at the sign of the White Hart 14½d."

The town kept a neighbourly eye on the doings of the University and noted that "the Proctors in their accounts charged two several sums of 20[d] and 18[d] as paid to the Vicar of Trumpington for letters written by him to the King's mother", from which it would seem that she had a correspondent other than Fisher on the spot.

"Lifeless and impoverished" is how he, its Vice-Chancellor, describes the University at this time, and particularly the Grammar College of God's House founded in 1439 "because ther is so grete scarcitie of Maistres of Grammar", by William Bingham rector of St John Zachary (the Baptist) in London. Twenty-four scholars were to be "perpetually educated" in grammar, logic and rhetoric and then placed in schools throughout the country in order to prepare boys for the Universities. The first twenty-four in charge of a Proctor were lodged in Mill Street near Clare Hall and more or less under its authority, but when King Henry VI desired the site for his College Roial, he enabled Bingham to find a better one for God's House in Preachers' Street in the parish of St Andrew on the other side of the Market. Bingham had captured the King's interest in his foundation; Henry gave it a charter, some endowment with hopes of more and took on himself the character of founder. His successors confirmed the charter and King Henry VII gave the society a licence to hold property. Alcock approved it and, when Bishop of Ely, proclaimed indulgences for any who should benefit it. Though to this there was a fair response, the condition of God's House was such as to challenge the instincts of a nursing mother like the Lady Margaret besides that holy Henry had fostered its beginnings. There is no doubt that she deemed herself "heir to all his godly intentions" when on May Day of the year 1505 God's House with the new name of 1505 Christ's College "was augmented, finished and established by Margaret Countess of Richmond and Derby, Mother to King Henry VII". The letters patent were confirmed in the following year on October 3rd, which date is taken as the birthday of the 1506 new College.

By this time she was again a widow, Thomas Stanley, Earl of

Derby, having died in the summer of 1504, one of those men whom the world both envies and despises for his successful mastery of its methods. But however we may judge him, she did not who was his loyal wife for twenty-one years. "Of mervyllous gentylness she was unto all folks, but specially unto her owne whom she trusted and loved ryghte tenderly" was Fisher's observation of her. "Unto the upright there ariseth light in the darkness; they are merciful, loving and righteous", said another wise man before him.

In a letter telling her of his intention to give Fisher a bishopric the King, after making it clear that he had thought of this all by himself, goes on to say "I have in my days promoted many a man unadvisedly and I wolde now make some recompencion". If there is here a trace of the anxious mind for ever like Lot's wife looking back and misdoubting itself, there may be also a glance at his mother's habit of letting her heart misguide her head. For instance, there was her stepson, James Stanley, whose rapid promotion in the Church was due to her; Erasmus had refused as a pupil this fashionable young cleric, whose favourite pastime was cock-fighting and of whom it is written in the Stanley family chronicle that it was a pity he was not a soldier like his brothers rather than a priest "as he had not the gift of continence". As Bishop of Ely one of his few respectable acts 1506 was licensing the chapel of Christ's College for divine service.

This was in the winter of 1506 by which time the buildings of God's House (one of which was originally acquired by Bingham from the Abbess of Denny) had been enlarged and adapted to the needs of the new society. Its numbers were double those of God's House; the fellows were twelve like Christ's disciples. There were forty-seven scholars in whose election preference was given to the poorer sort and to natives of the Northern Counties, particularly Lancaster, York and Richmondshire (then a separate division of the Kingdom); the master was John Sycklyng the last governor of God's House. Their lot was cast in a fair ground amidst green fields and running waters, by the Barnwell Gate of the town looking over the Nuns' Close—now the Christ's Fellows' garden—to Jesus College and half-way between the Franciscans or Grey Friars where now is Sidney Sussex and the Dominicans or Black Friars where now is Emmanuel.

How closely the Lady watched over this child of her old age has been adequately and indeed illustriously told by more than one of its sons. She is the only foundress of a college who is known to have resided within the walls; in the Master's Lodge "the first floor rooms built for our use" (we may note the possessive pronoun is in the royal plural) were comfortably furnished and frequently occupied by her. Some of that "goodly Cupboarde with grete plentith of gold and silver gilte", one of the glories of her Spanish party, was given to the College and may still be seen there; upon one cup are the names of her great-uncle Humphrey of Gloucester and his last duchess Eleanor Cobham. Nothing touching the College from the framing of the Statutes to the particular material, fashion and even laundry of the garments of the scholars was hid from the Lady. She advised about their recreations and arranged for their comfort in health and sickness, allotting her manor of Milton by Orwell as a house of retreat and refreshment. Another gift which recalls her own early years was the advowson of Manobra or Manorbere in Pembrokeshire; her beautiful signature may be seen on the document of conveyance which is in the possession of the College.

"Although his mother was never so wise (as she was both

witty and wise) yet her will was bridled and her doynges restrained to the intent", the King said, "he worthily might be called a King whose office is to rule and not be ruled." The same good sense on both sides prevailed in the Lady's relations with the University of her choice and the College of her foundation.

As in the Universities generally the rule of living was simple, almost austere (though we know that Sycklyng the first Master of Christ's was addicted to a feather-bed). "There is more piety and temperance in the colleges in Oxford and Cambridge than in any houses of religion" was the observation of Erasmus when he was Lady Margaret's Reader in Cambridge.

April 22 1506   It was the Eve of St George in the year 1506 when the King being on his way to the shrine of Our Lady at Walsingham visited Cambridge, accompanied by his mother. "The Universitie and the Mayor and his bredern met him two or three mile out of the Towne. Within a quarter of a mile ther stode first all the four Ordres of Freres and other religious and ther stode all the graduatts after their degrees in all their Habits and at the end of them was the University Cross wher was a form and a Cushion as accustomed wher the Kyng did alight and then the Bishop of Rochester, Dr Fisher then being Chancellor of the Universitie accompanied with odir Doctors sensyd the Kyng and afterwards made a little Proposition" or sermon. One of the "odir Doctors" was the Chancellor's friend Erasmus who in that year was given the degree of D.D. by the University.

"The Kyng took his hors agen and rood by the Blackfriers through the towne to the Queenes College wher his Grace was at that tym lodged and ther rested the space of an hour and then did on his gowne and mantell of the Garter and all odir Knights of the Ordre ther being present gave their attendance in the habit of the Ordre as appertayneth and roode from the Kynge's logginge to the Chappell of the Kyng's Colledge which was for the same cause redy appointed with Socchins (shields) of the Knights Companions' arms as ys yearly accustomed. The Bishop of Rochester did the Divine Service both the Even the day both at Mattens and sang the Mass of Requiem on the Morrow."

To the glory of God was this done and in pious memory of King Henry VI, founder of the College Roial. So

"Your bright promise withereed long and sped
Is touched, stirs, rises, opens and grows sweet
And blossoms and is you when you are dead."

At this time the Chapel without and within was the skeleton of itself as we know it, only partially roofed, the windows empty of glass, no carving in wood or stone nor ornaments of any kind except the arms of the founder. Yet King Henry VII was proud to hold a chapter of the Order of the Garter within its stark and naked walls. Both his Yorkist predecessors had helped more or less generously with the good work of completing the Chapel, King Richard ferociously declaring that "all who stopped or delayed it should be committed to prison". But the son of Margaret Beaufort whom the stupidity of convention has labelled "the meanest of our monarchs" was the noblest donor of them all and this in spite of his preoccupation with St George's, Windsor and his own Chapel at Westminster. He made provision for the entire vaulting of the Cambridge Chapel, side-chapels and porches, and for building the four corner turrets, with instruction to his executors to supply what more might be needed if the Chapel were not finished in his reign. But, according to him, "deed of charitie done in life of man and wilfull departure and refusal from the possession and propertie of goodes to suche and other goode uses and intents be muche more meritorious and availeable for the weal of mannys soule than to be done after deth".

Provost Hacomblen of the College Roial whose duty it was to see that the King's will was done must have been a man possessing that valuable quality—a sense of continuity. One of the exquisite glass vignettes in his chantry is a figure of St John Zachary, commemorating William Bingham, founder of God's House; near it another shows a bunch of daisies, "the Lady's posay", for the King's mother. Souvent me Souvient.

In those days this was easy for she was taking note of the needs of the whole University. She gave another £10 towards the completion of Great St Mary's Church, probably at the instance of Richard Wyot who was overseer of the work and who succeeded Sycklyng as Master of Christ's College. How she and her friends benefited Jesus College has been told 1506 already; now she visited the Quenes College which soon afterwards received a grant of land from Edward, Duke of Buckingham, who had been brought up in her family and whose portrait is in Magdalene College, Cambridge, which also he 1519 benefited in the days when it was Buckingham House.

Having established Christ's College the Lady gave her attention to the House or Hospital of St John the Evangelist, an ancient monastic foundation that after much persistence had been "admitted into the body and society of the University and allowed to partake of its privileges". But the Brethren, having wasted their substance in riotous living and declined from the simplicity of their rule, which required them to serve God in caring for the sick and poor, had caused the Hospital—always an embarrassment, then a nuisance—to become a scandal in the University. To destroy it root and branch as Alcock did the degenerate nunnery of St Rhadegund when he founded Jesus College, seemed the only way and the Lady took it. By the advice of Fisher, the Chancellor of the University, only the name and the site—by King's Hall and Michael House now Trinity College—were to be retained for the new society she intended to found.

The consent of the bishop of the diocese was necessary for the suppression of the Hospital; James Stanley could not refuse this to his step-mother though by his manner of life he was openly showing his sympathy with the degenerate Brethren. The business of the King's consent (of which informally she was certain) took longer to achieve for he was ill and hampered in his doings by failing sight. It was eleven years since his friend d'Ayala had described him as looking "old for his years which are forty-two but young for the sorrowful life he has led". Now he was worn out at fifty-three. Before his mother's business about her new foundation could be carried through he died at his palace of Richmond on St George's Eve. 1509

When he was borne through the City on his last pilgrimage, it is said that a figure wizened and dim of aspect like one whom Death has forgotten to claim stole to the bier and threw on it a handful of flowers. The bystanders muttered that this must be Shore's wife to whom, dishonoured and persecuted by his two predecessors, this King had given the chance to lead an honest and good life.

"Scarcely for a righteous man will one die." Henry of Richmond excelled in the virtues which men honour and strive to emulate; but it was not given him to win the love of his people. That they kept for his son "our divine young prince" as they called him to whom at this time the only drawback seemed that which was in the mind of the wise man when he said "Woe unto you when all men speak well of you".

When the evil days came the Lady Margaret beheld them June 29 "with larger, other eyes than ours". She died two months 1509 after her son, having served her country for over sixty years under six kings, two of whom had their life from her.

> "Once I was awakened by Thy light.
> Long years have passed and now the night
> Takes me to Thee. I am content.
> So be it in thy perfect plan
> A mansion is where I am sent
> To dwell among the innocent."

The death of the Lady Margaret and the press of business consequent on the accession of her grandson gave opportunity for her unworthy stepson James Stanley to take back the consent he, as bishop of the diocese, had given her for the suppression of the Hospital of St John. Though he was forced to keep his word to the dead by a mandate from the Pope Julius II (whose portrait by Raphael is familiar to us), fresh opposition and more craftily conceived came from another bishop—Wolsey—who was gaining the ear of the King. The Lady's splendid bequest for her second College was declared to be legally unsound and was claimed by the Crown. Even-1511 tually, through Fisher's unceasing travail, a mere remnant was restored by which, two years after the Lady's death, the foundation of the College of St John the Evangelist was accomplished by the man whom now we hail St John of Rochester, supremely enabled to endow it with the imperishable inheritance of her spirit so that it grew and flourished exceedingly.

CHAPTER VIII

FRANCES SIDNEY

Countess of Sussex

I

She was not a King's daughter. Her father claimed descent from a William Sidney, said to have been Henry II's chamberlain; but it is more likely that a yeoman family settled in the time of Edward I at Alfold in Surrey, where the name may still be heard, was that which bred the Sidneys. Her mother was Ann daughter of Sir Hugh Pagenham and widow of Thomas Fitzwilliam.

By the time the Tudors ruled the land, the Sidneys appear as gentlemen with cool heads and a certain amount of the spirit of adventure who could be trusted with the King's business. Before he was thirty William the father of Frances went to Spain to fight as a volunteer against the Moors; thereafter he remained at Madrid hospitably entertained by King Ferdinand who offered him knighthood which he refused. On his return to England (after taking part in a naval engagement at Brest), he commanded the right wing of the army at the battle of Flodden, for which he was knighted by his own King Henry VIII and had from him large grants of land and lordship in Yorkshire. 1513

With his brilliant cousin the King's friend Charles Brandon he then went to France in the suite of the King's sister Mary and was present at her marriage to the aged King Louis XII who died soon afterwards. Next summer he was sent to

France to announce her marriage with Charles Brandon who, after King Henry had protested enough, was forgiven and created Duke of Suffolk. Sir William now an esquire of the royal body attended it to the Field of the Cloth of Gold and afterwards took part with Suffolk in the French war. His Court service would necessitate residence in London; he seems to have had the use of Baynard's Castle, one of the royal houses on the river near Paul's Wharf, and here it is supposed his 1531 daughter Frances was born in 1531. Her godmother, daughter of the Princess and Charles Brandon, was Frances Duchess of Suffolk, the lady who six years later became the mother of Lady Jane Grey.

The first ten years of Frances Sidney's life were full of change for her country. The King declared himself Head of the Church and Clergy, not without protest from them, and ordained in Parliament "that the obedience of him and the people be withdrawn from the See of Rome". The most religious and 1533 gracious Queen Catharine was expelled from the Court and separated from her daughter; then followed her divorce and the King's second marriage, the birth of Princess Elizabeth on whom the Succession was settled, the beheading · of John Fisher and Thomas More because they opposed this and the Act of Supremacy, the death of Queen Catharine and, not many months later, the execution of her supplanter; then the King's third marriage, the appearance in the churches of an English translation of the Scriptures, the birth of a prince on Oct. 12 St Edward's Day, the death of his mother, the final dissolution 1537 of the monasteries and the assumption of all their properties by the King, his fourth and fifth marriages, the fall of Thomas Cromwell and the execution at the age of seventy of that steadfast woman Margaret Plantagenet Countess of Salisbury,

Clarence's daughter, Reginald Pole's mother, cousin to the King and the last of the protesters against his manifold iniquities.

In the next year died James V King of Scots, son of King 1542 Henry's sister Margaret, leaving only a daughter of one week old to succeed him. Before a year had gone, a marriage treaty between her and Prince Edward of England was forced on the reluctant Scots which was only the beginning of sorrows.

Through all the tragedies and perplexities trusty Sir William Sidney kept his own counsel and his place at Court. In exchange for his properties in Yorkshire he had lands in Kent and Sussex; when the King's son was born he was appointed Steward of the Prince's household and then his tutor. Sir William's only son Henry the King's godson was put in charge of the little Prince; though Henry was the elder by eight years, the brotherless boys loved and suited each other: "as he grew in years and discretion so grew I in favour and liking of him" was how Henry Sidney put it. Athwart the terrors and triumphs of his splendid father's reign and the little ease of his own the Prince had gleams of happiness "reading, playing or dancing and suchlike pastimes answerable to their spirits and innocence of years" with the children and grandchildren of his tutor. "Now, Jane, your King is gone I shall be good enough for you", he said over a game at cards to little Jane Dormer, the child of Sir William's eldest daughter Mary. The other daughters were Lucy wife of Sir James Harington and Ann who married Sir William Fitzwilliam. Frances was the youngest and became her father's companion after her mother's 1542 death in 1542.

In that year the King having disposed of his fifth wife, married a young but experienced widow Katherine Parr, Lady

Latymer; she was related to him by her descent from the daughter of John of Gaunt Duke of Lancaster and Katherine Swynford. Her influence was good and made for peace both in the King's family and realm. But the dissolution of the monasteries and the consequent rapacity of his favourites had alarmed the universities for their own survival; a humble deputation sent to wait upon him was received by the Queen who not only allayed their fears but gave indication of favours to come. Hence the foundation of Trinity College and five new professorships in Divinity, Hebrew, Civil Law, Greek and Physic at Cambridge. "I tell you sirs", so King Henry is said to have answered the protests of some of his courtiers, "I judge no lande in England better bestowed than that which is given to our Universities; for by their maintenance shall our realme be well governed when we are dead and rotten."

This Queen was gentle, pious and not a little learned, a quality which almost proved her undoing, for to be a bore is unforgivable whether in man or wife. But, intelligent enough to realise this in time, she contrived to survive the King and even to take to herself a fourth husband.

1547   Once again there was a child on the throne and "the Kyng's symplesse", causing feuds and intrigues. At first his uncle Seymour Duke of Somerset held the power with the misleading title of Protector till gradually the star of John Dudley rose and prevailed. He was the son of Edmund, Speaker of the House of Commons in Henry VII's reign, "who did proceed secretly to the Outlawery against men and then did seize their estates for himself; an eminent man", says Lord Bacon with hardly concealed admiration, "and one that could put hateful business into good language". It was supposed that he and Empson his accomplice had a plan to seize the King's person and assume the Government; for this they were beheaded in the second year of Henry VIII. Nevertheless, thirty years on, we find Dudley's son John Lord High Admiral of England with the title of Viscount de l'Isle and a place at Court as Master of Horse to the Lady Anne of Cleves. He is described as "a person very comely and of a spirit highly aspiring neither wanting skill, industry nor resolution to attempt great matters". One of those who have the art of impressing—and sometimes imposing upon—others, he was trusted and his word taken by both King Henry and his son who made him Earl of Warwick (so did history seem to repeat itself) and then Duke of Northumberland. It did not take him long to compass the end of the Protector Somerset nor to acquire the post of Earl Marshall and then Steward of the Household in succession to Sir William Sidney with whom, however, he had no quarrel having married his daughter Mary to Henry Sidney.

Sir William had begun to feel his age and now retired peace- 1553 fully "to hold of the King's gift without account the Palace of Penshurst with the park called Northlands containing two hundred and fifty acres and all the goods, Chattells and Household Stuff in or about the said Capital Mansion" and a great deal more in the way of manors and advowsons. He did not have long time given him to enjoy them for he died and was gloriously buried at Penshurst five months before the death of Feb.–July King Edward. 1553

II

Penshurst "the caput" of the family was Frances Sidney's home till her marriage. "Marry thy daughters in time lest they marry themselves" was cunning old Burghley's counsel which he followed himself to his daughter Ann's undoing.

Frances Sidney may be said to have married herself as she was
1555 at the advanced age of twenty-four when she became the
wife of Thomas Radcliffe, Lord Fitzwalter, son and heir to the
Earl of Sussex, "a goodly gentleman of a brave noble nature
and constant to his friends"; but keeping "a tong at liberty to
utter what he thoughte" about those he disliked such as the
Dudleys with whom by his marriage to Frances Sidney he was
now nearly connected. Robert (afterwards Earl of Leicester)
he called "that gypsy and upstart that had but two ancestors—
his father a traitor and his grandfather a publican", not that the
Radcliffe family history was untainted politically, one of them
having been concerned with Perkin Warbeck. But Thomas
was a pricker of other men's bubbles; his family badge was a
porcupine.

He himself was of ancient lineage and could if he chose
trace descent from Charlemagne through Jacquetta of Luxembourg whose daughter Katherine Wydville was his great-
grandmother. Thus he was nearly related to Elizabeth
Wydville's grandson King Henry VIII, by whom he was
knighted. Before he was twenty he held a command in the
expedition sent to Scotland to enforce the marriage treaty between the infant Queen of Scots and the Prince of Wales, of
which the result, despite the English victory at Pinkie Cleugh,
was to drive the Scots more surely into the arms of France.
At King Henry's funeral Lord Fitzwalter was one of the six
knights to carry the canopy. Though he was a signatory to the
royal letters patent by which King Edward gave the succession
to Lady Jane Grey, Queen Mary made him Captain of the
Gentlemen Pensioners and allowed him "to wear his cappe,
coyfe or night-cappe or two of them in our presens" wherein
the poor lady seems to have shown a rare gleam of humour.

He and Henry Sidney were of the embassy sent to Spain for the negotiation of her marriage with another of her cousins, King Philip, ten years her junior. The young men were about the same age as the King who was pleased to renew with Henry King Ferdinand's friendship with his father. To Fitzwalter the King gave "five precious stones" of which Thomas was very proud; they may be those that compose the interesting ornament worn by his wife Frances in each of her four portraits; the pendant looks like a small edition of the famous black pearl that Philip gave the Queen.

As Captain of the Guard Fitzwalter took Princess Elizabeth, attainted of treason, to the Tower "on Palm Sunday so that 1554 everie one might keep the churche and carie their palms that she might be conveyed without all recourse of people". "Full courteous and favorable", he protected her from the harshness of one of his band, whose name is withheld by the timid chronicler though not the indignities to which he sought to submit the Princess. "And, swearing, the Captain said to the others My lords let us take heed and do no more than our commission will bear us whatsoever shall happen hereafter. She was the King our maister's daughter and therefore let us use such dealing that we may answer for it hereafter if it shall so happen for just dealing, quoth he, is always answerable." Lord Fitzwalter had studied the law at Gray's Inn.

Having proved him a good soldier and diplomat, his grateful sovereign Mary sent him to Ireland as her Lord Deputy, a position which, before and since, has availed for the ruin of many a good reputation. On Whit-Sunday of the year 1557, 1557 he and his wife landed in Dublin accompanied by her brother Henry and the Fitzwilliams, her sister and brother-in-law.

To Sir Henry Sidney it seemed "there was never people that

lived in more misery as the people of this land—such misery as in troth hardly any Christian with dry eyes could behold". Yet, as an Oxford scholar of the time observed, "there is no lack of genius in Ireland", which Sidney also recognised for later he had visions of founding a University there. But these did not concern the Lord Deputy though he too had a love of good learning. His commission was "to establish the true Catholic religion, to have due regard to the administration of justice and to punish and repress all heretics, lollards and rebels". So he put forth into "the bogs, fens and marshes" of the North in pursuit of a particularly rebellious couple of brothers, fighting, slaying, burning, leaving smoking ruins and keening widows behind him and the last state of that land was worse than the first. He could not be called a merciful man nor yet bloodthirsty; only one under authority interpreting his orders as he understood them. "Then shipped I over to Cantire where I landed and burned the whole country. From thens I went to Arran and dyd the lyk there and so to the Isles of the Cambries which also I burned." But that raid was not as successful as he had hoped and he begged the Queen not to tax him with lack of zeal. On the contrary, she gave him the Garter when he appeared in London on the death of his father and he had the thanks and commendation of her Council, among them some of the very men who a dozen years later repudiated with loathing the massacres in Paris on St Bartholomew's Day.

While the Lord Deputy ranged thus through the land his lady existed as best she might in Dublin Castle which in spite of her brother's efforts to render it habitable was half ruinous and scant of furniture. She had the company of her strong-minded sister Ann, Lady Fitzwilliam, who, wherever she was, could be trusted to make herself felt. Lady Sidney did not at this time bring the comfort of her presence to the family party; like many a gallant woman of our day whose husband is serving his country abroad, she abode by the stuff and the children, rightly and duly administering his affairs, and, in spite of ill-health and lack of money, keeping a home for him and a warm, wholesome family life. Daughter of Northumberland, sister of Leicester, men without character or principle, she had escaped her family's taint; though most of her life was spent in the atmosphere of a Court she was marvellously unworldly. "Among whiche friendes before God there is none proceeds either so thoroly or so wisely as my lady my mother. For my owne parte, I have had onely Light from her" was what her son Philip thought of her.

Then Queen Mary died an old woman at forty-two and her sister came to the throne in the vigour of a virgin youth which she never put off. Lord Sussex came speedily to England to take his hereditary office of sewer at the coronation of the Sovereign. "Because he is our cousin and an Earl of this our land" and mindful perhaps of that Palm Sunday when he comforted her on her way to the Tower, the Queen promoted him to be Lieutenant-General in Ireland; back he went with much the same commission as before except as regards "the true Catholic religion". For the celebration in Dublin Cathedral of the Queen's accession the Protestant ritual was used, the Te Deum and Litany being sung in English.

If "it is required of stewards that a man be found faithful", it is the blessing of kings to be attended by servants who do their bidding without question or remark. In that they seem never to have protested (about religion at least), Sussex and the elder Sidneys cannot be called Protestants so much as con-

Nov. 1558

formists for whom the House of Rimmon had no problems. Sussex was a friend of Cardinal Pole, welcomed him on his return from exile and was present at his consecration as Archbishop. Though the other leaders of the Catholic party were never very sure of Sussex, Queen Mary made him one of her executors and left him five hundred marks. As her Lord Deputy, one of the first measures he introduced in the Irish Parliament was the repeal of her father's Act of Supremacy; but he was a member of Queen Elizabeth's first Parliament which restored the Act and gave all ecclesiastical jurisdiction to the Crown. When the Act of Uniformity in Religion was enforced, it would be a satisfaction to him to find himself on the other side from Robert Dudley who opposed it.

Though Henry Sidney and his wife were supporters of his cousin Jane Grey, and intimately concerned with her affairs, they managed to keep out of the closing tragedy. Two ladies, Mabelle and Elizabeth Sidney (said to have been his sisters but it is more likely they were his aunts), were in Queen Mary's service and valued by her "for their rare virtue and zeal in the Catholic religion". This fact and the ancient kindness between the Sidneys and the royal family of Spain were of use to him and made him one of the embassy that arranged the Queen's marriage. That long-suffering woman was in some ways more tolerant than her sister. When Henry Sidney's first child was born King Philip came to Penshurst to be godfather and gave his name to the boy. Later the King was a witness to the marriage in the Chapel Royal of Frances Sidney with Lord Fitzwalter, Gentleman of the King's Privy Chamber.

"Foy est Tout" as it is written on the walls of her College. To her and her family the Christian faith was a reality and rule of life but they made neither talk nor trouble of it though

Marginal notes:
1586

St Andrew's Day 1554

April 1555

doubtless under Elizabeth they were more at ease in Zion. Like one of their contemporaries who also accommodated himself to the see-saw of religions, they were "tolerant and humane, wanting perhaps in the elements of heroism and greatness, aiming rather at the happiness of their species than at the assertion of any particular dogma in religion". It was for the next generation to provide in Philip Sidney, godson of the most Catholic King, a champion of the Protestants. But that was after his eyes had seen St Bartholomew's Day.

Lord Sussex returned to Ireland for three years; then, "sick in body and mind", he asked to be recalled. When the Queen was able to give the matter her attention, which was not for nearly another year, he left to Henry Sidney "the thankless task" of ruling Ireland and came back to the life he knew and liked best though the ascendancy at his cousin's Court of Robert Dudley must have worried him, particularly as it fell to him in the course of his duties to present him to her to receive 1564 the Garter and be made Earl of Leicester.

III

"Next Camus, reverend sire, went footing slow."

In the August following, the Queen went on a progress which began with Cambridge. The University, having suffered from the political upheavals, appealed to its Chancellor Mr Secretary Cecil for a solution of its difficulties. In spite of being what he called "a nursling" of the University he was not too anxious to come to its rescue, but at last he undertook to induce the Queen to visit it. It seems that she needed persuasion. She liked and looked for entertainment on a lavish scale in the houses of her nobles—and dearly did it cost them; gone were the days when the great ones of the earth went on pilgrimage for their souls' health and were content with the hospitality of the religious houses. But Cambridge was the Alma Mater of her old friend and family tutor Ascham; and, what lay nearer her interest, Robert Dudley had recently become its High Steward.

So she consented and in town and University there was drilling and rehearsing and diversity of preparations. Inquisition was taken as to whether any in the town were dead or sick of the plague, that hovering menace, and efforts were made to cleanse the ill-paved streets from the filth of ages, loads of sand being hastily thrown down to smother what had to be left. Carpets and curtains and bedding were sent from the Queen's Household to replenish the resources of the College Roial where she was to lodge. Though a martyr to the gout, Mr Secretary Cecil himself came some days in advance to see that all was ordered fairly and his lady of the eagle eye came with him.

The Queen "with a great companie of ladies and maids of honour" appeared on a Saturday afternoon riding by Grant-chester from Haslingfield where she had lain the previous night at the house of one of the Gentlemen Pensioners. She was then a comely young woman of thirty-two "in a gown of black velvet pinked, a caul upon her head set with pearls and precious stones and a hat that was spangled with gold and a bush of feathers". Yet was there ever an age whose fashion of garments for both men and women was so ugly and perverse? It was the era of whalebone and starch—to this day one of mankind's dearest foes—by which the free natural lines of the human figure were deformed and disguised from head to foot.

The Mayor and his Council met the Queen at Newnham where, as the day—and her dress—were hot, she rested in the miller's house, then changed her horse and rode with the whole company to the Queens' College to be greeted by the Chancellor and acclaimed by the University; then she was conducted to the West Door of the King's Chapel where the Provost "Mr Dr Baker and all the Fellows and scholars in their capes standing in their order" received her. On entering the Chapel "the Queen knelt at a place appointed between the North door and the South and prayed privately. Afterwards the quire sang in English a song of gladness and so went orderly into their stalls in the quire the Queen following and going into her travys and marvellously devising at the beauty of the Chapel greatly praised it above all other in her realme." Then Evensong, "which being ended the Queen's Majesty came forth of her travys and went towards the Provost's lodging by a privy way. And as she went she thanked God that had sent her to this University where she altogether against her expectations was so received that she thought she could not be better."

The admission was timely and well deserved for, used as they were to entertaining kings who are but men, the celibate Provost and Fellows had literally to put themselves out for the Queen and her train of women. The porch of the Provost's Lodge (then at the South-East end of the Chapel) was called for the time being the Court where the Queen held audience; behind it was the Guard Room. She was lodged "above in the gallery" the whole of that floor being given up to her use; her ladies were in the Fellows' solar Chamber or Parlour—in fact, the Combination Room—on the other side of the Chapel; the Maids of Honour were in the neighbouring Gonville Hall recently refounded by Dr Caius. The Choristers' School of the King's College was used for the Buttery; the royal kitchens smoked in the open "against St Austin's wall".

The Earl of Sussex who brought a hundred servants was lodged in St Catharine's Hall; whether there was room left for his Countess also is not recorded. It is likely she was with "divers other ladies" in the Fellows' Chamber of the College Roial over against Clare Hall in which she took an interest as the future was to show. And at this time she met John Whitgift the Lady Margaret Professor, an earnest young Calvinist of her own age, not long emerged from a controversy that was agitating the University about the wearing of surplices in the College Chapels.

But one discord had been silenced: gone were the Friars who were wont to claim equal rank and notice with the University on the occasions of royal visits. Even their local habitations were disappearing. The Carmelite buildings had long been absorbed by the Queens' College; the Benedictines had died as Buckingham House and revived as the College of St Mary Magdalene; the stones of the great Franciscan Convent that once had housed the Parliament of England were being used for the new buildings of Trinity College over the way. The Dominican Monastery without the Barnwell Gate was now desolate and laid in heaps, which was noted and held in memory by the Queen's Lord Treasurer Sir Walter Mildmay, a son of Christ's College. He knew all about it, having been one of the Commissioners for the dissolution of the monasteries; he had profited—but honourably—from that work and used most of his wealth for the endowment of learning in the University.

Such was the Queen's complaisance that "order was taken her Majesty should remain one day longer than at first it was appointed and if provision of beer and ale could have been made her Grace would have remained till Friday she was so well pleased with all things". She made a tour of the Colleges noting the Great Gate-house of Trinity, the Chapel newly roofed, the Master's Lodge and the turret that lodged the Earl of Leicester. At Christ's College she received a pair of gloves "in remembrance of her Grand-dame the Lady Margaret Beaufort". At Peterhouse Sir Walter Mildmay's son "was much commended by the Queen because he being but a child made a very neat and trim oration pronounced very aptly and distinctly".

But the sun was hot and she began to remark that "some of the habits and hoods were too much torn and soiled" and, though she herself discoursed in Latin at some length, she thought she could dispense with certain of the disputations by the doctors. On Latin, Greek and flattery did she dine, sup and break her fast; but of music and dancing, two noble arts in which the Tudors as a family most excelled and delighted, there was little or no exercise.

The last act, very early in the morning, was the conferring of degrees on many of the distinguished guests; "and why some Regents went in white silk and others in mynever great inquisition was made as well by the Prince as by other of the nobility". And still the wonder grows in the childlike minds of visitors to the University as to the curious habits of the aborigines.

The Earl of Sussex was so content with his honorary degree that, as he said later, "I am ready to plesure the Universitie to my powre. I am a Master of Arte of that Universitie and have been twice to Oxford and there that degree hath been twice offered me but I have refused the same for I mean not to have two strings to my boe"—a dark saying.

IV

"Sweet Thames run softly till I end my song."

Some time after he returned to England Lord Sussex bought from Sir Thomas Pope "the goodly house built of stone and timbers" out of the ruins of the ancient Cluniac monastery at Bermondsey in the Borough of Southwark on the south bank of the Thames. It was in the new fashion of domestic architecture which Henry VII and his minister Reginald Bray began in England, and, except for the old gateway which was retained, it was in no sense a house of defence but a home, open and agreeable with rooms of gracious proportion that could never seem either too large or too small and wide embrasured windows whence one could look with ease both out and in. Queen Elizabeth came to visit her cousin Thomas once when "he lay very sick at his house in Barmsey". Though she liked to refer in a large way to "my ancestors", it is not clear that her interest in them reached farther back than her father, or that, on this occasion, she realised that she passed under the same gateway and trod the same stones as two of them who had spent their last days in the Clare Guest-house of the monastery—Queen Elizabeth Wydville whose name she bore and that Queen Katherine who first ushered in the Tudors.

The neighbourhood had become fashionable early in the century when Charles Brandon Duke of Suffolk built "a large and sumptuous house in grounds" where he entertained the Emperor Charles V; King Edward VI, when visiting the Archbishop who had it afterwards, remarked on the sweet air and pleasing prospects of the suburb.

It may be supposed these did not include the lazar-house or

the prisons of which there were five, Clink—the name of the oldest of them—having survived in our language as a generic term for a house of bondage. That they were dens of horror could not be ignored by any who lived near them as the Countess did; we know that she took pity on their miserable and often innocent inmates. Nor did she forget the poor at her gates; her contemporary Stow the Chronicler mentions that Bermondsey was noted for its beggars.

Behind the High Street was Paris Garden where was the bear-baiting; "there you have the shouting of men, the growling of bears, the barking of dogs and the bellowing of bulls mixed in a wild natural harmony", sweet to the ears of a sport-loving people. But the Garden had other uses; in parts "it was so dark with trees that a man must have lynceous oculos or els cattes eyes if he woulde behold his fellowes in it"—hence good for the meeting of those who liked not to do their business within four walls. Lord Sussex, busy as he was about the Queen's affairs, had sometimes to deal with such persons.

He was of the party that favoured the Queen's marriage though with whom did not seem to matter so long as it was not Robert Dudley; there are who hold that for a woman any marriage is better than none. Having refused his friend King Philip, she enjoyed herself hailing and then checking the advances of one and another foreigner though she and everybody knew that by Order of Parliament "no foreign potentate should exercise any power or authority in this kingdom". She sent Lord Sussex to Vienna with the Garter for one of them; when he returned, he found to his disgust that the Presidency of Wales on which he had counted was given to Sir Henry Sidney while he was fobbed off with the Governorship of the North. There he again harried the Scots and earned their hatred (though his mistress thought him too lenient) and found reason to distrust their queen who also was related to him. When she cast herself on the mercy of England, he was one of the judges who urged her imprisonment as a political necessity and condemned to death her champion the Duke of Norfolk— yet another of his relatives. The trumpet of Thomas Radcliffe gave forth no uncertain sound.

He vented his private discontents in quarrels with Sir Henry Sidney and, while Lord Chamberlain of the Household, in a petty persecution of Lady Sidney (Leicester's sister) about her lodgings at Court when she came to take her turn of waiting on the Queen. Sussex was childless while the Sidneys were the parents of children of whom the praise was in every mouth. But it was not in any of them really to enjoy or to prolong family quarrels; the Sidneys' latest born was named Thomas and Lord Sussex stood godfather with Lord Burleigh "though indeed" as Sir Henry wrote to the latter, "I have not my Will for I left order that if it were a boy it should have been a William and if a wench a Cecyll".

There is no reason to suppose that the Countess suffered other than vicariously from her husband's frowardness except the look of endurance tempered by a melancholy composure which appears in more than one of her portraits. Though "a man's roar's neither here nor there", it becomes wearisome; but her relations never let it affect their regard for her. She was intimate with her sisters' children, Haringtons, Fitzwilliams, Montagus; Philip Sidney the Queen's Cupbearer and his lovely sister Mary, one of the Maids of Honour, came about her. Nor would uncle Thomas's pronounced opinion of their other and favourite uncle Leicester discourage them at all.

Protesting to the last against "that gypsy" then at the height of his glory, Lord Sussex died at the age of fifty-seven, having 1583 spent himself in his country's service without fear or favour. Sir Henry Sidney and his wife died two years later, not many months before their eldest son "the light of our family" as his father called him when he was yet a boy. But that light has never died. Philip Sidney is still for his countrymen one of the shining ones who from time to time are sent into this world to "anoint and cheer our soiléd face".

In the "house in Barmsey", practising a dignified frugality, the Countess led a life secluded yet not dull. Something of "the rumour of the world" would reach her through her relations in high places; Sir William Fitzwilliam, husband of her sister Ann, was the Keeper of Fotheringay Castle, "a wise, grave man", who showed the captive Queen of Scots the kindness her kin denied her. There are certain families to whom interest in the things of the mind comes as a natural inheritance; "by these things men live and in all these things is the life of the spirit"; so was it with the Sidneys, men and women, from one generation to another. The inspiration that "Sidney's sister, Pembroke's mother" gave in her time to men of genius is an oft-repeated tale, but that her aunt Frances had a share in it should not be forgotten. "Loved of wise men was the shade of her roof-tree." There was her nephew John Harington, of Christ's College, Cambridge, the translator of Ariosto. There was John Whitgift whom the Queen treated with alarming freedom, Archbishop though he was, calling him her "little black husband" and punning upon his name—a grave liberty for even a queen to take. There were the two Deans Gabriel Goodman of Westminster, worthy of his angelic name, and his brother of St Paul's Dean Nowell, a keen fisher not of men only but verily of fish also and that, spite of everything, in "the sweet river Thames"—though those who so called it wisely abstained from drinking its waters. But the Dean was able to show them a more excellent way; he was the discoverer (though by accident) of bottled ale and, being Nowell, spread the good news and became a benefactor of the human race. According to his admirer Izaak Walton, he had a hand in the authorship of "that good plain, unperplexed Catechism printed in our good old Service book". Indeed Izaak's enthusiasm misled him into crediting the Dean with the whole of it.

A pluralist like many another, he was Vicar of Hoddesdon in Hertfordshire when the son of Dame Jocosa Frankland, one of his parishioners, was killed by a tragic accident at the age of twenty-three. The Dean shall tell the rest of the story: "She fell into sorrowes uncomfortable whereof I, being of her acquaintance, having intelligence did with all speed ride to her house near Hoddesdon to comfort her the best I could and I found her crying continually O my sonne, my sonne. And when I could by no comfortable words stay her from that cry and tearing of her hair God, I think, put me in mind at last to say Comfort yourself, Good Mistress Frankland and I will tell you how you shall have twenty good sonnes to comfort you in your sorrows which you take for this one sonne. There are in both Universities many pore toward youths that lack exhibition for whom if you would found certain fellowships and scholarships they would be in love to you as dear children."

Five years later the mourning mother left the bulk of her property "to be bestowed upon studious young men in Gunville and Keys College and in Emmanual College at Cambridge". Also and very properly she endowed the Colleges of Lincoln and Brasenose in the Dean's University and founded the school still existing at Newport in Essex. Among the executors of her will were Sir Walter Mildmay, founder of Emmanuel College, and Dean Nowell.

Surely that tender-minded man told Jocosa's story to his childless friend the Countess of Sussex who, as it happened, was her exact contemporary and who made her will at the same time, in the end of the year that saw the defeat of the 1588 Spanish Armada.

The noble lady had not as much to leave as Jocosa, the daughter of a London goldsmith, nor, loyal as she was to her husband's preference for Cambridge, did Dr Nowell persuade the Countess to share her favours between the two Universities.

"And where sithence the Decease of my Lord the Earl of Sussex, I have in Devotion and Charity purposed to make and erect some Goodly and Godly Monument for the Maintenance of Good Learning and to that Intent have yearly gathered and Deducted out of my Revenues so much as conveniently I could, I do therefore now in accomplishment and performance of the same my charitable Pretence what with the ready money I have so yearly reserved and with a certain portion of Plate and other things which I have purposely left Will and Ordain that my Executors shall bestowe and employ the Sume of five thousand Pounds for the erection of a new College in the University of Cambridge to be called the Lady Frances Sydney Sussex Colledge...for the maintenance of a Master and of ten Fellows and twenty Scholars Students there according to the laudable Custom of the said University....

"But if it be thought not sufficient to erect and found a new Colledge in her name...then that the said five thousand l. etc. be employed for the enlarging of Clare Hall in the said

University which Colledge from thenceforth shall be called Clare and Lady Frances Sydney Sussex Colledge or Hall."

She willed also that her Executors "should purchase a perpetual annuity of twenty l. a year to the use of a Godly and learned Preacher who for and in her name should read two lectures in Divinity weekly, every week, for ever in the Mynster unto the Collegiate Church of St Peter in West-minster on such several days as no other Sermons or Lectures were to be read there...and that her Executors also bestow one hundred Pounds amongst poor and Godly Preachers in London and the Suburbs thereof".

When from these high solemnities she condescends to the devising of her personal possessions she shows, Calvinist though she was, the healthy interest in clothes that springs eternal in the human breast. "A trained gown of black velvet embroidered all over with broken trees, a large Kirtle embroidered and a Suit of Aiglets inamelled with a Suit of Buttons with Garnets and Pearls of 120" went to the Montagus. Lady Montagu was her sister Lucy's daughter and with her husband Edward must have been a favourite for he had "the Plate in the Cupboard in her bed-chamber with a suit of Hangings with the story of Holofernes and Judith and much rich furniture in the Chamber therto belonging". But all of them—Haringtons, Fitzwilliams and the executors of her will were copiously remembered. There is, however, no mention of the diamond for a ring left by Sir Philip Sidney to "My very good lady the Countess of Sussex in token of my very dutiful love". Very likely it never reached her; both her brother and his eldest son died in debt and great poverty.

"We brought nothing into this world, and it is certain we can carry nothing out." But we often seek to evade the discomfort of that reminder by forecasting the manner of our exit, and this also has an enduring human interest. The Countess who did not fancy her husband's splendid tomb in Essex ordered a fine one for herself alone in the Chapel of St Paul within the Church of St Peter at Westminster. Very likely she saw its beginnings for "if her tomb should not be finished in her life-time, her Executors should bestow 200 l. or more if need required for the making therof with her Picture in Alabaster stone and other Garnishing".

It is unexpectedly beautiful and, what is rare in such monuments, gives an effect of repose in spite of the fretful porcupine at the feet of the figure; the face, sweet and womanly, is far more lifelike than in any of her painted portraits. Dean Nowell who was in demand on such occasions preached the funeral sermon whereof the substance is preserved in her epitaph:

> "Here lyeth ye most honourable ladye
> Frances sometime Countess of Sussex
>   daughter of Sir William Sidney of Penshurst, Kt.
> wyfe and widowe to ye most Noble most wyse and
>   most martiall Gent
>   Thomas Radclif Earl of Sussex
> A woman while she lived adorned with many
>   most rare Gifts both of mind and body
> Towards God truely and Zealously religious
>   To her friends and Kinsfowke most liberall
> To the Poore to Prisoners and to the Ministers
>   of the Word of God always most charitable
>   Pietate et Prudentia   Come Lord Jesus
>   Fide Conjugali   Come Quicklye."

In the Confessor's Chantry over the way lies Eleanor the Queen who first provided for the poor scholars of Cambridge and befriended also the Preachers of the Word of God. The two might be in sight of each other were it not for the stupendous monument a grateful people has set up in the Chapel of St Paul to James Watt. Might not his mother country claim this brooding figure and enshrine it more suitably where "the palpitating engines snort and steam about her acres"?

The Preachership endowed by the Countess was in operation till 1905 when it was decided that "the benefaction shall be devoted to the spiritual care of the Almsmen, Almswomen, Workmen and any other dependents of the Collegiate Church of St Peter for whom at present no definite provision of the sort is made".

The noble army of her executors included four doctors of divinity—one of them the Vice-Chancellor of Oxford—two Masters in Chancery, Henry Grey the Earl of Kent, her nephew Sir John Harington—all "for the great honour Zeal and Religion in Vertue and fair dealing that she had noted in them"—and her cousin Mr Henry Bosseville whose vertue, etc. we have to take for granted. The Earl of Kent and Sir John Harington did most of the work, which was not easy (it never is) nor swift of fulfilment. But they were spared the difficulty of pouring their new wine into old bottles for Clare College refused to adopt the new College, having not long recovered from the threat of absorption by Trinity Hall and remembering the decree of the Lady of Clare that the College should be called by her name "and by no other".

So a site was acquired in Bridge Street where was the Grey Friars' Monastery; and seven years after the Countess's death

the foundation stone of the College of Sidney Sussex was laid April
by James Montagu who was descended from her sister Lucy 1589
Lady Harington and who at the age of twenty-seven became May 20
the first Master of the College.   1596

Thus Frances Sidney takes her place among our honourable
women sponsored by Elizabeth de Clare and Margaret Beaufort who more particularly would seem to have inspired and
enabled her. "As sparks among the Stubble so shall they run
to and fro."

Six years after Sir Henry Sidney's death his dream of a
University for Ireland was realised by some Oxford and
Cambridge scholars in the foundation of Trinity College, 1591
Dublin, "for the combatting of ignorance, barbarism and
sedition". And because the depredations of Sussex as Lord
Deputy in Ireland have been told, it should be noted that the
first College of the University to open its fellowships to 1606
Scotsmen and Irishmen as such, was that one that bears his
name. So came the wheel full circle.

PEDIGREE I

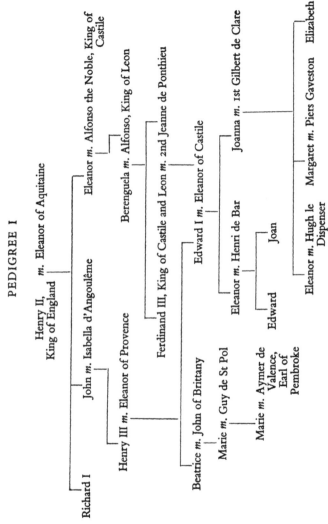

PEDIGREE II

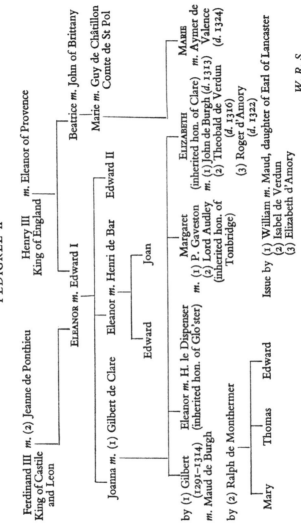

W. R. S.

PEDIGREE III

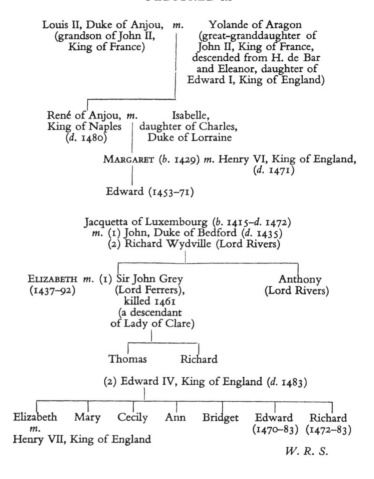

Louis II, Duke of Anjou, *m.*   Yolande of Aragon
(grandson of John II,   (great-granddaughter of
King of France)   John II, King of France,
descended from H. de Bar
and Eleanor, daughter of
Edward I, King of England)

René of Anjou, *m.*   Isabelle,
King of Naples   daughter of Charles,
(*d.* 1480)   Duke of Lorraine

MARGARET (*b.* 1429) *m.* Henry VI, King of England,
(*d.* 1471)

Edward (1453–71)

Jacquetta of Luxembourg (*b.* 1415–*d.* 1472)
m. (1) John, Duke of Bedford (*d.* 1435)
(2) Richard Wydville (Lord Rivers)

ELIZABETH *m.* (1) Sir John Grey   Anthony
(1437–92)   (Lord Ferrers),   (Lord Rivers)
killed 1461
(a descendant
of Lady of Clare)

Thomas   Richard

(2) Edward IV, King of England (*d.* 1483)

Elizabeth   Mary   Cecily   Ann   Bridget   Edward   Richard
m.   (1470–83) (1472–83)
Henry VII, King of England

W. R. S.

270

PEDIGREE IV

Edward I, King of England *m.* (1) Eleanor of Castile, (2) Margaret of France

Edward II, King of England *m.* Isabelle of France

Thomas

Edmund, Earl of Kent *m.* Margaret, Lady Wake

Joan, Fair Maid of Kent *m.* (1) Sir Thomas Holand

Thomas de Holand *m.* Alice of Arundel

Edward III *m.* Philippa of Hainault

Edward, Black Prince

Lionel of Clarence

John of Gaunt *m.* (3) Katherine Swynford

Henry

John, Marquis of Somerset *m.* Margaret Holand

John, Duke of Somerset *m.* Margaret Beauchamp

Margaret Beaufort *m.* (1) Edmund Tudor, Earl of Richmond

Henry VII, King of England

INDEX

ABBREVIATIONS

Abp.	= Archbishop.		K.	= King.
Bp.	= Bishop.		Pr.	= Prince.
Cts.	= Countess.		Q.	= Queen.
Dch.	= Duchess.		s.	= son.
Dk.	= Duke.		d.	= daughter.
E.	= Earl.		Ped.	= Pedigree.

18-2

For EU product safety concerns, contact us at Calle de José Abascal, 56–1°,
28003 Madrid, Spain or eugpsr@cambridge.org.

www.ingramcontent.com/pod-product-compliance
Ingram Content Group UK Ltd.
Pitfield, Milton Keynes, MK11 3LW, UK
UKHW012335130625
459647UK00009B/298